catalogue

back with diff...... ...se... to

that quoted by yo...........

may not be required edition)

STUDIES IN ECONOMICS
Edited by Charles Carter
Vice-Chancellor, University of Lancaster

5

Industrial Organization

COMPETITION, GROWTH AND STRUCTURAL CHANGE
IN BRITAIN

Industrial Organization

Competition, Growth and Structural Change in Britain

BY

KENNETH D. GEORGE

Professor of Economics, University College, Cardiff

REVISED EDITION

London
GEORGE ALLEN & UNWIN LTD
RUSKIN HOUSE   MUSEUM STREET

First published in 1971
Second impression 1972
Second edition (revised) 1974

© *George Allen & Unwin Ltd 1971, 1974*

ISBN 0 04 338070 0

Printed in Great Britain by
Alden & Mowbray Ltd
at the Alden Press, Oxford

To Elizabeth

Preface to the Second Edition

The writing of textbooks in applied economics is a hazardous business. Research workers and politicians are continually at work undoing past efforts. The field of industrial organization is certainly no exception to this problem. Although this book was first published only three years ago much has occurred in the meantime which necessitates the publication of a second edition. A great deal of research has been undertaken on the structure of industry and on the effects of policy. In particular, more information is now available on the position of large companies and on international comparisons of industrial structure and performance. Much has also been done in evaluating the effects of regional policy. A number of important institutional changes have also occurred such as the abolition of S.E.T. and the passing of the Fair Trading Act 1973. These developments account for many of the changes found in the second edition. In addition most of the chapters incorporate revisions of a more general nature designed, it is hoped, to clarify exposition and improve understanding.

In preparing this edition I have been fortunate to receive advice and assistance from Terry Ward and John Rhodes of the Department of Applied Economics at the University of Cambridge.

K.D.G.

Editor's Note

Economics is a large and rapidly developing subject, and needs, as well as elementary works for the beginner, authoritative textbooks on special subjects. This book belongs to a series of such textbooks (more than forty titles are planned): the general level is that of the second or third year in a British university course, but the books are written so as to be intelligible to other readers with a particular interest in the subject concerned.

C.F.C.

Acknowledgments

The first draft of the book was read by A. B. Atkinson, Z. A. Silberston, G. Whittington and J. C. G. Wright. I am most grateful to them for their comments and suggestions which were most useful in preparing the final manuscript. I am also grateful to the Editors of the *Economic Journal*, the *Review of Economics and Statistics*, and the *Journal of Industrial Economics*, for permission to reprint parts of articles which I have published in these journals. Finally it is with great pleasure that I record my thanks to Mrs. Lilian Silk and her staff for typing the manuscript.

June 1970

K.D.G.

CONTENTS

INTRODUCTION

This book is intended as an introductory text for a course in industrial organization with particular reference to Britain. Although our main concern is with the British economy, the general issues relating to competition, growth and structural change which are dealt with are relevant to all advanced capitalist economies. These issues include various elements of structural change, such as the changing relative importance of the 'goods' and 'services' sectors of the economy and the regional problem; the process of the growth of firms; the inter-relationships between market structure, business behaviour and market performance, and issues of public policy. The subject-matter of the book is organized along the following lines.

In Chapter 1 an empirical examination is undertaken of the main changes which have occurred in the structure of British industry since the inter-war period. We not only observe the changes that have taken place, but also test some hypotheses relating to growth and structural change. Thus we are concerned with such questions as the relationship between changes in output and changes in productivity at both the national and international level, and with the economic implications of the growing dominance of large companies in the economy. This is followed in Chapter 2 by an analysis of the process of change and for this purpose attention is focussed on the firm. A large part of the changing structure of industry is brought about by the continuous adaptation of successful firms to changes in their environment—to changes in demand conditions and in technology. Of course changes in industrial structure are accompanied by the birth of new firms, some of which subsequently achieve large size, and by the death of unsuccessful ones. Our concern in Chapter 2 however is with certain aspects of the growth of existing firms—with diversification and vertical integration, research and development effort, and acquisitions and mergers.

The results of research and development expenditure—the introduction of new products and processes of production—is of course one of the main aspects of *market performance*, by which we mean the outcome of the process of competition between firms in a market. Chapter 3 examines the other main aspects of performance, namely, efficiency, profitability and the importance of selling costs. It is in fact with the explanation of the quality of market performance in these various dimensions that much of the subject-matter of industrial organization is concerned. Chapters 4 and 5, therefore, examine the basic determinants of market performance—market structure and business behaviour.

11

Market structure refers to the organizational features of a market which have an important effect on the extent and nature of competition within the market. The main aspects of structure which are examined in Chapter 4 are seller concentration—that is, the number and size distribution of firms operating in a particular market; the conditions of entry of new firms into an industry—which refers to the obstacles facing new firms when entering an industry; and product differentiation—or the extent to which units of a product which is produced by competing firms are regarded as imperfect substitutes by buyers because, for instance, of the effects of advertising and differences in packaging and design. There are other environmental factors in addition to the organizational ones just mentioned, which exert an important influence on market performance. In particular, there is the importance of the rate of growth of demand for an industry's products. This factor has to be included in any empirical analysis which seeks to explain the quality of market performance.

The examination of business behaviour in Chapter 5 is concerned with the way in which firms adapt themselves to their environment and to changes in their environment. Clearly, the motivations or the objectives pursued by firms are important in explaining their behaviour. Do firms maximize profits or do they maximize some other variable such as sales revenue? Indeed can the objectives of firms be adequately described in terms of any form of maximizing behaviour? A sufficiently competitive situation in product markets and/or in the capital market would tend to force firms towards profit-maximizing behaviour. But to what extent do these markets operate in such a way as to bring about this result? These are some of the questions which are looked at in this chapter. In addition there is a brief account of the process of managerial decision-making, and an examination of some aspects of the price and output policies of firms.

Having examined some of the main aspects of market structure and business behaviour, our next task is to see to what extent differences in structure and behaviour can offer a useful explanation of variations in the quality of market performance. Thus, for instance, to what extent can persistent excess profits be explained by high levels of industry concentration and high entry-barriers to new competition? Again, are excessive sales-promotion expenses systematically associated with any aspect of market structure? What is the evidence concerning the relationship between market structure, business behaviour and the rate of innovation? It is clear that empirical work in this field has to contend with a formidable battery of problems— problems which relate both to the compilation of suitable data, and to the interpretation of the results of the research work. It is the purpose of this chapter to illustrate some of these problems as well as to give the results of some of the empirical work.

The empirical evidence concerning the relationships between market structure, business behaviour and market performance is clearly relevant to issues of public policy and particularly to policy towards monopoly and competition. Before turning to a critical examination of policies in this field, however, it is important to put them into perspective by taking a more general look at issues of public policy at the industry level. This is done in Chapter 7. This chapter sketches the main problems associated with the concept of an optimal allocation of resources—such problems as dynamic adjustment, externalities and the choice of goods. There is also a discussion of the range of problems with which monopoly policy should be concerned. Should it, for instance, be concerned with such issues as the balance of payments and regional policy as well as with efficiency? The general point is that the government has several goals which it must pursue and also has at its disposal a variety of policy weapons. The problem is to choose the set of policy weapons which will be most effective in attaining the goals. The policy weapons which are relevant to our analysis include not only monopoly and restrictive practices policy, but also discriminatory fiscal policy and direct government intervention in industry. Chapters 8–10 examine some of the issues related to these policy instruments, as they have been applied in Britain in the post-war period. Monopoly and merger policy is critically examined in Chapter 8. Chapter 9 looks at the effects of restrictive practices legislation including the effects of the abolition of resale price maintenance (r.p.m.) following the Resale Prices Act, 1964. The main effects of the abolition of r.p.m. is to be found on margins, productivity and structure in the distributive trades. Any attempt to measure these effects, however, is complicated by the introduction in September 1966 of the Selective Employment Tax (S.E.T.) which also affected the variables concerned. Chapter 9, therefore, also looks at the way in which S.E.T. could be expected to affect margins, productivity and structure in the distributive trades. It provides our first example of the government's use of discriminatory fiscal policy in its attempts to influence industrial structure. S.E.T. may well be abolished, but regardless of how long it lasts, a study of the effects of the tax is an interesting case study in the use of discriminatory fiscal policy.

A second example of the use of discriminatory fiscal policy is found in Chapter 10 with the examination of regional policy. This chapter also looks at some aspects of direct government intervention in industry and in particular at some of the main issues relating to the position of the nationalized industries in the economy.

CHAPTER 1

Changes in the Structure of British Industry

The development of an economy is characterized by changes in the structure of its industry. Some sectors of the economy grow faster than others, so that over time there are marked changes in their relative importance. Again, within individual sectors and industries there are changes in the relative importance of plants and firms of different sizes.

The causes of such change are complex but include changes in the pattern of demand, the invention of new products and processes and the differing opportunities for technical progress in individual sectors, the growing importance of the economic functions of the government, and the changing pattern of international competitiveness. These and other factors inter-react to bring about the changes in industrial structure. Thus, for instance, the growth in the importance of employment in the service sectors, which seems to characterize the later stages of development, is largely the result of two factors. First the increase in the income elasticity of demand for services relative to that of manufactured goods. Secondly, the general tendency for the rate of increase of labour productivity to be lower in services than in other sectors due, for instance, to fewer opportunities for technical advance.

Changes in industrial structure also often give rise to regional problems as large industries, which for economic reasons were concentrated in a few areas, go into decline.

This chapter is concerned with the way in which factors such as the above have worked out in the United Kingdom since the inter-war period. It is divided into three sections. The first examines the broad structural changes that have occurred since the 1920s with particular reference to the distinction between 'goods' and 'services'. The second examines the process of change more closely by looking at the relationship between changes in output, employment and output per head. The third looks at some of the changes which have occurred within the industrial sector in the relative importance of plants and firms of different sizes. The regional problem, with the

14

associated policy issues, is dealt with in Chapter 10.

A. GOODS AND SERVICES[1]

1. *Sector Shares*

A useful starting point in examining structural change is to look at changes in sector shares in terms, for instance, of manpower and output. Here we are concerned with changes over a long period and in particular with comparing the depressed inter-war years with the years of high demand in the post-war period. The use of comparative data over any long period of time is fraught with difficulties arising out of inaccuracies in the data. We must be cautious, therefore, in drawing conclusions. However, an analysis of sector shares since the inter-war period does seem to show a number of interesting features.

First, Table 1.1 shows the shares of the 'goods' and 'services' sectors in terms of net output at constant prices, and manpower. In terms of the volume of output there has been a general increase in the share of the goods sector since the 1920s, this share having increased in each of the periods shown in the table. Over the whole period, therefore, there has been a substantial increase in the share of output accounted for by the goods sector and a corresponding fall in the relative importance of services. In terms of current pounds, the changes in sector shares have been much less marked and indeed in the post-war period 1951–64 the changes are opposite to those found in terms of constant value output—a reflection of the higher price increases in the service sector of the economy.[2]

In terms of manpower the distinctive feature is the marked fall in the inter-war years in the share of the goods sector and a marked increase in the share of the service sector. During these years there was an increased concentration of resources in services which did not produce a corresponding increase in output; indeed, as we have already noted, the share of services output fell during the period. What seems to have happened is that some of the surplus labour of the inter-war years was taken up as under-employed labour in the low-wage industries in the service sector. This took the form not only

[1] The goods sector comprises agriculture, forestry, fishing, mining and quarrying, manufacturing, construction and public utilities. Services comprise transport and communications, distributive trades, insurance banking finance, and all other services.

[2] In terms of current pounds the share of the goods sector fell from 50 per cent in 1951 to 48 per cent in 1964, whereas that of services increased from 50 per cent to 52 per cent.

TABLE 1.1 *Distribution of Output and Manpower, Goods and Services Sectors, UK 1924–64*

| | (percentages) 1958 S.I.C. | | | |
	1924	1937	1951	1964
Net output at constant prices				
Goods	43	47	50	52
Services	57	53	50	48
Manpower[1]				
Goods	52	48	52	50
Services	48	52	48	50

Source: This table and also Tables 1.2, 1.3 and 1.5 are based on data compiled by Mr J. Odling-Smee as part of a research project sponsored by the Social Science Research Council of New York on the growth of advanced economies. The part of the project that is concerned wih Great Britain is being undertaken by R. C. O. Matthews, C. H. Feinstein, and J. Odling-Smee. I am grateful to them for permission to use the data in the above-mentioned tables. Some of the first results of their study were published in R. C. O. Matthews, *Some Aspects of Post-War Growth in the British Economy in Relation to Historical Experience*, paper read to the Manchester Statistical Society, November 1964.

[1] In the case of the net output figures various adjustments such as that for banking services have been allocated equally between the sectors. For both output and manpower the process of adjusting the figures for the first three years shown in the table so as to conform to the 1958 Standard Industrial Classification is always liable to lead to errors. These factors, however, are not likely to upset the very broad trends shown in the table.

of under-employed employees, but also of an increase in self-employment. During this period the rate of increase in labour input was greater than that of output so that there was a fall in labour productivity.[3] These manpower changes were reversed during the war and early post-war years when there was a marked increase in manpower in goods as compared to services, and by 1951 the sector shares seem to have been much the same as they were in 1924. Since 1951, however, there has again been a fall in the share of manpower in the goods sector and an increase in the share going to services.

The figures in Table 1.1 certainly suggest very strongly that

[3] See Table 1.5 below.

Britain has not yet reached the stage of economic development where services account for a substantially larger share of output and absorption of resources than goods. From this point of view it is interesting to compare Britain with the position in the United States. In the latter country the share of total persons employed in the goods sector decreased from 53 per cent in 1929 to 49 per cent in 1947 and 42 per cent in 1965. The share of the service sector on the other hand increased from 47 per cent in 1929 to 51 per cent in 1947 and 58 per cent in 1965.[4] Whereas then in Britain there has been relatively little change in these sector shares of total persons employed since the 1920s, in the US there has been a strong secular tendency for the percentage of manpower accounted for by the service sector to rise.

The second clear set of changes are those that have taken place within the goods sector. These are summarized in Table 1.2. There is

TABLE 1.2. *Distribution of Output and Manpower, the Goods Sector, UK 1924–64*

| | (percentages) | | | |
| | *1958 S.I.C.* | | | |
	1924	1937	1951	1964
Net output at constant prices				
Primary	12·0	9·6	8·3	7·0
Agriculture	4·4	4·0	4·3	4·3
Mining	7·6	5·6	4·2	2·7
Secondary	30·9	37·2	41·4	44·7
Manufacturing	24·5	28·5	33·9	35·7
Manpower				
Primary	14·3	9·6	8·9	6·3
Agriculture	7·8	5·7	5·2	3·7
Mining	6·6	3·9	3·6	2·6
Secondary	37·7	38·2	43·1	44·1
Manufacturing	31·2	30·5	34·8	35·0

Source: See footnote to Table 1.1.

a clear distinction between the declining primary sector and the expanding secondary one. The former shows a general long-term decline in terms of both manpower and output. The decline in the share of manpower has been persistent for both agriculture and mining. But in terms of output the fall in the relative importance of

[4] See Victor R. Fuchs, *The Service Economy* (National Bureau of Economic Research, New York, 1968), Chapter 2.

the primary sector has been due almost entirely to the decline in mining.[5]

Within the secondary sector the important feature has been the growing importance of manufacturing. Since 1937 it has employed more of the nation's labour resources and its share of output has increased in all the periods shown in Table 1.2. Again it is interesting to compare the manpower position with that in the United States. There, the share of labour in manufacturing was 22·8 per cent in 1929, 26·7 per cent in 1947 and 25·9 per cent in 1965. As compared to Britain, two things stand out. First the much lower share of manpower in manufacturing, and secondly, the fall in the share of the manufacturing sector in the post-war period.

There has of course been a great diversity of experience within the manufacturing sector which is only very partially disclosed by the figures for the industrial groups shown in Table 1.3. The industries

TABLE 1.3. *Distribution of Manufacturing Manpower by Industry Group, UK 1924–64*

Industry group	(percentages) 1958 S.I.C.			
	1924	1937	1948	1964
Textiles	22·6	17·8	13·0	9·5
Mechanical engineering and shipbuilding	13·6	13·4	18·0	18·0
Clothing	12·2	10·8	7·7	6·7
Food, drink, tobacco	9·6	10·1	8·7	9·5
Paper, printing, publishing	6·7	7·3	6·0	7·0
Other metal industries	6·3	6·9	8·1	7·8
Iron and steel	6·2	6·0	5·6	5·1
Vehicles	4·8	6·2	8·8	9·9
Timber, furniture	4·5	4·8	3·9	3·4
Bricks, pottery, glass, cement	4·0	4·6	4·1	3·9
Leather, rubber, etc.	3·9	3·9	4·1	4·2
Chemicals	3·7	3·8	5·4	5·8
Electrical engineering	2·9	4·9	6·6	9·2

Source: See footnote to Table 1.1.

are arranged in descending order of their share of manpower in 1924. The main features have been the marked decline of textiles and

[5] The primary sector's share of the capital stock in the post-war years, however, has been largely maintained because of the increased mechanization in both agriculture and mining.

clothing and the increased importance of electrical engineering, chemicals and vehicles as employers of labour. These expanding groups have been characterized by continuous technical advance, and the difference between them and other groups such as clothing, furniture, and shipbuilding has justified the broad distinction between 'science-based' and 'craft' or 'traditional' industries. The technical developments characteristic of the new growth industries have been of increasing importance in determining the pattern of structural change.

Although evidence such as that contained in Table 1.3 reveals substantial changes in the relative importance of different groups of industries, it also conceals much of the change that has taken place. In the first place a great diversity of experience is found *within* the industry groups which are identified in the table. Thus in the case of textiles, for instance, employment in the older industries such as cotton, jute and lace has shown a marked decline, whereas in the production of man-made fibres and knitted goods it has increased. Again, in the case of vehicles, motor-vehicle manufacturing has been a rapidly expanding industry while locomotives and railway carriages, etc. have declined in importance.

Secondly, the growing importance of technical improvements referred to above suggests another 'hidden component' of structural change. Over time, the nature of an industry's products may undergo radical alterations, and indeed completely new products may be produced to add to or supersede the old. Thus motor cars are very different products from what they were forty years ago, and the expansion of the chemical and electrical engineering industries has been characterized by a stream of new products.

Thirdly, the table does not show the interdependence that exists between industries and thus how the rapid growth of one industry can have effects on structure which are much wider than its own increasing share of total industrial output. The growth of the motor-vehicle industry for example has been of major importance to producers in several other industries, and Table 1.4 gives some idea of the quantitative importance of their interdependence. Columns (1) and (2) show the direct inputs of the motor industry from other manufacturing industries. Thus in the case of iron and steel the estimated direct input in 1963 was £204 million, or £128 per £1,000 of gross output of the motor industry. Column (3) expresses these direct inputs as a percentage of the total output of the supplying industries. Thus the motor industry's direct input of iron and steel accounted for 15 per cent of total iron and steel output. Columns (4) and (5) show the total inputs, direct and indirect. Again taking iron and steel as an example, the figures include not only iron and

TABLE 1.4. *Direct and Indirect Inputs of the Motor-Vehicle Industry, 1963*

Industry group	Direct inputs			Direct + Indirect inputs		
	Total £m (1)	Per £'000 gross output £ (2)	% of total output of suppliers % (3)	Total £m (4)	Per £'000 gross output £ (5)	% of total output of suppliers % (6)
Food, drink, tobacco	—	—	—	—	—	—
Oil refining, chemicals and allied trades	26	16	1	98	62	4
Iron and steel	204	128	15	260	164	20
Non-ferrous metals	48	30	8	86	54	15
Non-electrical engineering	76	48	3	109	69	4
Scientific instruments and electrical goods	79	50	4	100	63	5
Metal goods	158	100	13	182	115	15
Textiles, leather, clothing	22	14	1	43	27	2
Pottery and glass	12	8	5	14	9	6
Furniture, timber	27	17	4	33	21	5
Paper and paper products	11	7	1	40	25	3
Rubber	58	36	17	63	40	18
Other manufacturing	20	13	1	46	29	3

Source: Central Statistical Office, 'Input–output tables for the United Kingdom 1963', *Studies in Official Statistics* No. 16, Tables D and E, HMSO, 1970. The input-output data are based on information obtained by the Census of Production, 1963. Although taken in 1963 the full results of this Census did not become available until 1970. The last Census of Production was taken in 1968 and it is to be hoped that this time the time-lag before publication will be substantially reduced.

steel sold directly to motor manufacturers but also the iron and steel which is sold to engineering and metal goods industries and so on, which is used to make other inputs of the motor industry.[6] Column (6) which expresses these total inputs as a percentage of the total output of the supplying industries shows, as one would expect, that the industry groups most dependent on the motor industry are iron and steel with 20 per cent of its output going into motor vehicles, rubber with 18 per cent, and non-ferrous metals and metal goods both with 15 per cent.

Table 1.4 gives of course a static picture of interdependence, but similar tables for different points in time with the data expressed at constant prices can reveal changes in structural interdependence. Thus for each unit of vehicle output there was a fall between 1954 and 1963 in the inputs from the textiles, leather, clothing and timber groups and an increase in the inputs of plastics.[7]

2. *Growth Rates of Input and Output*

Another way of looking at changes in industrial structure is by examining the rates of growth in different sectors. Table 1.5 summarizes the position for broad sectors of the economy for the periods 1924–37 and 1951–64. The first three columns of the table will be familiar but the last one requires a word of explanation. The figures in this column measure the productivity of labour and capital combined. In measuring the productivity performances of a sector it is a useful supplement to the more familiar concept of labour productivity because it makes an allowance for the increased input of capital over a period.

For the whole economy the position is easily summarized. The rate of increase in gross domestic product was rather higher in the post-war period than in the inter-war one, 2·7 per cent per annum as compared to 2·3 per cent per annum. This increased rate of growth of output was attributable to a marked improvement in the productivity performance of the economy which more than offset the fall in the rate of growth of employment. The better productivity performance was reflected both in terms of labour productivity and after an allowance had been made for the input of capital.

The most interesting result shown in the table, however, relates to the sectoral contribution to this overall improvement in productivity performance. Apparently, all the improvement in the rate of growth

---

[6] See the source referred to at the foot of Table 1.4, for an explanation of how the figures in the table are compiled and the assumptions underlying the compilation.

[7] See A. G. Armstrong, 'The motor industry and the economy', *District Bank Review*, September 1967.

TABLE 1.5. *Annual Growth Rates of Output and Input by Sector*

Sector	Output		Employment		Labour productivity		Output per unit of total factor input	
	1924–37	1951–64	1924–37	1951–64	1924–37	1951–64	1924–37	1951–64
GDP	2·3	2·7	1·2	0·6	1·1	2·1	0·9	1·5
Industrial production	3·2	3·1	0·9	0·6	2·3	2·5	2·2	1·7
Manufacturing	3·3	3·2	1·1	0·6	2·2	2·6	2·4	1·8
Services and distribution	1·7	2·4	2·2	1·0	−0·5	1·4	−0·4	0·7

Source: See footnote to Table 1.1.

of output per unit of total factor input and almost all the improvement in the rate of growth of labour productivity, was attributable to the services and distribution sector. Whereas, for instance, the rate of growth in labour productivity in industrial production was only 0·2 percentage points higher in the post-war period as compared to the inter-war period, in the services and distribution sector it was 1·9 percentage points higher. In the inter-war period employment in services increased at a faster rate than output, and productivity, therefore, declined. In the post-war period there was a substantial increase in the rate of growth of output and a substantial decline in the intake of labour, which resulted in the negative gain in labour productivity of −0·5 per cent per annum in the inter-war period being converted into a positive gain of 1·4 per cent per annum in the post-war period. A similar result is found in terms of total productivity movements although it is less marked as a result of the much higher rate of increase in the input of capital in the services sector in the post-war period.

The evidence given in Table 1.5 is consistent with the view that a high level of demand has a favourable effect on productivity growth. A higher rate of overall productivity growth can be the result of an increase in growth rates in individual sectors or of the growing relative importance of the high productivity sectors. Both these factors have contributed to the improved performance of the post-war over the inter-war years. There has been a movement of labour from low-wage sectors of the economy to the high-productivity ones particularly the secondary industries, and there has been a more rapid rate of growth of productivity in the low-wage sectors themselves. The overall pressure of demand in the labour market in the post-war period is likely to have been an important cause of such changes, leading both to a movement out of low-paid jobs, including self-employment in services, and also to a greater inducement in all industries to introduce more labour-saving methods of supply.

There is the further question of whether the gain in productivity in services has been a once-and-for-all effect, or whether the change in the condition of the labour market in the post-war years led to continued advance. A study of the performance of the service sector in the United Kingdom within the post-war period found that the average annual productivity gain was much higher in the period 1956–63 than in the period 1948–56.[8] A better productivity performance after the mid-1950s seems in fact to be a feature of several broad sectors of the economy and applied, for instance, to manufacturing as well as to services. The movements in output and employ-

[8] B. M. Deakin and K. D. George, 'Productivity trends in the service industries, 1948–63; *London and Cambridge Economic Bulletin*, No. 53, March 1965.

ment underlying the improved productivity performance were, however, not the same in all sectors. In manufacturing the faster rate of increase in productivity over the period 1956–63 as compared to 1948–56 was largely the result of a marked reduction in the rate of increase of labour input. In several service industries, on the other hand, the rate of increase in employment was greater in the latter period but productivity increase was greater because of an even greater improvement in the rate of increase of output.

The differences between sectors in the rate at which they were increasing employment is worth looking at a little more closely because they became a matter of concern in 1966 and were a major factor underlying the introduction of the Selective Employment Tax. Table 1.6 shows the changes in employment by broad sector over the seven years leading up to the introduction of the tax. It is clear that the main part of the increase in employment went into services and construction. This fact was noted by the White Paper on the

TABLE 1.6. *Change in the Number of Employees in Employment, by Sectors: UK 1959–66*

Sector	Index 1966 (1959 = 100)	Change 1959–66 (thousands)	Total, at June 1966 (thousands)
Agriculture etc., mining and quarrying	70·8	−436	1,058
Manufacturing	106·3	+536	9,055
Construction	121·4	+304	1,725
Gas, electricity, water	112·8	+49	431
Transport and communication	96·7	−55	1,629
Distributive trades	109·7	+269	3,035
Financial, professional and scientific services	128·6	+717	3,222
Government services	107·3	+94	1,383
Other services	112·2	+244	2,246
Total employees in employment	108·1	+1,778	23,784

Source: Annual Abstract of Statistics.

Selective Employment Tax which described the tax as a 'scheme . . . deliberately to assist manufacturing'.[9]

The economic arguments for such discrimination in favour of

[9] *Selective Employment Tax*, Cmnd. 2986.

manufacturing were advanced by Kaldor.[10] His main propositions were first, that the growth of industrial economies is closely related to the growth of manufacturing output; second, that in manufacturing the growth of labour productivity is closely related to the growth of employment; third, that the increase in employment in manufacturing is secured by a transfer of labour from the agricultural and tertiary sectors, and that this transfer of labour would have no adverse effect on the growth of output in the sectors from which the labour was transferred. Given the small size, in terms of manpower, of the UK agricultural sector any marked transfer of employment into manufacturing would clearly have to come mainly from the service industries.

One should hasten to add perhaps that there is nothing 'wrong' about the growth of employment in services, which indeed may be expected as real income per head increases. This is not to say, however, that the increase in the output of the service sector could not, in the years before S.E.T., have been accomplished without a smaller input of labour had there been a greater incentive to adopt more labour saving methods.

The Selective Employment Tax was, then, a fiscal measure aimed at increasing the availability of labour to manufacturing industries so as to enable them to expand more easily and thereby to achieve a faster growth of productivity as a result of increasing returns to scale.[11] Unfortunately, shortly after the tax was introduced the economy moved into the deepest and most prolonged recession of the post-war years. From June 1966 to June 1972 the total number of employees in employment in the UK declined from 23·78 to 22·34 million. The fall was particularly marked in manufacturing, construction and distribution. The only broad sectors to show an increase in employment were government, and financial professional and scientific services. By 1972 the unemployment level had increased to nearly 4 per cent as compared to 1·4 per cent in 1966. Over the period from 1967 to 1972 a general labour shortage had ceased to be a major problem in manufacturing industries.

B. FURTHER EXAMINATION OF STRUCTURAL CHANGE

So far we have looked at changes which have occurred in broad sectors of the economy. We now turn to a more detailed analysis on the basis of a finer industry breakdown. We are concerned in

[10] N. Kaldor, *Causes of the Slow Rate of Economic Growth of the United Kingdom* (Cambridge University Press, 1966).
[11] The effects of the Selective Employment Tax on efficiency and structural change in one sector—the distributive trades—will be examined in Chapter 9.

particular with the relationship between changes in output and output per head. There is, of course, a well-known positive association between the two variables: that is, a tendency for industries with above-average increases in output also to have above-average increases in output per head. What is the explanation of this relationship, or Verdoorn's Law as it is commonly known? Does it apply only to the secondary sector of the economy or is it of wider application? Again, does any evidence of a strong positive correlation between the growth of output and productivity emerge when making comparisons between the performance of manufacturing sectors in different countries? It is to these questions that we now turn.

1. Changes in Output, Employment and Output Per Head—UK Industry

Table 1.7 shows for 28 selected industries the changes in output, employment and output per head for the periods 1924–35 and 1954–63. For both periods the industries are arranged in descending order of their increase in output. It is clear that industries with an above-average increase in output also tend to have an above-average increase in employment. For 1924–35 the correlation coefficient, which is a statistical measure of the strength of the relationship between the two variables, is +0·67 and for 1954–63 it is +0·75. There are some cases, for instance fertilizers in the post-war period, where the gain in productivity has been so great that a rapid expansion of output has required a less-than-average increase in employment. But this sort of situation has been the exception rather than the rule.

The high correlation between movements in output and employment is due to the high correlation that also exists between movements in output and output per head. A glance at the table shows that for both periods there is a general tendency for industries with above-average increases in output to have above-average increases in output per head, and vice versa at the other end of the scale. The correlation coefficient is +0·67 for the inter-war period and +0·69 for the period 1954–63. The square of these coefficients tells us that 45 per cent and 48 per cent respectively of the variation in one of the variables can be explained statistically by variations in the other.

Clearly the observed relationship is only a general tendency. For both periods rather less than half the variation in output per head changes can be 'explained' in terms of the variation in output changes, so that there are plenty of exceptions to the general association which exists between the two variables. Two further points of interest may be made.

First, the correlation is usually better for longer time periods than for shorter ones. For instance, for the period 1924–50 the correlation

TABLE 1.7. *Changes in Output, Employment and Output per head, 1924–35 and 1954–63, for selected United Kingdom Industries*

1924–35 (Index numbers 1924 = 100)

Industry	Gross output	Total employment	Output/head
Electricity	370	204	181
Rubber	263	117	225
Cutlery	238	109	212
Steel tubes	179	111	161
Cement	175	102	172
Paper and board	170	117	145
Chemicals	168	118	146
Bricks and fireclay	168	134	125
Glass	161	125	129
Cocoa and confectionery	147	95	154
Hosiery and knitted goods	143	121	118
Wallpaper[1]	143	134	107
Linoleum	139	101	138
Wire and wire working	133	94	140
Paint and varnish	131	134	98
Brushes and brooms	127	108	117
Boots and shoes	122	89	137
Spirit distilling[1]	118	66	177
Leather	114	100	115
Iron and steel	108	86	125
Coke-ovens	106	76	140
Matches[1]	106	77	138
Jute	98	69	140
Cotton	91	72	126
Blast furnaces[1]	87	59	148
Tinplate[1]	83	79	105
Coal-mining	83	64	130
Brewing	81	85	97
Median	**132**	**101**	**138**

1954–63 (Index numbers 1954 = 100)

Industry	Gross output	Total employment	Output/head
Electricity	210	118	178
Chemicals	187	117	160
Toilet preparations[2]	155	146	106
Fertilizers, etc.[2]	154	101	154
Misc. paper manufactures[2]	147	109	135
Glass	139	111	132
Paper and board	139	111	116
Hosiery and knitted goods	136	121	116
Linoleum, etc.	136	99	138
Wire and wire working	133	121	113
Rubber	127	112	118
Non-ferrous metal[2]	126	109	116
Steel tubes	126	103	123
Brewing and malting	123	119	105
Paint and printing ink	123	111	111
Cement	123	94	130
Footwear	117	112	105
Iron and steel	113	85	134
Bricks, fireclay, etc.	110	104	106
Dyestuffs[2]	106	85	125
Cutlery	106	84	126
Jute	104	95	109
Cocoa and confectionery	101	90	113
Brushes and brooms	98	94	104
Coal-mining	93	79	118
Coke-ovens	87	77	112
Leather	86	91	96
Cotton spinning	86	72	120
Jute	69	55	126
Median	**123**	**102**	**118**

Source: W. E. G. Salter, *Productivity and Technical Change* (Cambridge University Press, 1966), 2nd edn., Appendix A(4) and Table 33.

[1] Not included as separate industries in the period 1954–63.   [2] Not included as separate industries in the period 1924–35.

coefficient for the same industries as those shown for the inter-war period in Table 1.5 is +0·81. The reason for this is that the shorter the time period which is considered, the more likely it is that the forces which lie behind the association will be outweighed by special short-term factors.

Secondly, the correlation is better at the top end of the scale, i.e. for the fast-growing industries, than at the bottom end. In the inter-war period, with only one exception (chemicals) the seven industries at the top of the ranking order in terms of increases in output are also in the top seven for output per head, and in the post-war period five of the seven industries which showed the biggest gains in output are in the top seven for productivity gain. Amongst the slow growers, however, there are far more exceptions. For both periods only two of the seven which have the lowest gains in output fall in the bottom seven for productivity gain, and in both periods some of the industries at the bottom of the table have an exceptionally good productivity performance. In the inter-war years 'blast furnaces' and 'jute' which are ranked twenty-fifth and twenty-third respectively in terms of the output index are ranked seventh and ninth respectively in terms of productivity gain, and in the post-war period cotton spinning has the lowest output index but the tenth largest gain in productivity. Firms in industries which are facing conditions of adversity seem to be forced to adopt measures to increase efficiency, and over the sort of time periods considered in Table 1.7 such measures seem quite frequently to result in larger productivity gains than those observed for industries with medium rates of growth. In addition there are often special factors which help to explain the good productivity performance of declining industries, particularly government-sponsored rationalization schemes such as the one introduced for cotton spinning in 1958. These striking performances by declining industries however would be more difficult to sustain over longer periods, and it is interesting to observe that over the period 1924–50, although the correlation is again somewhat weaker at the bottom end of the scale than at the top, the difference is not so marked, and the good productivity performances amongst the slow-growing industries are not so striking. The best example is 'tinplate' which is ranked twenty-fourth on the output index and sixteenth on the output per head index, followed by 'jute' which is ranked twenty-eighth and twentieth respectively. The longer the period of time the more likely it is that all the growing industries will show greater productivity gains than the stagnating or declining ones because, for instance, of the greater opportunities for profitable investment and of benefiting from economies of scale.

There is abundant evidence, then, of a positive association between changes in output and output per head in the industrial sector of the economy. There is also growing evidence which suggests that the relationship is found elsewhere. In the retail trades, for instance, a high correlation has been observed between movements in the volume of sales and the volume of sales per person engaged for twenty different kinds of business over the period 1957–66.[12] Again there is evidence of a positive correlation between changes in output and changes in productivity in the transport sector.[13]

The positive correlation between changes in output and productivity is not, then, peculiarly associated with the secondary sector of the economy but appears to be of quite general applicability. The direction of causation can of course run either way. On the one hand, above-average increases in output may be the cause of above-average increases in productivity. In this case the gain in output is the autonomous factor and it causes gains in productivity by allowing an industry to take fuller advantage of economies of scale. On the other hand, the alternative explanation takes productivity as the autonomous factor and argues that industries which are experiencing rapid improvements in technology show continually falling costs relative to other industries, which makes possible falling relative prices and rapidly expanding output. It is unlikely that either of these explanations can be selected as the causal process with any consistency, but whichever variable occurs first, once the process of interaction gets under way changes in one variable will facilitate changes in the other. Of course, conditions are especially favourable to exceptional gains in both output and productivity for those products where, because of, for instance, rising incomes, there is a big increase in demand, and where there are also many opportunities for technological improvements.

2. International Comparisons of Changes in Output and Productivity

The positive relationship between output and productivity changes in the manufacturing sector is also observable when making inter-country comparisons of performance. Thus for twelve countries over the period from the early 1950s to the mid-1960s the square of the correlation coefficient between changes in output and changes in output per head is $+0\cdot89$. The three countries with the fastest rate of growth of manufacturing output (Japan, West Germany and Italy) also had the fastest rate of growth of labour productivity, and two countries which were at the bottom of the list for output growth

[12] K. D. George and T. Ward, 'Productivity Growth in the Retail Trade', *Bulletin of the Oxford Institute of Economics and Statistics*, February 1973.
[13] B. M. Deakin and T. Seward, *Productivity in Transport* (Cambridge University Press, 1969).

(USA and UK) were also at the bottom in terms of productivity growth. Over this period the faster growing countries also had the fastest growth of manufacturing employment. During the second half of the 1960s this ceases to be so. There continues to be a positive correlation between changes in output and productivity but there is no longer a positive correlation between changes in output and changes in employment. The countries with the fastest growth of manufacturing output and productivity had, in general, no faster a growth of manufacturing employment than slow growing countries.[14]

TABLE 1.8. *International Comparison of Growth and Investment in Manufacturing, 1960–70*

	Growth of output (% p.a.)	Gross investment–output ratios
Japan	12·5	30·5
Netherlands	6·4	18·8
France	6·3	17·4
West Germany	5·8	15·9
Belgium	5·4	18·7
UK	3·1	13·0

Source: OECD, *National Accounts of OECD Countries.*

At the international level, the positive association between changes in output and changes in productivity may again reflect the process of 'cumulative causation', with fast growth leading to high productivity gains, due in part to a high rate of investment, which in turn means faster structural change and greater competitiveness, which sustains the high growth rate. Table 1.8 shows that as compared to some of our main competitors the UK has had, during the 1960s, both a slower rate of growth of manufacturing output and a lower ratio of gross investment to output in the manufacturing sector.

As well as the indirect effect which it has on efficiency, gross investment is also an extremely important component of demand for a number of industry groups, as is shown by the industrial input–output table in the 1971 National Income and Expenditure Blue Book. It is particularly important, of course, for mechanical and electrical engineering and vehicles. For mechanical engineering gross domestic investment accounted in 1968 for 54 per cent of the demand of final

[14] For further details see T._F. Cripps and R. J. Tarling, *Growth in Advanced Capitalist Economies 1950–70* (Cambridge University Press, 1973).

buyers and 41 per cent of total output including intermediate output. A period of low investment can clearly have a very damaging effect on the efficiency of a sector of this kind, since it means a low demand for the output of the sector, falling profitability, and thus a weakening of the process of structural change whereby old plants are replaced by new. There is nothing to impede the closure of *old* plants but low profitability means that there is little inducement to invest in new capacity. The long-term competitiveness of the industry therefore weakens. It is interesting to observe that in a recent study of the consequences of entry into the EEC for different British industries, mechanical engineering is one of the sectors which, it is thought, will be most adversely affected.[15] While the revival of demand and the consequential increase in output will have some effect in inducing greater investment it is doubtful whether this mechanism alone will be sufficient. When an industry has shown low output and productivity gains for a considerable period of time and has become uncompetitive in world markets, private finance may be difficult to attract. In industries such as machine tools there is a strong case, therefore, both from the point of view of growth and of efficiency, for major government participation in the finance of investment.[16]

The relatively weak productivity performance of UK manufacturing has not, of course, been uniform in extent across all industries. The picture in a little more detail is given in Table 1.9 which shows comparative output and productivity growth rates for UK and West German industry groups for the period 1953–69. For all fifteen industry groups the output growth rate is substantially lower in the UK. In broad terms, however, the pattern of structural change has been similar in both countries. The industry groups are arranged in descending order of their output growth rate in the UK and it can be seen that the ranking is similar for West Germany, the Spearman coefficient of rank correlation being 0·88. The major difference, at least at this level of aggregation, is not in the pattern of change but in the rate of growth, the average growth rate for manufacturing being twice as high in West Germany as in the UK. Of course, the table shows industry groups and there is a great deal of scope within each group for differences in the pattern of structural change and in the degree of specialization. Two other points of interest arise from the table.

First, the biggest proportionate differences in productivity growth

[15] S. S. Han and H. H. Liesner, *Britain and the Common Market: The Effect of Entry on the Pattern of Manufacturing Production* (Cambridge University Press, 1971).

[16] The Industry Act 1972, with its provisions for selective financial assistance for industry is a step in this direction.

are, in general, found in those industries with relatively poor output
growth rates in both countries, and where in proportionate terms
the differences between the output–growth performance are greatest.
Thus taking the bottom six industry groups, in four cases the productivity gain in West Germany is at least twice as high as that in
the UK and only in one case (footwear, wearing apparel) does the
UK performance come near to the German one. If we compare the
productivity performance of the top six industry groups, on the other

TABLE 1.9. *Growth Rates of Output and Labour Productivity by Industry
Groups, UK and West Germany, 1953–69 (% p.a. compound)*

Industry group	Output		Labour productivity	
	UK	WG	UK	WG
Electrical machinery	5·90	10·39	3·42	3·64
Chemicals	5·84	10·33	5·11	6·94
Printing and publishing	4·54	6·57	3·03	3·11
Paper and paper products	4·33	6·65	2·67	4·77
Rubber products	4·10	7·30	2·61	3·10
Beverages	4·04	6·01	3·99	3·74
Non-electrical machinery	3·27	5·92	1·52	2·01
Other non-metallic mineral products	3·21	5·68	3·14	4·99
Transport equipment	2·87	8·00	2·60	3·16
Food products (exc. beverages)	2·25	5·03	1·63	2·83
Basic metal industries	1·98	5·79	1·93	4·38
Footwear, wearing apparel	1·42	5·25	2·46	2·99
Tobacco	1·39	5·19	1·55	10·22
Textiles	−0·17	4·63	1·86	5·64
Leather and fur products	−1·31	2·39	0·15	3·64
Average for manufacturing	3·41	7·13	2·97	4·63

Source: United Nations, *The Growth of World Industry.*

hand, the general impression is one of greater similarity between
the figures, with four out of the top six industry groups showing a
similar productivity gain. Thus although our fastest growing industry
groups grew significantly less fast than their counterparts in West
Germany the rate of growth was nevertheless high enough to maintain a high productivity performance.

Second, and as a reflection of the differences just mentioned,
the correlation between the growth of output and output per head
is much stronger in the UK than in West Germany, the square of

the correlation coefficient being +0·67 in the former and virtually zero in the latter. In West Germany the relatively slow growing industrial sectors have, by comparison with the UK, achieved a high absolute rate of growth. This seems to have enabled the industries concerned to produce a productivity performance similar to the faster growing industrial sectors. What this suggests is that there is a threshold effect in the relationship between output and productivity growth with productivity growth responding to faster growth rates at the lower end of the growth scale but with little extra benefit when growth rates exceed some critical level.

Finally, it is important to note that the interaction between growth, investment and productivity performance involves the growth of demand in world markets not just domestic ones. During the 1950s and most of the 1960s the export performance of the UK was hampered by a pegged exchange rate which, as our productivity fell increasingly behind that of our main industrial competitors, meant that the margin of profit on exports was being increasingly squeezed. Throughout the 1950s and 1960s the countries with the biggest increase in exports also in general had the biggest increases in productivity which, given the fixed exchange rates that existed over most of the period, meant that they were more successful in maintaining the profitability of their exporting industries. And higher profitability means greater ability to compete effectively in the widest sense especially in terms of the number and quality of sales outlets.

There is little doubt that the competitive position of UK industry has been badly eroded over the post-war years. Over the period 1968–72 productivity increased very markedly by means of plant closures and increased internal efficiency, but unless growth is sufficiently high to induce a higher level of gross investment there is a danger that the UK will end up with more efficient but smaller industries and still lower level of activity in the private manufacturing sector relative to that of our main competitors. If our performance in terms of growth continues to be unfavourable relative to other EEC countries, then within the enlarged EEC the position will be aggravated by the fact that private investment will tend to gravitate more strongly towards the faster growing areas.

C. THE SIZE OF PLANTS AND FIRMS

Another important aspect of structural change since the inter-war years has been the greater concentration of production in large plants and firms. This has been encouraged by the increased size of markets, new developments in transport and by technological and organizational changes which have generally tended to favour the large unit. ⊐

Table 1.10 shows the distribution of employment by size of plant for UK manufacturing industry in 1935, 1951 and 1963. The general pattern is clear. From 1935 to 1963 there has been a steady decline in the percentage employed in smaller plants and a steady increase in the percentage employed in larger ones. Thus in 1935, 51·8 per cent

TABLE 1.10. *Distribution of Employment by Size of Plant British Manufacturing Industry, 1935, 1951 and 1963*

Number employed in plant	Percentage of total employment[1] 1935	1951	1963
11–49	13·9	11·5	9·0
50–99	11·7	10·4	8·3
100–299	26·2	22·2	20·3
300–499	12·8	11·6	11·4
500–999	13·9	13·6	14·6
1,000–1,499	6·3	7·2	8·2
1,500 and over	15·2	23·6	28·2

Sources: Alan Armstrong and Aubrey Silberston, 'Size of Plant, Size of Enterprise and Concentration in British Manufacturing Industry, 1935–58', *Journal of the Royal Statistical Society*, Series A, Vol. 128, Part 3, 1965.

Board of Trade, *Report on the Census of Production*, Part 131, Table 4, 1963.

[1] Excluding plants employing ten or less.

of employment was in plants employing less than 300. In 1963 the percentage of total employment accounted for by these plants had fallen to 37·6 per cent. Plants employing 1,500 or more, however, accounted for 15·2 per cent of manufacturing employment in 1935, and this percentage had risen to 28·2 per cent by 1963.

The same general movement towards the greater importance of larger plants is found in most of the individual industry groups. Some of the information is summarized in Table 1.11. From 1951 to 1963 there were only two industry groups—footwear and rubber—where there was a decline in employment in the largest plants, and in both cases the percentage employment in the largest plants in 1951 was also less than it was in 1935. Over the whole period 1935–63, clothing was the only other group with less employment in the largest plants at the end of the period. For nine out of the fourteen industry groups for which information is available employment in the largest plants was greater in 1963 than in 1935, the movement towards these plants being most marked in chemicals, metal industries, bricks, etc., and paper manufacturing.

TABLE 1.11. *Percentage Employed in Largest Plants, by Industry Group, British Manufacturing Industry, 1935, 1951 and 1963*

Industry group	Size of largest plants	Employment in largest plants as percentage of total employment[1]		
		1935	1951	1963
Food, drink, tobacco	1,500+	18	14	22
Chemicals	1,500+	18	25	30
Metal industries	1,500+	13	23	30
Engineering	1,500+	22	23	25
Shipbuilding	2,000+	n.a.	44	45
Electrical goods	1,500+	n.a.	47	51
Vehicles	1,500+	52	56	67
Aircraft	1,500+	52	67	77
Textiles	750+	19	16	19
Clothing	500+	19	16	18
Footwear	1,000+	15	11	8
Bricks, etc.	1,000+	10	18	22
Timber	400+	10	12	14
Paper manufacturing	500+	28	40	43
Printing and publishing	500+	33	33	33
Rubber	1,500+	44	41	38
All manufacturing industry	1,500+	15	24	28

Sources: Alan Armstrong and Aubrey Silberston, op. cit.; Board of Trade *Report on the Census of Production*, 1963.

[1] Excluding plants employing ten or less.   n.a. = not available.

In terms of employment, therefore, there has been a clear tendency towards the greater importance of large plants in most industries. A similar result would also be found on the basis of output data. Thus between 1935 and 1958 for instance 'the movement towards larger plants was very similar in terms of both output and employment'.[17]

The increased importance of large plants has been accompanied by the increased importance of large enterprises. In 1935 enterprises

[17] Alan Armstrong and Aubrey Silberston, op. cit., p. 400.

employing 10,000 or more accounted for 14 per cent of manufacturing employment. By 1958 the proportion had increased to 25 per
cent and in 1963 it was 32 per cent. A similar picture is shown in
terms of net output. The proportion of net output accounted for by
the same size-class of enterprise in 1935, 1958 and 1963, was 15 per
cent, 28 per cent and 36 per cent respectively. Over the same period
there was a marked decline in the importance of small enterprises—
those employing fewer than 1,000. Their share of employment fell
from 59 per cent in 1935 to 37 per cent in 1963, and of net output
from 56 per cent to 32 per cent.

If we look at the hundred largest manufacturing firms over the
post-war period we find that their share of manufacturing net output
increased from approximately 20 per cent in 1948 to 38 per cent in
1963. By the end of the 1960s the figure was almost certainly around
45 to 50 per cent, so that over the period 1948–70 the share of the
100 largest companies in manufacturing net output has almost certainly more than doubled.

This finding of a large increase in the degree of dominance of the
largest companies based on Census of Production data is also
revealed by data on the balance sheet value of net assets of the 100
largest industrial companies whose ordinary or preference shares
were quoted on UK stock exchanges. As well as manufacturing,
companies in construction, transport and communication, distributive trades and miscellaneous services are included. The details are
shown in Table 1.12. In 1948 the share of the 100 largest companies
was 46·5 per cent, in 1968 it was 63·7 per cent. The 1968 share of
the 10 largest and 50 largest companies also showed a big increase
over the 1948 figure.[18] To say the least, there has been a striking
increase in the degree of dominance of the largest companies.[19]

· But the rate at which the dominance of the largest companies has
increased is even greater than a comparison of the years 1948 and
1968 suggests, because as Table 1.12 shows quite clearly, most of the
increase took place after 1957. Thus in the case of the 100 largest
companies, for instance, their share of total net assets showed a
relatively small increase between 1948 and 1957, from 46·5 per cent
to 50·7 per cent, but a marked increase between 1957 and 1968,
from 50·7 per cent to over 60 per cent.

The distribution of the top 100 companies by industry group has

[18] The inclusion of the non-manufacturing sectors has the effect of reducing the
level of aggregate concentration in all years. For manufacturing alone the share
of the top 100 companies in 1968 was over 70 per cent.

[19] A more detailed analysis of the top 100 companies over this period has been
undertaken by G. Whittington. See his article in the November 1972 issue of
the *Journal of Industrial Economics*.

not of course remained constant. The biggest changes over the period were the decline in numbers in the 'Drink' 'Textiles' and 'Metal manufacture' industry groups, the first two reflecting mergers and the last the nationalization of the steel companies. The industry group which showed the biggest increase in the representation of its companies among the top 100 was 'Bricks, pottery, etc.' followed by 'Electrical engineering' and 'Transport and communication'.

TABLE 1.12. *Aggregate Concentration and Net Assets in the Industrial Sector, UK 1948, 1957 and 1968*[2]

Group of companies	Total net assets					
	£m			as % of all quoted companies		
	1948	1957	1968	1948	1957	1968
10 largest	765	2,017	4,992	16·5	18·7	23·7[1]
50 largest	1,626	4,314	10,694	35·0	39·9	50·8[1]
100 largest	2,157	5,473	13,409	46·5	50·7	63·7[1]
All quoted companies	4,641	10,805	16,057	100·0	100·0	100·0

Sources: The 1948 figures are from *Company Income and Finance, 1949–53* (The National Institute of Economic Research, London, 1956), Appendix C; those for 1957 from *Company Assets and Income in 1957* (HMSO, London, 1960); and those for 1968 were compiled by the Statistics Division of the Department of Trade and Industry.

[1] Slightly exaggerated because of the exclusion in 1968 of small quoted companies from the population. The removal of small companies by the Board of Trade in 1960 resulted in a reduction in total net assets of 2 per cent.
[2] Excluding: companies whose trading activities were primarily outside the UK, consolidated subsidiaries of companies which are already included in the list, and companies engaged primarily in insurance, banking, finance, investment, property and shipping.

Table 1.13 summarizes the situation with regard to the turnover of the 100 large companies. Of the top 100 companies in 1948, 52 survived in the same group in 1968, but 48 had disappeared. Of the top 50 in 1948, 25 survived in that group in 1968 and of the top 10, 6 were still in the top 10 in 1968. These were Unilever, ICI, Imperial Tobacco, Courtaulds, Distillers, and Guest Keen and Nettlefords. Vickers, Dunlop, J. & P. Coats and Odeon Theatres were replaced by GEC, British Leyland, Bass Charington and Allied Breweries.

The high rate of turnover might be taken as a sign of intense competitiveness among leading companies, but before jumping to this conclusion we have to examine the way in which the companies disappeared. The argument that a high rate of turnover is a reflection of a high degree of competitiveness would be strongest if it were found that the majority of disappearances from the top 100 was due to lower ranking brought about by the entry of new firms which had overtaken some of the previous leaders. However, Table 1.13

TABLE 1.13. *Turnover of the Largest 1948 Companies*

	1948 top 50	1948 top 100
Number surviving in group in 1968	25	52
Number of exits	25	48
Due to: lower ranking	7	12
death by take-over or merger	12	27
death by nationalization	6	9

shows that this has not been the case. Looking at the 1948 top 100 we see that as many as 36 out of the 48 companies which disappeared from the group did so because of take-over or merger, or nationalization. Only in 12 cases was a company displaced or 'relegated' from the top 100 without losing its independent identity, and as one would expect the majority of these were at the lower end of the top 100 ranking in 1948. The high rate of turnover of companies in the top 100, therefore, has been associated in the main with the process of take-over or merger and of nationalization, which has greatly increased the dominance of the largest companies.

Once again, however, it is interesting to distinguish between the two sub-periods 1948–57 and 1957–68. Of the 48 disappearances from the top 100 over the whole period, 24 occurred during the nine-year period 1948–57 and another 24 occurred during the eleven-year period 1957–68. The causes of the disappearances, however, differ markedly. In the earlier period 19 of the disappearances were due to 'relegation', there were 4 cases of death by merger or take-over and one by nationalization. In the latter period, however, all the 24 disappearances were accounted for by death by merger or take-over or by nationalization.

The leading companies have also greatly increased their dominance in the United States. Thus the hundred largest manufacturing firms held 38 per cent of total manufacturing assets in 1941 and 50 per cent in 1968. In both the UK and US then the growing dominance of the largest companies is one of the most striking features of modern industry.

A major characteristic of these firms is the great diversity of their activities, and the extent of this diversification seems to have been increasing significantly in recent years. In the United States the average number of four-digit industries engaged in by the 200 largest firms increased from 13 in 1960 to 20 in 1968. The level of diversification is of course very much greater for the larger firms in the top size-bracket. In 1968 nine of these firms each operated in over 50 four-digit industries and 39 of them operated in over 30 industries. Furthermore, it appears that the diversification of the largest firms is resulting in a larger number of them holding leading positions in several industries.[20] What are the implications of all this for structural change and the competitive process?

It is clear that the integration of economic activity has come to depend more on the planning of activities within firms and less on competition in the market. Thus managerial decision making and the allocation of resources within the firm have become much more important matters for investigation. A key issue to the economist is that of the relative efficiency of resource allocation within the firm and by means of the market mechanism—to what extent is the competition for investment funds in the market adequately replaced by competition for funds between the various product branches within the firm, and to what extent is the large firm forced, or indeed able, to maintain a high level of efficiency in the use of existing assets in each of its wide range of activities? A great deal obviously depends on the form of organization, the extent to which the internal transactions of the firm are based on 'arms length' prices, and the extent to which individual branches or departments are tightly controlled on a profit and loss basis.

From this point of view it may be argued that the multi-divisional form of organization has the advantage over more centralized or unitary forms. In the unitary form of organization the operating divisions are organized along functional lines (e.g. manufacturing, marketing and finance) with the chief executive co-ordinating the activities of the divisions and also planning the overall strategy of the firm. In the multi-divisional form on the other hand the operating divisions, based on the production of different products or the same

[20] See Federal Trade Commission, Bureau of Economics, *Economic Report on Corporate Mergers* (Washington, 1969).

products in different geographical markets, are semi-autonomous, each organized along functional lines. The operating divisions report to the general office which is responsible for overall enterprise activity and is assisted by a specialist staff.

Because of the superior organization, and because the operating divisions form profit centres which can be meaningfully compared, the multi-divisional form of organization will tend, it has been argued, to display greater internal efficiency. Furthermore, it may also have the advantage over a system of several specialist unitary form organizations in being able to reallocate resources more quickly from low to high profit centres.[21] Given the importance of internal funds in the finance of investment this form of organization may then speed up the process of resource reallocation.

However, there are several problems to be considered. First, the efficiency of resource allocation within the firm still depends on the control exercised by top management. Even though the decentralized form of organization has facilitated the diversification of the firm's operations it has not eliminated the problem of coordination and of adaptation to change. The basic strategic decisions such as the hiring of key management personnel and the allocation of investment funds remain in the hands of top management. Furthermore, when the large diversified firm has monopoly power in individual markets management is not *compelled* to be as efficient as possible. And in the field of invention and innovation, which is a particularly important aspect of structural change, it has been pointed out by several investigators that the contributions of the large corporations have often fallen far short of what might be expected of them, given their resources. Outside a small number of areas such as electronics and chemicals large firms have been accused of concentrating the bulk of their research and development on projects which result in modest advances rather than on the introduction of radically new products and processes.[22] Indeed it has been suggested that 'if inventiveness and innovation are to be accelerated the need is for less emphasis on the large corporation'.[23]

In relation to these questions of efficiency one can safely say that while the form of organization will undoubtedly affect the performance of large firms, a great deal will also depend on the excell-

[21] For the details of an argument along these lines see O. E. Williamson, *Corporate Control and Business Behavior* (Englewood Cliffs, New Jersey: Prentice Hall, 1970).

[22] See R. R. Nelson, M. J. Peck and E. D. Kalachek, *Technology, Economic Growth and Public Policy* (The Brookings Institution, Washington DC, 1967), p. 54.

[23] John M. Blair, *Economic Concentration, Structure Behavior and Public Policy* (Harcourt Brace Jovanovish, June 1972), p. 251.

ence of a few top managers, and for large firms as a group this means reliance on the widespread and continuing availability of high quality management. However, experience shows that the quality of top management in large firms varies greatly. Examples of efficiently run, highly diversified firms can certainly be found, but there is also no shortage of the other type.

The process of growth in firms, including the role of diversification and research and development will be considered in more detail in the next chapter. For the moment we simply note the fact that over the last twenty years the structure of industry has been radically altered by a very large increase in the dominance of big companies.

CHAPTER 2

The Size and Growth of Firms

In the previous chapter we have examined the broad structural changes which have occurred in the British economy since the 1920s. This chapter is concerned with a more detailed examination of the *process* of change, and attention is focussed therefore on the firm. It is clear why this must be so, for structural change has been associated with the varying fortunes of individual firms. In declining industries firms which have failed to adapt themselves and move into new growth areas have declined and often passed out of existence. In expanding industries existing firms have been able to increase in size, and capacity in the industry has also been expanded by the birth of entirely new firms and by the extension of the activities of firms whose main interests lie in other fields. Little needs to be said about the unsuccessful firm which finds itself in a declining market and, because of its failure to adapt to changing circumstances, ultimately passes out of existence. Our concern is rather with those firms that make a more positive contribution to structural change; that is, with the way in which the successful firm adapts itself to changing circumstances.

In this chapter, therefore, we examine some of the main characteristics of expanding firms, and in particular, diversification, vertical integration, research and development, and mergers. These various aspects of growth are not of course of equal importance to all firms, and for the same firm they are likely to change in relative importance at different points in time. Thus, for instance, diversification is more likely to be an important feature of the growth of established firms in mature oligopolistic industries than for young firms in new industries. Again some large firms have grown largely by internal growth whereas for others acquisitions have played a crucial role in their development. Some firms are leaders in the process of invention and innovation, others are content to follow. Further elaboration is unnecessary in order to emphasize the diversity of experience which is likely to characterize the process of growth of any randomly selected group of firms.

A. DIVERSIFICATION AND VERTICAL INTEGRATION

A major feature of many firms, and especially the larger ones, is

42

the wide range of their activities. One way in which a firm may increase the range of operations is by vertical integration. A firm may integrate 'backwards' and thus produce products which it formerly purchased from others; it may also integrate 'forwards' and thus extend its range of operations towards the final consumer. Thus a producer of iron and steel products may integrate backwards and acquire its own source of iron ore, and also integrate forwards by, for instance, acquiring shipbuilding yards and engineering firms which will use as inputs some of the products of the iron and steel works. In this case the firm is increasing the range of its operations by integrating successive stages in the production of particular products.

A firm may also extend its interests by the production of new commodities which are not vertically related to its existing operations. This type of expansion we call diversification. Of course vertical integration is in fact a special form of diversification. It is convenient however to distinguish between the two not only for ease of exposition but also because although the motives for the two types of expansion are not entirely different they are not entirely the same either. Thus although the search for profitable growth opportunities may be an important factor explaining both diversification and vertical integration, a desire to reduce the variability of profits due to fluctuations in demand for final products is a motive for diversification but not for vertical integration.[1]

1. Diversification

Risk and uncertainty. One important motive for diversification is associated with risk and uncertainty. A highly specialized firm will, in the event of a sharp downturn in the demand for its products, be faced with a drastic and perhaps fatal decline in profits. It is to guard against this sort of outcome that firms very often move into new product lines. To see what is involved in this sort of decision-making it may be worth taking the analysis a little further. Decision-making by firms is of course carried out under conditions of

---

[1] In both cases there are problems of measurement. The degree of diversification, for instance, depends on how narrowly a product is defined. The narrower the definition the greater the degree of diversification and vice-versa. Clearly a mere count of the number of industries in which a firm produces is inadequate without at least a measure of the absolute size of the firm's interests in each industry. Furthermore, Census of Production data will not give a good measure of diversification. The Census classifies *establishments* to individual trades according to their principal products. There is the problem therefore not only of the appropriateness of the official product classification but also of the 'hidden' diversification that exists within each establishment. These problems of measurement however need not detain us, but they are clearly extremely important in any empirical work in this field.

uncertainty. Under such conditions profit-maximization has no precise meaning, in the sense that any action taken by the firm is associated not with a unique outcome but with a range of potential outcomes. Thus take, for instance, the case of a firm which specializes in the production of a particular product and which is deciding on whether to invest a given sum in the integration of a previous stage of production or in establishing facilities for the production of an entirely different final product. In the case of the former assume that the firm's assessment of the most likely outcome is a return on investment of 15 per cent but that the range of possible outcomes envisaged is from 0 to 25 per cent. Assume further that in the case of the alternative investment project the most likely return is thought to be 12 per cent and the range of possible outcomes is from 8 to 15 per cent. As compared to the first project, then, the most likely outcome is less favourable and the range of possible outcomes is much less. It is not possible to decide which way the decision will go without knowing something about the attitude of the decision-maker towards risk, but clearly the distribution of possible outcomes associated with the diversification project may be preferred because of its effect in reducing the variability of the firm's profits.

In a world characterized by change and uncertainty, there will be some businessmen who are sufficiently confident about the future course of demand to concentrate all their resources on the production of one commodity. But the general effect of an uncertain future is to cause firms to modify their choice of products towards producing more products rather than less.

Some fluctuations, such as seasonal ones, are foreseen by the firm which can therefore plan its production to allow for them. This is not the case with erratic or irregular fluctuations which are particularly likely to occur in industries in which goods are made to individual orders and specifications. Under these conditions the production of the firm's main line will commonly be supplemented at times of low demand by the production of secondary products. The function of the latter is to make some contribution to overhead costs and particularly to keep together a skilled work-force. For this purpose a firm may be prepared to produce the secondary products at very little above their prime costs of production.

Diversification may not, however, offer an effective solution to individual firms if in a general area of activity each firm diversifies into the main activity of others. Conditions may then arise with competition in all lines of activity tending to depress prices below the level of full costs of production. The problems are particularly acute where fixed costs form a big proportion of total costs so that the prime costs per unit of output are well below the full unit costs of production, and where excess capacity is substantial at times of low demand as a result of a high level of investment during the previous boom. The situation may be eased after a time by firms leaving the industry, but an alternative solution to the problem is a series of mergers and acquisitions.

Growth. A second motive for diversification is found in the profit and growth objectives of firms. In terms of growth, for instance, diversification will be induced because it will often be difficult for the firm to grow at a faster rate than the rate of growth of the industry which it finds itself in at present even though it has the resources to do so. In other words for the firm with growth as an important goal to seek to diversify it is not necessary that its existing markets be declining but only that they are not expanding quickly enough. Similarly, the existing fields of operation of a firm may be profitable ones but the most profitable use of new investment funds may still entail diversification.

What direction is this diversification likely to take? There are some instances, of course, of diversification with no technical or marketing links between the various activities. But in the majority of cases the direction of diversification is dictated by the advantage which established firms have in the production of goods in which they have special experience in marketing and technology. In some cases the amount of technological experience is great but the degree of marketing skill required is small. In other cases the reverse situation holds. But in most instances the diversification of a firm's activities is related to its special advantages in one or both of these fields. Diversification based primarily on a high degree of competence and technical knowledge in specialized areas of manufacture is characteristic of many of the largest firms in the economy, particularly those in the chemicals and engineering fields. The diversification of other companies such as those in the tobacco industry, on the other hand, seem to be based mainly on their special advantages in the large-scale marketing of consumer goods.

Somewhat more specifically we would emphasize the following factors as important in explaining the extent and pattern of diversification.

First, the success with which a firm tackles the problem of controlling separate divisions has an obviously important bearing on the extent to which it can handle the production and marketing of several products. In fact, as they grow larger, firms often adopt a decentralized form of organization, each division being operated very largely like independent firms. There is no doubt that the development of decentralized forms of organization has greatly facilitated the process of diversification.

Secondly, the selling efforts of the firm may provide a basis for diversification. In certain industries, and especially in the production of consumer goods, sales effort, including advertising, forms an important part of inter-firm rivalry. The selling effort of the firm is usually associated with a brand name which establishes the identity of the producer, so that in advertising a product the firm is also advertising itself. It follows that success in the marketing of one product enhances the reputation of the firm, and this in turn gives it an important advantage when diversifying into new product lines.

Thirdly, the motivation of management, and in particular the importance of the desire for size or growth in the preference function of management, will affect the extent of diversification. This is most clearly seen in the case of the 'empire-builders' who see in diversification the quickest way of building up a large organization.

But the most important factor of all perhaps is the possession of technical know-how. Firms with competent research and development teams have a built-in tendency to diversify. These teams are needed to develop new products or processes, but once they are established and the initial teething troubles are ironed out the research and development staff are free to pursue new ideas. In addition, of course, the possession of qualified technical personnel places the firm in a favourable position to take advantage of new opportunities arising from the research and development work of other organizations.

The importance of technical know-how and also of growth are emphasized by Gort in a study of diversification in 111 of the largest US manufacturing firms.[2] He found that the ratio of technical personnel to all employees was an important determinant of diversification and also that in most cases firms diversified into industries with a higher growth rate than that of their primary activities.

Although in principle we can distinguish between the risk and uncertainty motive for diversification and those motives such as growth which would exist even without uncertainty, in practice it is difficult to do so. Diversification to guard against future adverse changes in the demand for existing products will be difficult to distinguish from diversification based on the growth motive, for the latter is also a question of the relative growth rates of demand for different products. There is also another way in which the two motives are interrelated. Growth and the attainment of larger size in itself adds to the security of the firm. One of the important reasons for this is that, over some size-range at least, larger size means a greater

[2] Michael Gort, *Diversification and Integration in American Industry* (Princeton University Press, 1962).

ability to undertake research and development work. This provides
some safeguard to firms from a fall in the demand for its products
brought about by obsolescence caused by technical change.

Diversification and competition. The most important issue concerning diversification is its relationship to the competitive process.
The relationship is a complex one. Competition both encourages
diversification and sets limits to it. Diversification in turn may
increase the degree of competition or may reduce it.

We have already drawn attention to the fact that in industries
where advertising and other selling costs form an important aspect of
competition diversification may be encouraged because of the market
advantage which a firm may have in producing a range of products.
Thus, in the case of domestic electrical appliances, for instance, if a
firm develops a reputation for producing a 'good value for money'
appliance it will have a market advantage in producing other appliances. Each new appliance will be backed in advertising campaigns
by the 'good name' of the firm. Diversification of this kind will, for
any particular firm, tend to be the natural outcome of the growth
process, and in particular of the technical and marketing advantages
of the firm. But once one firm has developed in this way it tends to
force other firms in the same field to follow suit in order to maintain
their competitive position.

But competition also serves to set limits to expansion by diversification, because the diversifying firm must expect to meet competition in each of its basic areas of production. It must have the resources both to maintain its competitive position in existing fields and
also to establish itself and improve its position in new ones. The
strength of the competitive constraint on diversification is related to
the importance of economies of scale and technical change in the
production of the firm's existing products. Assuming that competition exists, the more important are economies of scale the greater
must be the output of the firm in order for it to be competitive in
existing markets. Similarly, if there is rapid technical change in the
production of existing products a greater part of the efforts of
management will be taken up in maintaining competitiveness in
existing areas of production. For a given volume of investment
funds and a given supply of managerial services, therefore, the more
important are economies of scale and the more rapid the rate of technical change in existing areas of production the more effective will be
the competitive constraint on diversification.

As far as the effect of diversification on competition is concerned
there are again several possible outcomes. Diversification itself may
take place either by the establishment of entirely new facilities or by
the acquisition of an already existing firm or part of a firm. In the

case of the former there is an increase in productive capacity and in the number of decision-making units in the industry which is being entered. In this case the degree of competition in the industry is likely to increase. Diversification by acquisition, however, leaves the number of decision-making units unchanged and also, initially at least, has no effect on capacity. This does not mean, however, that diversification by acquisition will not result in more competition. It may result for instance in the replacement of an inefficient management by an efficient one, or simply in a change in management goals which in itself may increase competitiveness. Furthermore the acquisition of a firm in another industry is often intended to form the basis for future expansion, so that the growth of the acquired firm may be greater than what it would have been had it remained under separate ownership.

There are also wider issues concerning the relationship between diversification and competition, relating in particular to the *direction* of diversification. It has been argued that one of the main factors inducing diversification is the fact that a firm is unable to realize its full growth potential in its existing industry. This is most likely to be the case in high concentration industries which have advanced beyond the stage of rapid growth, and where competition is between a few large firms so that it is difficult for one firm to increase its share of the market at the expense of the others. It might be expected that firms in such industries are most likely to look for new opportunities in growth industries with a low concentration where the prospects for successful entry and expansion are highest. There is in fact evidence that diversification is positively associated with the level of concentration in the diversifying firm's main industry.[3] It does not appear, however, that the industries into which large firms diversify are distinguished by having low levels of concentration. In part, the reason that high concentration is not an important obstacle to the diversification of large firms is the fact that they can enter such industries by acquisition or merger. In addition, however, the rate of growth of demand and the rate of technological change are also important. Where there is a high rate of growth and a high rate of technological change a firm may still find that diversification by acquisition is the most profitable method of entering an industry. But under such conditions it is also unlikely to be deterred from establishing *new* facilities in the industry even when the latter is dominated by a small number of established firms.

It is clear why industries characterized by rapid growth and technological change are attractive to firms which are seeking new outlets for their investment funds. First, diversification in the

[3] See Michael Gort, op. cit.

direction of such industries is most likely to satisfy the growth and profitability objectives of firms. Second, a high rate of growth of market demand and rapid technological change are factors which ease the problems of entry into new industries. A high growth rate means that a firm can set up new units of production in an industry with a smaller risk of a response from established firms than would be the case where the growth of market demand is low. And under conditions of rapid technological change some innovations are likely to be made by firms outside the industry which will be able to enter with a product or cost *advantage* over established firms.

Although diversification may have the result of increasing competition by increasing the number of markets in which the large firms are competitors, the picture would not be complete without pointing to the monopoly dangers of the situation.

The most familiar is the danger of cross-subsidization. Thus, the large diversified firm can use its financial power to discipline specialist rivals who engage in price cutting. More important perhaps is the use of excess profits in one market to engage in heavy advertising in another so as to extend a firm's sphere of monopoly influence. The danger is particularly great where marketing rather than production skill is the main basis of diversification. It is in the field of marketing that large firms have perhaps the main advantage over smaller ones—especially where such factors as brand names, national advertising and style changes are important.

A further danger is that as large diversified firms increase their dominance of industry they will tend to develop 'spheres of influence', deliberately reducing the extent to which they compete in order to avoid spoiling the markets. The increasing dominance of these firms will also increase their interdependence as buyers and sellers. There will be a tendency, therefore, for an increasing proportion of inter-firm transactions to be based on bargaining power rather than on a close comparison of price and quality from several alternative sources of supply.

Where the balance of advantage and disadvantage lies in relation to the large diversified company is difficult to determine. On the one hand, it is argued that the increase in diversification has strengthened competition by increasing the number of markets in which large companies confront each other. In addition there is the argument pointed out in Chapter 1, that large diversified firms organized on multi-divisional lines may facilitate more rapid resource reallocation. On the other hand, there are the monopoly dangers just outlined which become greater as the large companies come increasingly to dominate individual markets. Furthermore, the profitability performance of large diversified companies does not always suggest that they are superior to the more specialized firms. Indeed, if anything, the balance of empirical evidence suggests the opposite conclusion.[4]

2. *Vertical Integration*

In explaining the reasons for vertical integration the usual emphasis has been placed on the firm's search for greater security. 'Vertical integration is sometimes the consequence of a reuniting of separated processes of production. It is more often the consequence of a search for security.'[5] From this point of view the incentive to integrate will be influenced by the state of trade, the structure of markets and the efficiency and reliability of suppliers. Thus when demand is at a high level it may pay a firm to own its own sources of materials, both in terms of the benefits of higher profits and of the greater reliability of supply. In times of low demand, however, the integrated firm may be at a disadvantage in so far as it may not be free to purchase materials from the cheapest source of supply. The number of firms on both sides of the market and their relative size is also important. If, for instance, there is a high degree of concentration on both sides of the market but the consuming firms are large relative to their suppliers, they will be in a strong bargaining position and are not likely to have to pay much more than the competitive price.

Similar considerations apply to forward integration. Here again the state of trade is important. But whereas the incentive to integrate backwards is greatest at times of high demand, the incentive to integrate forwards will be greatest when demand is falling. Again the size of firms is an important factor. Thus, for example, in several industries the inducement to manufacturers to acquire distributive outlets has been increased by the growth of the large multiple retailers which has eroded the dominance which manufacturers have traditionally had over the small 'independent' retailers.

Efficiency considerations, however, are also important in explaining changes in the degree of vertical integration. The basis for the efficiency explanation rests on two factors. The first rests on the fact that there is a cost involved in co-ordinating resources by means of market transactions. Secondly, our observations of changes in the degree of integration take place within the framework of a set of industry boundaries which have been determined by past production methods and organizational know-how.

[4] For a further elaboration of these arguments see J. M. Blair, *Economic Concentration: Structure, Behaviour and Public Policy* (Harcourt, Brace, Jovanovich, 1972), pp. 185–95; and K. D. George, 'Concentration and Specialization in Industry', *Journal of Industrial Economics*, April 1972.

[5] E. A. G. Robinson, *The Structure of Competitive Industry* (Cambridge University Press, 1958), p. 110.

The cost advantages of integrating processes are most obvious in cases, such as the production of iron and steel, where important economies are to be achieved in having the processes performed in quick succession one after the other. But apart from technical links of this kind there are other costs of using the market and thus potential cost reductions available as a result of integration. These costs include the cost of obtaining information on relevant prices, the cost of negotiating and concluding separate contracts for each transaction, and costs resulting from delays in delivery. Given these costs, 'a firm will tend to expand until the cost of organising an extra transaction within the firm becomes equal to the cost of carrying out the same transactions by means of an exchange on the open market or the cost of organising in another firm'.[6]

The balance of advantage between co-ordinating transactions within the firm and by means of the market will, however, change with changes in technology, in organizational techniques and in the size of markets, so that traditional industry boundaries become inappropriate to the most efficient organization of production. An increase in the size of markets has often been a cause of vertical disintegration, but the first two factors mentioned—technological and organizational change—have usually worked in the opposite direction. In particular it has been emphasized that the complicated nature of modern industrial production means that many highly specialized processes and skills need close co-ordination and that this results in an increase in the extent to which the co-ordination of resources takes place by planning within firms rather than by means of the market mechanism.

At the same time there are plenty of reasons to expect that the degree of vertical integration will vary a great deal from one firm to another even in the same general field of activity. Managerial ability to co-ordinate the different stages of production varies, and in the face of uncertainty as to future supply and demand conditions, and with only very limited knowledge about the costs of other firms, there is room for a difference of opinion as to the merits of integrating activities. Furthermore, even though vertical integration may be profitable there is also the question of the availability of funds for investment and the alternative uses of these funds. Thus the fact that one firm in an industry is more highly integrated than another may reflect differences in the supply of investment funds. Again managements will have different views about new investment opportunities. Some will see vertical integration as the most profitable use of funds, others will choose to diversify into new products or to extend their production 'horizontally' in existing markets.

[6] R. H. Coase, 'The nature of the firm', *Economica*, November 1937.

An important example of vertical integration is the integration of the retailing and wholesaling functions—an important feature of the development of the large multiple retailer. The position of the latter as large-scale buyers has enabled them very often to take the initiative in deciding what to produce, and has also permitted manufacturers to achieve the advantages of long production runs. The growth in importance of the large retailer–wholesaler firm has also destroyed the security of the manufacturer and independent wholesaler and forced them in many cases to change their own organization. Thus in the food trade in particular the reaction of the independent wholesaler has been the formation of voluntary chains of retail shops in order to achieve the same sort of benefits of large-scale buying as the multiples. The manufacturers have also been active. In the textile field Courtaulds, for instance, has bought some Marks & Spencer suppliers and has also acquired several wholesaling firms, some of them associated with voluntary groups of retailers.

Vertical integration then is often a natural part of the growth of firms. A particular example, although it does not involve full-scale vertical integration, is the growth of Marks & Spencer. The success of this company has been due in large measure to the reputation which it has established for supplying the consumer with a range of goods of high quality which conform to precise and detailed specifications. It has secured this standard by establishing production and technical services so as to offer advice and guidance to supplying firms on technical and production problems. 'Through its technical services and its merchandising departments Marks & Spencer undertook to ensure that at every stage of production back to the primary producer of the raw fibre, the needs of the consumer were represented and at each stage of production its specialists and technologists collaborated with the firms responsible.'[7] Here then is a field where rapid technical progress has been made in the development of new fibres and where the involvement of a retail firm in the production of the goods has been an integral part of the firm's strategy of development.

A final aspect of vertical integration which requires some comment is the fact that it may have monopoly consequences. A firm which initially has integrated backwards or forwards on the basis of efficiency considerations alone may continue to do so in order to increase its market power. The integration of the retailing and wholesaling functions by the large multiple retailers although based on economies of integration has almost certainly reached the stage where part of the special terms which they are able to arrange

[7] Goronwy Rees, *St. Michael, A History of Marks and Spencer* (Weidenfeld & Nicolson, 1969), p. 163.

with the manufacturers is due to their market power rather than to real economies of size.

Vertical integration by one or more established firms in an industry can clearly have a profound effect on structure and on the degree of competitiveness. By refusing to supply or to purchase from unintegrated firms, or by supplying and purchasing from them on unfavourable terms, the integrated firms may be able to achieve a dominant position in the market. To survive, other firms may be forced to integrate, and to be successful any new entrant may have to start operations as an integrated concern. But this raises capital requirements which in turn means that the possibility of new entry is restricted to a much smaller number of firms. The larger capital requirements now necessary for successful entry will not be a barrier to entry for large firms in other industries, but it will be for all firms which are either unable to obtain the amount of capital required or can only obtain it on unfavourable terms.

The Monopolies Commission reports give several examples of monopoly power resulting from vertical integration. In flat glass, for instance, about a fifth to one-quarter of the product of the monopoly producer (Pilkington) is used, after being turned into safety glass, by the motor industry. The dominant manufacturer of safety glass (Triplex) became a subsidiary of Pilkingtons in 1965, but since the 1930s there had been agreements between the two companies that Pilkingtons should supply all the flat glass required. In 1967 Triplex acquired its only competitor and the vertical link was complete. Another important case of monopoly power resulting from vertical integration is found in the development of Courtaulds. This company has 'interests in fibres and textiles ranging from the production of raw material to the retail distribution of madeup garments'. The Monopolies Commission found that, in relation to cellulosic fibres, Courtaulds' vertical integration forward into the textile industry was done for the purpose of preserving its monopoly position by increasing the entry barriers to new competitors, limiting the entry of imports, and reducing the seriousness of competition from other fibre producers.

B. RESEARCH AND DEVELOPMENT

The importance of research and development expenditure in the process of diversification has already been noted in the previous section, where it was seen that the research and development efforts of the firm give it one of its main opportunities for expansion. In this section we look at some further aspects of research and development and in particular its association with the size of firms.

How far should we expect research and development activity to be associated with size? A number of arguments have been advanced which suggest that the large firm has certain crucial advantages. First, the high costs involved in modern-day research are such that only large firms have the necessary resources to carry on the work. Second, there are the risks associated with research and development work, and where both costliness and riskiness are combined only the large firm has the resources to afford a sufficient diversity of research projects to reduce the risks to acceptable levels. Third, large firms have a further advantage in so far as there are economies of scale in research and development work associated with the employment of specialist staff and equipment. Fourth, and most important perhaps, there are the advantages which large firms have in the marketing of new products. Because they have a major advantage in terms of established links with distribution outlets and large-scale advertising, large firms can expect a new product to achieve a much faster speed of market penetration. A given proportion of a potential market will be attained over a shorter time period thus increasing the expected rate of return on the investment.

The evidence on the distribution of R & D expenditure by size of firm certainly shows that a large proportion is concentrated in firms in the large size-classes. In the UK in 1959 over 90 per cent of total expenditure was accounted for by firms with an employment of more than 2,000. Furthermore, whereas 90 per cent of these large firms spent money on research only 18 per cent of firms employing less than 300 did so. A similar picture applies to the US where, in 1958, firms with 5,000 or more employees accounted for nearly 90 per cent of all R & D expenditure in the manufacturing sector. And whereas over 90 per cent of these large firms recorded R & D spending, less than 20 per cent of those employing fewer than 1,000 did so.

A study of the process of innovation, however, cannot be adequately undertaken simply by comparing the research and development expenditure of firms in different size classes. The following factors are also important.

First, there is a very great variation in the size of firms in the large size-class, and the observation that a high percentage of R & D work is concentrated in this class does not tell us whether within this population of firms there is a correlation between size and R & D effort. The evidence suggests that although in most industries the absolute level of expenditure is correlated with size, there is no strong and systematic relationship between size and the intensity of R & D effort as measured by R & D expenditure as a percentage of sales or net output. In most industries the positive correlations found have been weak and in some the correlation has been negative. In the United States the general picture seems to be that, 'While in most (but not all) industries the R & D to sales ratio rises as one moves from the group of firms with less than 1,000 employees to the group in the 1,000–5,000 range, there is no clear tendency for these ratios

TABLE 2.2. *R & D Expenditure as a Percentage of net Output, UK 1964–65*

Industry	R & D as per cent of net output	Output as per cent of all manufacturing industry, 1963
Aircraft	39	3·1
Electronics	14	3·7
Petroleum products	13	0·7
Scientific instruments	6	1·5
Chemicals	5	9·3
Motor vehicles	4	7·1
Electrical engineering	4	5·6
Rubber	2	1·7
Mechanical engineering	2	14·5
Glass, pottery, bricks	2	4·1
Primary metals	2	7·9
Ships and marine engineering	1	2·0
Textiles	1	8·0
Food, drink, tobacco	1	12·2
Timber, furniture	} < 0·5	2·7
Paper, printing, publishing		8·5
Clothing, footwear, leather		4·5

Source: Technological Innovation in Britain, Report of the Central Advisory Council for Science and Technology (HMSO, 1968).

to be larger for the giants in the above 5,000 range than for the firms in the 1,000–5,000 range.'[8] Figures of R & D intensity are of course a measure of the *input* of R & D and should be used with caution. A high figure is not necessarily a good thing and indeed may reflect inefficiency in the organization of research and development programmes.

Secondly, the intensity of R & D expenditure is closely related to the type of product. Table 2.2 shows R & D expenditure as a percentage of net output for industries in the UK. There is a close similarity

[8] R. R. Nelson, M. J. Peck and E. D. Kalachek, *Technology, Economic Growth and Public Policy* (The Brookings Institution, Washington D.C., 1967).

between the intensity of R & D effort by industry in the UK and that in the US, and an important part of the explanation is found in the differences between industries in the opportunities and pressure to carry out R & D work. The opportunities for such work are much higher in the science-based industries, such as aircraft, electronics and scientific instruments, and here the pressure to innovate is also great because competitiveness is largely a function of technological advance.

One further aspect of the industry pattern of R & D work deserves mention. Whereas the UK is similar to the US in concentrating a high percentage (about 35 per cent) of its R & D effort in aircraft, Germany for instance has a much lower concentration of resources in aircraft and a much higher concentration in machinery, chemicals and metals. The argument that Britain needs to change the pattern of its R & D effort so that it becomes more similar to the German one, and also should be more selective in R & D work in the science-based industries has much to commend it. It also leads us on to our next point, which is the importance of the size of the market.

The size of the market is relevant because the larger it is, the more obvious are the rewards for success and the greater the inducement to R & D effort. Although a firm can widen its market by exporting, a sufficiently large domestic market is clearly an advantage. Some general support for the hypothesis that the rate of innovative activity is related to the size of the market is given by Schmookler in a study of patent statistics.[9] He finds that for capital goods industries, the number of inventions in a field varies directly with sales. The explanation given for this result is that the pattern of innovative activity is governed mainly by considerations of profitability and that the latter is dependent mainly on expected sales of the improved capital goods which in turn is largely determined by sales of existing goods.

The rate of growth of a market is important, of course, as well as its size. A large market will offer little inducement to R & D if it is declining, particularly if decline is accompanied by intensive price competition. In such industries innovation is likely to be inhibited by uncertainty about future demand, and management is likely to be preoccupied with short-run problems of a defensive nature. The quality of management will also tend to decline as it becomes difficult to attract new talent and this will have a further and marked adverse consequence on innovation. In rapidly expanding industries, on the other hand, the position is reversed. They can attract the best management, above-average profitability supplies the finance for research work, and above all the prospects of a rapid growth of

⁹ J. Schmookler, *Invention and Economic Growth* (Harvard University Press, 1966), Chapters 6 and 7.

demand promise high rewards for the successful innovator. For seventeen industry groups in the UK manufacturing sector a close positive association was in fact found between the growth of output from 1935 to 1958 and the intensity of R & D effort.[10]

Although some degree of safety has been emphasized as a factor which has a favourable effect on R & D, the role of competition has also been stressed. This does not require the existence of large numbers. The number of competing firms in industries with a high level of research and development expenditure may be small, but the intensity of competition is often great, especially where it is important to be first in a particular field and to gain a head start over competitors. Where there are important economies of scale in research it may appear to be wasteful to have several research teams conducting experiments to solve the same kind of problems. However, there are two considerations which favour this state of affairs.

The first is the advantage of flexibility. There will usually be different views about the best way of tackling a particular problem and all of them are not likely to be favoured by one organization. Indeed, a single organization may commit itself to one line of approach, and where large sums of money are involved it may be slow to take up new ideas which might render the initial approach obsolete. An illustration of alternative systems in developing a new technology, one emphasizing competition and a variety of approaches and the other monopoly and development on a narrow front, is found in the design and development of nuclear power stations in the US and the UK. In the US the emphasis has been to encourage the development of all promising systems and to attract private companies to design and develop different systems competitively to the prototype stage. In the UK, on the other hand, effort has been concentrated on the development of one system—the gas–graphite reactor—and the Atomic Energy Authority has had a monopoly in the development of new systems to the prototype stage. In a recent study of the development of nuclear power it has been suggested that these organizational differences, together with those on the electricity supply side (where in contrast to the US the Central Electricity Generating Board in the UK has a near monopoly position in the market for nuclear plants) have been major factors in explaining the more rapid development of low-cost nuclear power systems in the US.[11] It is certainly arguable that the greater flexibility of approach and the

[10] See C. Freeman, 'Research and Development, a comparison between British and American industry', *National Institute Economic Review*, May 1962.
[11] Duncan Burn, *The Political Economy of Nuclear Energy* (London, Institute of Economic Affairs, Research Monograph 9, 1967).

competitive development of different systems have been of major importance in explaining the greater success of the US programme.

The second consideration is the distinction between research, and the development of an idea to the stage of full-scale commercial application. The latter is both expensive and risky and without some strong pressure on the firm the natural tendency is to delay full-scale industrial application. To some extent the necessary pressure will emanate from inside the firm, from the research and development team anxious to see the practical application of their ideas. But more powerful and more reliable is the external pressure provided by competition and the fear, therefore, that another firm will 'get in first'. Thus although firms require some degree of safety before they will be prepared to invest in innovative activity, competition is also important in influencing both the speed and the direction of that activity.

Another question relating to the competitive aspect of research and development is whether firms that do take the lead in the development of new products and processes stay ahead or are replaced by those which, for the time being, have fallen behind. One point of view which has been advanced is that 'it seems highly probable that the next advance in technique will be made by some other firm than the one which by means of the last advance made itself into the most efficient in the industry'.[12] There is, however, no inevitability about this outcome as there are conflicting forces at work. To the extent that success breeds success, especially by providing more finance to undertake further research, and to the extent that a leading firm has an internal pressure group which is always on the lookout for new opportunities, there are forces at work which favour the firm that initially forges ahead. Furthermore, firms that fall behind may run into financial difficulties which will put them at a further disadvantage. On the other hand these firms will be under greater pressure to make technical or organizational changes, whereas the firm which made the last advance will be under less pressure to look urgently for further improvements because it will be able to expand successfully on the basis of its existing technology and organization.

The relative efficiency and profitability of firms within an industry certainly do change over time, but the strength of this tendency varies and will depend not only on the relative importance of the factors which have just been mentioned but also on such factors as the initial number and size distribution of firms, and the importance of entry by large established firms.

The distinction which has been made between invention and inno-

12 J. Downie, *The Competitive Process* (Gerald Duckworth & Co., 1958).

vation brings us again to the relative performance of the small and large firms. Because of the different amounts of expenditure involved and the different types of skill and organization required, the contribution of the individual and the small firm is likely to be greater in the case of invention than it is in improving upon an initial idea and developing it to the stage of commercial application. Jewkes, Sawers and Stillerman, for example, in tracing the origins of 61 major inventions which occurred mainly between 1930 and 1950 found that only 12 could be clearly attributed to large firms. Thirty-eight were due to the work of individuals and small firms, and eleven were unclassifiable. In a review of new evidence which has appeared since their original work was published the authors conclude that there does not seem to be a need for substantial modification of their earlier views relating to the importance of individuals and small firms.[13]

Similar research in the US has also shown the importance of the individual and the small firm in inventive activity. Apart from numerous case studies their importance is also revealed by patent statistics. Thus although there has been a long-term decline in the percentage of patents issued to individuals the average figure for the years 1956–60 was still 36·4.[14] In addition to this many of the patents assigned to firms originate from work done by individuals outside the formal research and development programmes.

There can be little doubt about the importance of individuals and small firms in inventive activity, and especially as a source of *major* inventions. Indeed it has been suggested that apart from a small number of areas, the bulk of R & D carried out by large firms is relatively safe and aimed at modest advances, 'Outside defense and space related R & D, however, and possibly some segments of the civil electronics and chemical industries, the bulk of corporate R & D is modest design improvement work not reaching very far—the type of work that results in yearly changes in automobile design, gradual improvement in refrigerators and vacuum cleaners, and steady improvements in the automaticity, speed and capacity of machine tools, rather than radically new products and processes.'[15]

The major advantage of large firms seems to lie not as a source of major inventions but in developing proven ideas. It is in development, and particularly the later stages of development when a new product or process is introduced on a full commercial scale, that the resources

[13] J. Jewkes, D. Sawers and R. Stillerman, *The Sources of Invention* (Macmillan, 1969), 2nd edn.
[14] J. Schmookler, op. cit., p. 26.
[15] R. R. Nelson, M. J. Peck and E. D. Kalachek, op. cit., p. 54.

of the large firm give it an advantage. But how big a firm needs to be, to be a successful innovator, again varies greatly from one industry to another. Thus in mechanical engineering, for instance, there are a large number of opportunities for small-scale, low-cost innovations, and here the small firm can hold its own. In fields such as heavy chemicals, however, the advantage is overwhelmingly with the large firm. But even this is too simplified a view. Perhaps it is more accurate to say that within most industries there is a range of research and development work both in terms of cost and the degree of risk involved. Under these conditions an important contribution to research and development can be made by individuals and small firms as well as by the larger corporations.

The final point I wish to make is to stress that successful R & D effort is a management technique that must be considered as an integral part of the total activity of the firm. This brings out two points of great importance. First, the task of the successful research manager is not simply to solve technical and scientific problems but to solve those which are relevant to the production and marketing objectives of the firm. This involves a clear view as to what these objectives should be, the time period involved, and the finance which is likely to be available for research and development work. There has to be effective communication, therefore, between the various departments of the firm, particularly between research and development, production and marketing. This again is well illustrated by the development of Marks & Spencer. It has been 'an essential side of Marks & Spencer's approach to retailing that its scientists and technologists were not advisers or consultants, "back-room boys" who operated in mysterious isolation. They were fully integrated into the commercial organisation of the business, so that they were active and indispensable members of its buying departments.'[16] In addition it is extremely important to get an appropriate balance between R & D expenditure investment and marketing. It is a common criticism of British industry that the effective development of R & D projects into profitable innovations is seriously hampered by weaknesses in production and marketing. The fundamental weaknesses here seem to be inadequate capital investment and the relatively small number of professionally trained people in management, production and marketing.

The problem of deciding on the most appropriate level of research expenditure and on the choice of projects in terms of choosing those which are most likely to have usable results is, of course, an extremely difficult one. The outcome of research and development work is by its very nature highly uncertain, and it is hardly surprising therefore

[16] Goronwy Rees, op. cit., p. 170.

that firms of much the same size, even in the same industry, reach very different conclusions as to how much money it is worth spending in this field. It does not appear to be true either, that the largest firms are the ones which invariably make the most efficient use of resources. Thus in his study of the iron and steel, petroleum refining, and chemical industries of the US, Mansfield found that inventive output per dollar of expenditure was lower in the largest firms than in the large and medium-sized ones.[17]

A second important role of the managerial function is that of keeping open the lines of communication with sources of technical knowledge external to the firm, and of being aware of their relevance to the firm's own position. These external sources include developments in other industries and countries, research associations and technical and scientific journals. One way of keeping abreast with the latest technical advances is by using or producing under licence the processes or products developed by other companies at home or abroad. Countries like Japan and Australia have made great use of such licensing agreements in their industrial development. In general, however, British firms have spent much less on royalties and licences than, for instance, firms in France and Germany.

The availability of outside information also means that it is quite possible for small firms to be technically progressive. So long as the management of small firms keeps in touch with the various outside sources of technical knowledge, and of course has the ability to understand the relevance of such knowledge to the firm's position, then they will be able to participate effectively in the results of research. It may be in the form of using developments made in industries which supply it with inputs, or in the form of licensing arrangements with larger companies, or in the form of making use of the results of research associations. As we have seen the actual role of small firms in research and development has in fact been much more positive than this. Numerous studies both in Britain and America testify to the historical importance of the individual and the small firm in this field. It remains to be seen whether their role will be as important in the future.

C. ACQUISITION AND MERGER

So far in this chapter we have examined the importance of diversification and research and development in the expansion of firms. This expansion can take place either by the firm building new plants or by acquiring the plants of existing firms.

---

[17] Edwin Mansfield, *Industrial Research and Technological Innovation: An Econometric Analysis* (New York, W. W. Norton & Company, Inc., 1968), p. 42.

Mergers are an important feature of the growth of many firms and of most large ones. It is not possible, however, to make an accurate assessment of the contribution of mergers to the overall growth of the firm. After a merger has occurred, information is available on the growth of the whole unit but separate information is not generally available for the firm which has been acquired. As a result, the initial contribution of the acquired unit to the growth of the firm can be measured but not its continuing contribution. For the latter we can only make a number of alternative assumptions; for example, that the acquired company would have expanded at the same rate as the average rate of expansion of all firms in the industry, or that its rate of expansion would have been equal to its own rate over a previous period of time. No assumption is entirely satisfactory. There is no reason, for instance, why the past growth performance of a firm should be repeated in the future, and even if it would have been, had it remained independent, the fact that it has been acquired may affect not only its own growth performance but also that of the acquiring company.

In spite of the measurement problems, however, the empirical studies in this field are agreed on the importance of mergers in the growth of large firms. In a study of US companies, for instance, Weston concluded that mergers made a significant contribution to growth in all firms.[18] In the UK, Evely and Little drew attention to the major importance of external expansion in the growth of leading firms in high concentration trades, and that there were few firms among the leaders which were not created by amalgamation or had not resorted to acquisition or merger at some stage.[19]

More general information which shows the growing importance of expenditure on acquisitions in the post-war period is given in Table 2.3. Over the years 1959–66, 15 per cent of the total capital outlay of non-financial quoted companies took the form of expenditure on acquisitions as compared to 8 per cent over the years 1953–58 and 4 per cent in the period 1949–52.

Most of the literature on mergers has been concerned with its relation to the monopoly problem. Some studies, however, have been more concerned with the part played by mergers in the growth of firms. 'Whenever merger is considered to be the most profitable way to expand, there will surely be a tendency for merger to occur. Economic analysis that treats it only as a means of reducing competition, or establishing monopolistic dominance, is placing the wrong

[18] J. F. Weston, *The Role of Mergers in the Growth of Large Firms* (University of California Press, 1961).
[19] R. Evely and I. M. D. Little, *Concentration in British Industry* (Cambridge University Press, 1960).

emphasis on one of the most significant characteristics of the firm in the modern economy.'[20] As we have already noted, mergers are clearly an important part of the growth of firms, and there are several situations where they reduce the difficulties of expansion. This will be the case, for instance, in static or declining industries where economies are available to larger firms but where firms do not feel confident enough about future demand to invest substantially in new equipment. Competitive investment programmes carry the danger of over-capacity, and mergers will be the most effective way of achieving the necessary market adjustments.

TABLE 2.3. *Acquisitions by Non-financial Quoted Companies, 1949–66, Manufacturing, Distribution, Construction (average annual expenditure or %)*

	Total capital outlay	Expenditure on acquisitions	
	£m	£m	% of total
1949–52	984	38	4·0
1953–58	1331	108	8·0
1959–66	2519	351	15·0

Source: H. B. Rose and G. C. Newbould, 'The 1967 takeover boom', *Moorgate and Wall Street*, Autumn 1967.

Another circumstance in which merger may often reduce the difficulties of expansion is when the firm seeks to diversify. It is likely to be particularly important when a firm is diversifying into areas where there are difficulties in obtaining market connections because of patents and the attachment of consumers to established brands, and where perhaps different management skills are required. Here, the acquisition of an existing firm means that the costs of building up a competitive business in the new field are reduced as compared to the alternative of internal expansion.

As a final example of the profitability of acquisition as a means of expansion, take the case of the development of a new technology which threatens the position of an established firm. There are a number of alternatives open to the threatened firm. It can do nothing and suffer a decline in its market share; it can attempt to develop a similar or even better technology so as to restore its competitive position; or it can attempt to acquire the innovator. The last response is likely to occur most often when the threatened firm is substantially larger than the innovator. The larger firm may of course be in a position to make a quick counter with the introduction of its own new technology. But where it is not, acquisition may be

[20] Edith T. Penrose, *The Theory of the Growth of the Firm* (Basil Blackwell, 1966) p. 155.

seen as the most profitable, and certainly the safest, course of action. Because of the difference in the size of the firms, the profits which the small firm will make at its existing scale of operations may well be much less than the losses which the large firm will suffer as a result of its weaker competitive position. Under such circumstances, the large firm may be prepared to pay a price for the innovator which is higher than that which represents the present value of its expected stream of profits.

There are, of course, more general factors than the power of big business which make small firms susceptible to take-over bids. Apart from personal considerations which explain the existence of many willing sellers amongst the ranks of small firms, the pattern of their growth also indicates that there are critical points in their development at which a major reorganization of management and finance has to occur in order to form a sounder basis for sustained growth. Even where management has recognized and accepted the need for organizational changes substantial difficulties may face the firm attempting to grow when it is in a transitional phase, difficulties which, in particular, relate to recruiting new management personnel and in raising capital through outside finance. Firms in such a position are obviously susceptible to a take-over bid.[21]

Mergers, then, can be looked at as part of the process of the growth of firms, in that firms will presumably resort to external expansion where this is the most profitable course open to them. On the other side of the coin, some mergers may best be explained by the difficulties which firms encounter in the process of expansion. All this, however does not get us away from the monopoly issue. Indeed, mergers will be especially profitable where they result in substantial increases in market power. In the example given above, for instance, the acquisition of the innovating firm will not only increase the profitability of the acquiring company over what it would have been in the absence of the acquisition, but it will also give it a greater control over future technological advances in the industry. The monopoly issue must, therefore, remain of central importance in an analysis of the economic effects of mergers and we will be returning to it in later chapters.

D. PROFITABILITY AND THE SIZE AND GROWTH OF FIRMS

We have now examined some of the main aspects of the growth of firms. It may be useful to end the chapter by seeing 'how it all works

[21] Professor E. A. G. Robinson has defined the 'pessimum' size of firm as that size 'which combines the technical disadvantages of smallness with the managerial disadvantages of being too large for individual control'. See *The Structure of Competitive Industry* (Cambridge University Press, 1958), pp. 105–6.

out', particularly in terms of the relationships between profitability and the growth and size of firms.

We would certainly *expect* to find a positive association between growth and profitability. In terms of the *ability* to grow the link between the two is clear. A growing firm requires finance for expansion, and the supply of this finance, whether originating internally from ploughed-back profits or externally from new issues, is related to the firm's profit record. In so far as the firm's growth is financed from retained profits then clearly the greater the profit the more growth it will be able to finance. In so far as growth is financed 'externally' by the issue of new shares, the profitability of the firm is again important because the ease of raising outside funds depends upon the prospects of dividends.

The firm's *desire* to grow is also related to profitability. In an expanding economy in particular, growth is an essential ingredient of the forces of competition. The growing firm has an advantage over stable or contracting ones in attracting and holding good management because of the increased opportunities and resources available for members of the organization. The rise in productivity in the firm is also likely to vary positively with the rate at which its output is expanding. The faster the increase in output the faster the accumulation of new machines and the scrapping of old ones. We would expect the age distribution of the capital stock of the growth firm to have a lower mean age and a lower variance than firms of stable or declining size. As Meyer and Kuh have noted, 'firms that are on the downgrade as indicated by an aged capital stock typically do not reverse the trend while the more dynamic firms continue to "rejuvenate" their capital stock by investing at higher rates'.[22] The faster growing firms in an industry are, therefore, likely to have a higher productivity than rivals, and will tend to be more competitive in terms of price and quality of product and/or more profitable. Whether its advantage shows in the form of greater price-product competitiveness or higher profitability the firm will have an advantage in striving to increase its share of existing markets or in diversifying into new lines of activity.

The empirical work that has been done in this area falls into two main groups. The first group examines the relationship between changes in output and output per head, differential changes in the latter being a measure of relative efficiency and in the former of relative growth. On an industry basis the positive association between these two variables is well established (see Chapter 1). On an individual

[22] J. Meyer and E. Kuh, *The Investment Decision* (Harvard University Press, 1957), pp. 99–100.

firm basis there is less evidence. However Downie found that on an individual firm basis there was '... a very definite association in most industries between changes in productivity and growth' for the period 1935 to 1948.[23] These statistical results do not tell us whether it is high output increases which cause high productivity gains or whether it is the latter which induces the former. But either direction of causation is consistent with the behaviour of a firm operating under a goal structure in which growth is a significant factor.

The second group of empirical studies has examined the relationship between profitability and the rate of growth of firms in terms of assets. These studies have, in general, found a strong positive association between growth and profitability. For instance, Singh and Whittington find 'a fairly strong association between growth and profitability with profitability "explaining" on an average about 50 per cent of the variation in growth rates'.[24] It is also pertinent to note that about 50 per cent of the variation in growth rates is *not* 'explained' by variations in profitability. This is not surprising because there are other important factors at work, notably differences in the quality and goals of management and in the degree of competition. Furthermore the general relationship between profitability and growth which is shown in these studies does not say anything, of course, about the *direction* of expansion of the most profitable firms. The evidence is consistent with a wide range of growth patterns. Thus, in some cases, high profitability will be associated with rapid expansion in existing lines, in others with a rate of expansion which has been achieved mainly by diversification.

Another interesting point about these studies is that neither productivity nor profitability was found to be related significantly to the size of the firm. Downie found that 'no association [between size of firm and productivity] can be distinguished when size is measured by employment' and the 'result is in most cases not much stronger when size is measured by net output'. Again Singh and Whittington found that 'average profitability was on the whole [with some exceptions] lower the larger the size of the firm, but the differences in average profitability of firms between size-classes were not found to be statistically significant at the 5 per cent level, by the usual tests, for most of the populations of firms considered'. This conclusion was based on a study of four broad industries only, but an extension of the analysis to cover 21 industry groups also finds that with the possible exception of one group there was no systematic relationship

[23] J. Downie, op. cit., p. 181.

[24] A. Singh and G. Whittington, *Growth, Profitability and Valuation* (Cambridge University Press, 1968).

between size and profitability for the period 1948–60.[25]

Another finding which is relevant to the analysis of this chapter is that as between different size-classes of firm there are significant differences in the *dispersion* of profit rates, the tendency being for the degree of dispersion to vary inversely with the size of the firm. A number of reasons may be advanced to explain this finding. First, large firms are much more diversified than small ones, and their reported profit is an average which may conceal wide variations. Second, the management of large firms may be more skilful in avoiding projects which result in losses, but at the same time are less adventurous and so lose many opportunities of making exceptional gains. Third, there might be greater scope in large firms for offsetting falling profits caused by adverse changes in conditions external to the firms, by increasing internal efficiency.

Large firms also have a lower dispersion of growth rates than small ones. Again this can be explained by the fact that the greater diversification of their activities allows them to offset poor performance in some markets against good performance in others.

As far as average growth rates are concerned some early studies suggested that there was no significant difference between the growth rates of large and small firms. This was one of Hart's findings for a sample of UK companies over the period 1950–55.[26] Later work by Samuels, however, revealed a strong positive association between size and growth for a sample of 400 companies over the period 1951–60.[27] A positive but weak association between size and growth has also been found by Singh and Whittington for the period 1948–60.[28] Such findings may be explained by the argument that the growth motive is stronger the larger the firm. But a more likely explanation is that whatever dis-economics of management a firm might face as it gets larger tend to be outweighed by economies of scale and/or market power advantages in finance, production and marketing.

Finally, there is the important question of the relative efficiency of internal growth and growth by acquisitions. It has been argued that internal growth is likely to result in the greatest efficiency gains[29] and indeed there is some evidence mainly in the US which shows that firms that grow predominantly by internal growth tend to have a

[25] I am grateful to Mr G. Whittington for giving me some of the results of his analysis covering the 21 industry groups.

[26] P. E. Hart, 'The Size and Growth of Firms', *Economica*, February 1962.

[27] J. M. Samuels, 'Size and the Growth of Firms', *Review of Economic Studies*, 1965.

[28] A. Singh and G. Whittington, 'The Size and Growth of Firms', unpublished paper, Cambridge, 1973.

[29] K. D. George and R. M. Cyert, 'Competition Growth and Efficiency', *Economic Journal*, March 1969.

superior profitability performance than those that have resorted
a great deal to mergers and acquisitions.[30]

[30] See J. M. Blair, loc. cit.

CHAPTER 3

Market Performance

A. INTRODUCTION

Our attention so far has been concentrated on structural change in the economy and the process by which such change comes about. As far as the latter is concerned we have been particularly concerned about the searches of existing firms for new opportunities, which for the successful ones means not only adaptation to changing external conditions but also the use of resources within the firm, particularly in the form of research and development, to *create* new opportunities. From this discussion of the growth of firms it is clear that large firms in particular cannot be correctly allocated to one industry. Yet the concept of an industry is useful in understanding the behaviour of firms. How then, may an industry be defined?

One approach is to define an industry as all those firms producing the same commodity, or as a group of firms producing commodities which are 'close substitutes'. Here, an industry is defined from the demand side, and the method has the merit of grouping together those firms which are closely interdependent in terms of market behaviour in relation for instance to price determination and advertising policy. The problems involved in such an approach are those of defining a commodity and of deciding where to draw the line when attempting to group together those products which are close substitutes. Furthermore because of the diversified nature of many firms it will often be impossible to allocate whole firms to a particular industry.

In fact it is establishments and not firms which are classified by industry.[1] This means that the definition of industries is likely to be based mainly on supply factors rather than on market considerations since it is technical and other supply factors which basically determine the products which are produced within an establishment. This emphasis on the supply side will sometimes result in industry boundaries which are not wholly appropriate to a study of the competitive process. Thus, for instance, in the Standard Industrial Classification the manufacturing of cloth, leather and fur gloves is

[1] In the case of one-establishment firms there is, of course, no distinction.

69

classified into a different industry from the manufacture of knitted gloves, although in terms of the degree of substitutability to buyers they would undoubtedly be grouped together. In other cases the Census industry will be 'over-inclusive'. This may occur where products, which are not close substitutes to buyers, are grouped together because they are produced by a common process. Again the Census industry refers to national production whereas, because of high transport costs in relation to the value of the product, the products of sellers in different regions or even towns may not be close substitutes to buyers. Finally, the use of the establishment as the basis of classification does not solve the problem of the multi-product firm. In many cases several products are produced within the same establishment. The latter therefore have to be classified according to its principal products. But the principal products of the trade will not always be produced exclusively by the establishments allocated to it, and these establishments may also produce the principal products of other trades.

In many instances, therefore, the Census definition of an industry will not approximate at all closely to the theoretical industry defined in terms of a group of products that are close substitutes to buyers. Given these shortcomings, then, it is clear that the more detailed the breakdown of activities shown by the Census the better, for the more detailed the classification the greater the scope for the reclassification of industries on to a basis which is more appropriate for the conduct of a particular investigation. The difficulties which arise from the Census emphasis on technical rather than market considerations should not, however, be overemphasized. The use of common raw materials or similar technical processes do in many ways provide a sensible basis for grouping firms, and our discussion of diversification in the previous chapter shows that such similarities on the supply side are frequently the basis of potential if not actual competition between firms.

Given the fact that a satisfactory definition of industries can be arrived at, our main concern is with an examination of the main aspects of industry structure, the behaviour of firms and market performance, and of any systematic relationships which might exist between structure and conduct on the one hand and market performance on the other. Economic theory suggests that the structural features of an industry strongly influence the competitive interaction among its constituent firms, and the prices, profits and output levels resulting in its markets. But only under narrowly specified theoretical conditions has it been possible to deduce market performance entirely from structural factors. Beyond the limiting case of perfect competition theory serves best as a guide to the identification of potentially significant variables and to the development of hypotheses about the relationship between them. In this chapter we look at some aspects of socially acceptable market performance and to the evidence relating to these aspects. This is followed in Chapters 4 and 5 by an examination of industry structure and business behaviour. Chapter 6 then looks at some relationships between industry structure, business behaviour, and market performance.

B. ASPECTS OF SOCIALLY ACCEPTABLE MARKET PERFORMANCE

It is not possible to outline the aspects of socially acceptable performance without the intrusion of personal values, but the following would probably command general agreement.

First is efficiency in the production of a given set of outputs. Production should be optimally allocated between plants which, where the market is large enough, means that production will be carried on in plants of minimum optimal size. Furthermore the cost advantages of vertical integration should be realized and there should be no prolonged under- or over-capacity. There is also the question of the internal efficiency of firms. That is, with a given capital stock, a given technology and a given set of resource prices, firms should be producing goods and services with a minimum expenditure of the economy's resources. This condition implies that firms should utilize capital embodying the latest technological improvements as soon as it is economical for them to do so. It also implies that there must be resources devoted to improving the production processes through technical research and development, or that there is an information system which has access to such activities in other countries. In addition, resources should be devoted to the improvement of the management and administrative processes within the firm so that progress in the techniques of co-ordinating keeps pace with technical advances in production.

A second aspect of performance relates to the need for the system to devote resources to product innovation. This objective includes the improvement of existing products and the development of new ones in both the producers' and consumers' markets.

A third aspect is that the fruits of the efficiency gains and innovative activity in the economy be passed on to society as a whole. This means that the gains should not result in a persistent tendency towards excess profits or excess selling costs but should rather be converted to benefits to the consumer in the form of lower prices and improved quality. This does not mean of course that excess profits are never justified. In particular they would be justified, for instance, where demand has increased relative to capacity and where there is, therefore, a short-run condition of excess demand. Here excess profits provide the desired spur to increase capacity. Again, excess profits are justified as a reward to the successful innovator, although exactly how much excess profit is needed as a reward is difficult to determine. The issues involved are complex ones and we shall return to them in a later chapter. The same applies to selling costs. These are an essential part of business activity but in certain cases the costs incurred are undoubtedly excessive.

This outline of some of the main aspects of acceptable performance relates of course only to the enterprise section of the economy. In terms of the *aggregate* performance of the economy it is obviously only a part of the overall picture. The aggregate performance relates to such factors as the level of employment, the degree of stability in the level of output and its rate of growth, the allocation of resources and the distribution of income and wealth. They are affected not only by the behaviour of firms but also by the behaviour of trade unions and particularly by government policy. Furthermore, wider issues relating to welfare are ignored. Thus, for instance, we do not take account of such factors as the extent to which the organization of the enterprise system allows individuals to participate in decision-making. An increase in the degree of democratization might be considered a worthwhile prize even if it entails some loss of efficiency.

But even when we are concerned only with an examination of the evidence relating to those aspects of performance which have been outlined we have to begin with the recognition of the limitations which an analysis of this kind inevitably faces. A complete assessment across industries of performance in relation to any of the aspects outlined is impossible, either because of lack of evidence or because we do not have adequate criteria for evaluating the performance observed. In the latter case even if relevant data are available difficulties are encountered in interpreting the evidence because of the absence of clear-cut standards of desirable performance. The problem here very often takes the form of having to 'trade-off' one goal against another with no universal agreement on what is the socially most desirable rate of exchange between the two goals. Two examples will suffice to illustrate the difficulties. First there is the problem of evaluating the progressiveness of industries in invention and innovation. A comparison of industry research and development expenditures reveals nothing. An industry's progressiveness can be evaluated only in terms of how progressive it has been relative to its opportunities. The difficulties in relation to invention are obvious, for the potential rate of discovery against which the actual rate

might be measured cannot in any way be systematically approximated. But even in the case of the commercial application of previously discovered techniques the amount of evidence needed to
evaluate performance is complex and of a kind which is not readily
available. Secondly, there is the question of the choice between
variety and standardization. Buyers will generally have different
tastes regarding the quality–design–price combination which they
most prefer. Differences in tastes may be great but standardization
may result in economies of scale and therefore lower unit costs. The
problem of choice in this context is particularly important where
there are substantial economies of scale and where the size of the
market is such that it can support only a very limited number of
plants producing the standardized commodity.

With these problems in mind we proceed to examine some of the
evidence on market performance. Some of this evidence, especially
that relating to innovation, has already been dealt with in Chapter 2.
Here we focus attention on three other aspects of performance—
efficiency, profitability and selling costs.

C. EFFICIENCY

One of the most important elements of efficiency is the extent to
which an industry is composed of plants of efficient scale. In a detailed
study of twenty manufacturing industries in the United States Bain
concluded that typically, 'enough plants are so near optimal or
larger scales that the bulk of industry output is provided by plants
suffering no serious cost disadvantage because of scale'.[2] For the
UK the evidence is more scanty. There have, however, been attempts
at measuring the importance of economies of scale in some industries which suggest the existence of gross structural inefficiencies.[3]

Further information on plant size is obtained by international
comparisons of industrial structure. In one such study Bain found
that, on the basis of data on the average number of employees in the
largest 20 plants for a sample of 34 industries, large UK plants are
on average almost one-quarter smaller than their US counterparts in
terms of employment, and thus smaller by a more substantial margin
in terms of output because of higher US productivity.[4] With US

[2] Joe S. Bain, *Barriers to New Competition* (Harvard University Press, 1962),
p. 111.
[3] C. Pratten, R. M. Dean and A. Silberston, *The Economies of Large Scale
Production in British Industry: An Introductory Study*, University of Cambridge,
Department of Applied Economics, Occasional Paper 3 (Cambridge University
Press, 1965).
[4] Joe S. Bain, *International Differences in Industrial Structure* (Yale University
Press, 1966).

average employment per plant in each industry equal to 100 the indexes of plant sizes in the UK varied from 24 to 131. As compared to non-US countries, however, the scale of plant in the UK is on average very favourable. Thus, for instance, with the US average employment per plant again equal to 100, the median plant size in France was 39, in Japan 34, and in Italy 29. These results are based on data relating to the mid-1950s and the position since then may have changed significantly, although it is unlikely that the UK position relative to that of our non-US competitors has on average become unfavourable. There will certainly be a number of instances, however, where it has. A comparison of the UK iron and steel industry with that of Japan's is a good case in point.

Even for those industries where the average size of plant is less than that in the US this does not mean of course that all plants in the UK are of sub-optimal size. Typically there will be a range of plant sizes part of which will be classified as inefficient, and the various scraps of evidence available suggest that this tail of inefficiently small plants is typically larger in the UK than in the US. A number of explanations have been put forward to help account for this difference.

First, in so far as newer techniques have in general favoured larger plants, the difference may be partly accounted for by the higher standards of obsolescence in the US induced by the higher level of real wages there. The reasoning behind this argument is roughly as follows. Assume a competitive industry in which there are no differences in labour and managerial efficiency between firms, where all plants are operating at full capacity, and where each plant consists of indivisible capital equipment embodying the best available technique when it was built and which cannot be adapted to subsequent techniques. Any industry will be made up of a number of plants embodying a range of techniques, such a range existing because whereas new plants embodying the latest techniques will not be built unless total revenue is expected to cover total costs, plants already in existence will not be scrapped until revenue is insufficient to cover *operating* costs, or replaced until the operating cost of the old plant is equal to the total costs of a new plant.[5] Clearly, then, the rate of scrapping and replacement, i.e. the standard of obsolescence, is influenced by relative factor prices. The higher the level of real wages the higher are operating costs of old plants

---

[5] This formulation ignores the site value of the plant, working capital and scrap value. Taking account of these factors the formula for scrapping is that plants will be scrapped when the surplus earned over operating costs is just insufficient to earn a normal return on the present value of the site, the working capital and the scrap value of the fixed capital.

relative to new ones, and the greater the disadvantages of retaining out-of-date methods of production. The higher, therefore, will be the standards of obsolescence and the more up-to-date will be the capital stock. This argument suggests, then, that as compared to the US, a longer tail of plants in the UK using out-of-date methods of production is due to the lower level of scrapping and replacement which in turn is due to the lower level of real wages.

A second argument is that restrictive agreements have been far more prevalent in the UK and that these agreements to restrict competition have protected inefficient firms and allowed a wider dispersion of efficiency to persist than would otherwise have been the case.

A third part of the explanation may be that there is a greater amount of product differentiation in the UK reflecting in part a different pattern of consumer preferences but also the different reactions of management to uncertainty. The production of specialities is, of course, a frequent explanation of the survival of small firms in an industry dominated by much larger units, and in so far as their existence means that cost savings associated with a more standardized production pattern are foregone this is the price which is paid for greater variety.

More serious, however, from the point of view of efficiency is the situation where several product lines are produced in the same plant. We saw in Chapter 2, for instance, how the process of competition in industries experiencing fluctuations in demand may result in a group of firms diversifying into each other's main lines of activity. In a situation of this kind there may be very little excess capacity but a great deal of technical inefficiency in the sense that the products would be produced more efficiently if each firm was more specialized and had a larger share of its more specialized output. Although there is little detailed evidence available it is commonly supposed that the typical British plant of a given size turns out more product lines than its US counterpart. It may be possible, therefore, to achieve substantial economies by standardizing production so as to allow individual firms to increase the output of particular products and so to extend production runs. How much is possible along these lines depends on the number of firms and the size of the market. It has been argued that in some cases at least the size of the UK market may be too small to induce the existing number of firms to invest in the most up-to-date technique for the production of a standardized product.

Most economic analysis has concentrated on allocative efficiency assuming that there is no problem of internal efficiency since each output is produced at the lowest possible cost. We have already suggested one reason why this may not be so, i.e. where a number of competing firms are producing two or more products within the same plant so that economies would be achieved by increased specialization. But the possibilities for internal inefficiency are much wider than this. In surveying the evidence relating to the relative importance of allocative and internal efficiency (or 'X-efficiency' as he calls it) Leibenstein concluded that 'the data suggest that in a great many instances the amount to be gained by increased allocative efficiency is trivial while the amount to be gained by increasing X-efficiency is frequently significant'.[6] In other words the evidence suggests that many firms operate with a significant degree of 'organizational slack' which is assumed not to exist in short-run profit-maximizing theories.

If the Leibenstein position is accepted it follows that efficiency should be viewed not only as a function of the market but also as a function of management. There are a number of ways in fact in which it is possible to explain the existence of organizational slack. First, it may exist in the case of an expanding firm where the goal is to maximize the expected stream of discounted profits. Such a firm will for instance be tending to train people for positions in *anticipation* of a continuing increase in demand, and its staff will at any moment of time therefore be in excess of what is needed for *current* operations. Secondly, organizational slack may be due to the pursuit by management of goals other than profit maximization—thus management may be viewed as operating a firm with the aim, subject to a minimum profit constraint, of maximizing a utility function an important component of which is the size of the management team.[7] Thirdly, the achievement of a *satisfactory* performance, in relation for instance to profitability and growth, may be a more accurate description of a firm's goal. Here again there is no presumption of internal efficiency.

There are two other elements of efficiency that need to be mentioned before we turn to other aspects of performances. The first is the degree of vertical integration. In this case, however, it is not possible to reach any general conclusions. We saw in Chapter 2 how the

[6] H. Leibenstein, 'Allocative efficiency versus X-efficiency', *American Economic Review*, vol. 56, 1966.

The importance of internal inefficiency is revealed by the results achieved by firms which, following perhaps the failure to attain a set of goals, have instituted a search procedure to establish the reasons for failure and to improve performance. See for instance O. E. Williamson, *The Economics of Discretionary Behavior: Managerial Objectives in a Theory of the Firm* (Prentice-Hall Inc., 1964), and J. Johnston, 'The productivity of management consultants', *Journal of the Royal Statistical Society*, Series A, vol. 26, part 2, 1963.

[7] See O. E. Williamson, op. cit.

situation is constantly changing as techniques of production and organization change. There is need for detailed evidence in order to judge any case and even then it might not be possible to generalize for any one industry. One manufacturing firm may find it worth while to have its own wholesaling or transport division, another firm not. Such differences may be due to differences in the organizational abilities of management, to differences in the availability of funds or to different assessments of the most profitable use of funds. A further point is that in examining the degree of vertical integration consider-ations of monopoly enter into the reckoning as well as those of efficiency and it is often difficult to separate the two.

The second element of efficiency referred to above is the relation-ship of capacity to demand, and in particular whether certain indus-tries show conditions of persistent excess capacity or shortage of capacity. Industries experiencing fluctuations of demand will of course tend to have periodic excess capacity and under-capacity. Where the fluctuations are due to changes in the overall level of demand all industries will be affected to a greater or lesser extent, although conditions of a shortage of capacity may not materialize in industries which are experiencing a long-term decline or in those where capacity is expanding ahead of demand. Certain industries, however, are characterized by the problem of peak-demand and the associated problems relating to the amount of capacity which is desirable. Such industries include retailing, transport, and electricity. There is evidently here a great problem as to how much capacity is desirable. Should it be adequate to meet peak demand at existing prices or should the relationship of capacity to demand be such as to minimize unit costs over a period of, say, a year. The issues involved are complicated and a full discussion of them would take us too far afield, but the following points are nevertheless worth making.

First, the size of the peak demand is related to the price structure, and as such may be modified by price adjustments. To the extent that price adjustments are feasible, therefore, the problem of sup-plying capacity to meet the peak will be alleviated. The importance of price adjustments may be particularly great where there are two or more facilities for meeting demand as in the case, for instance, of public and private transport. Here the relative charges of the two agencies may have an important bearing on the demand for extra capacity. Secondly, within the existing institutional framework price adjustments may have very little effect on the pattern of demand and even if they did, in some cases they might not be acceptable on grounds of equity. In such cases an administrative 'solution' to the peak demand problem may be appropriate. Thirdly, the problem of peak demand, and the associated problem of how much capacity to build in a particular sector, cannot be discussed without an analysis of the effects of alternative courses of action on other sectors of the economy. For instance, in considering the case say, for sufficient steel capacity to meet peak demand without having to resort to sharp price increases, a relevant argument is that such a situation would allow conditions of buoyant demand to be more prolonged with consequent benefits to the level of employment.

Another important case of excess capacity arises as a result of lags in the adjustments of capacity to secular changes in demand. The problem is particularly great where, as in the case of railways and traditional textiles, downward adjustments of the capital stock are required. Upward adjustment of the capital stock can, however, take place much more quickly so that situations of long-term under-capacity are less likely to materialize unless they arise as a result of monopoly restrictions on the expansion of capacity. A situation of long-term excess capacity will also develop in sectors where small firms are being displaced by large ones, but where the process is a slow one because of product differentiation, including locational advantages, and easy entry conditions, which means that many of the small firms which are driven out of the market are replaced by new ones. Such a situation is approximated by the distributive trades where the small independent firm is losing ground to the large national multiple. The competitive process involved results in a measure of excess capacity which is in addition to that associated with peak demand.

D. PROFITABILITY

A second important aspect of performance is profitability, an aspect which is important in relation to the problem of judging the degree of allocative efficiency attained in the economy. Thus, as noted earlier in this chapter, industries should not show a persistent tendency towards excess profits or indeed losses. The former reflects misallocation of resources as a result of monopoly power and the latter misallocation as a result of the failure of the market mechanism to bring the level of capacity into line with demand. All this is of course perfectly consistent with short-run excess profits and losses since these deviations from zero excess profits are part of the adjustment mechanism by which efficient firms expand at the expense of the inefficient and by which the capacity of individual industries is brought into line with demand.

Ideally, we would like to have information on the relationship between price and long-run marginal cost for a cross-section of industries. This information is, however, not normally available and empirical work has to make use of the data on the ratio of profits to assets. One such measure, the pre-tax rate of return on net assets, is used in Tables 3.1 and 3.2 to indicate the sort of variability in profit

TABLE 3.1. *Average pre-tax Rate of Return on net Assets, 1948–60; for UK quoted Companies in Industry Groups*

Industry group	Pre-tax rate of return on net assets	Industry group	Pre-tax rate of return on net assets
Electrical engineering	20·5	Bricks, pottery, etc.	16·5
Non-electrical engineering	20·2	Cotton and man-made fibres	16·3
Metal manufacturing	20·1	Hosiery	15·8
Metal goods n.e.s.	19·8	Leather, etc.	15·5
Construction	18·2	Wholesale distribution	14·8
Retail distribution	18·0	Clothing and footwear	14·7
Food	17·6	Entertainment and sport	13·6
Chemicals and allied industries	17·5	Miscellaneous services	13·2
Woollen and worsted	17·4	Drink	12·8
Vehicles	17·3	Tobacco	12·0
Paper, printing, etc.	17·2	All industries	16·6

Source: Standardized company accounts prepared by the Statistics Division of the Board of Trade.

TABLE 3.2. *Average pre-tax Rate of Return on net Assets, 1959–66. Leading UK Companies in selected Manufacturing Industries*

Industry	Pre-tax rate of return on net assets	Number of companies
Drugs	25·5	6
Toys	20·0	7
Cement	15·0	4
Biscuits	14·2	5
General chemicals	11·3	7
Cotton	9·9	6
General rubber goods	8·5	4

Source: Standardized company accounts prepared by the Statistics Division of the Board of Trade.

rates which is observed. For twenty-one industry groups shown in Table 3.1, the average rate of return for quoted companies varies from 20·5 per cent for electrical engineering to 12·0 per cent for tobacco, the average profit rate for all industries being 16·6 per cent. These are average figures for broad industry groups and the variability of profit performances is more marked on a finer industry breakdown. This is illustrated in Table 3.2, which shows the average pre-tax rate of return on net assets for some of the leading companies in seven selected manufacturing industries over the period 1959–66. The variability of profit performance is of course even greater on an individual firm basis. Thus in the case of the seven manufacturers of drugs included in Table 3.2 the pre-tax rate of return on net assets varies from 77·9 per cent to 11·8 per cent, and for cotton the variation is from 19·9 per cent to 0·8 per cent.

It is apparent from such data that over a given period some firms are earning persistent excess profits of varying amounts whereas at the other end of the scale there are firms which are failing to earn a normal return on capital. This evidence does not in itself, however, give an indication of the extent of allocative inefficiencies. It would do so only to the extent that in the case of excess profits, for instance, such profits were due to monopolistic restriction of output, and not to other factors such as superior management and innovative activity. Clearly over any given period to which profit figures apply it is important to determine the causes of excess profits. Such an analysis is an essential part of the evaluation of the profit performance of industries or firms and thus an important aspect of anti-monopoly policy.

E. SELLING COSTS

As mentioned earlier in this chapter another aspect of performance is that of selling costs. Performance in this respect would be regarded as unsatisfactory if selling costs were judged to be excessive. The costs involved here include such items as the cost to manufacturers of employing salesmen, the cost of sales-promotion efforts, manufacturers' advertising expenses, and selling cost incurred at the wholesale and retail stages of distribution. Information, however, is readily available for advertising expenditure only, and Table 3.3 shows advertising expenses both in terms of the total amount spent and as a percentage of net output for the fourteen main Orders in the manufacturing sector as well as for certain industries within these Orders. The information relates to 1963. The most striking feature of the table is of course the very wide variation in advertising expenses. As a percentage of net output, for example, it varies from over 30

TABLE 3.3. *Advertising Expenditure in Manufacturing, UK, 1963*

Industry	Amount spent on advertising £'000	% of net output
Food, drink and tobacco	109,735	8·8
Cocoa, chocolate confectionery	13,159	11·8
Tobacco	18,818	15·9
Soft drinks	7,106	13·3
Spirit distilling	7,380	10·7
Chemicals and allied industries	74,661	7·3
Pharmaceutical preparations	16,737	15·4
Toilet preparations	14,371	33·9
Soap, detergents	19,962	34·8
Mineral oil refining	5,238	8·2
Lubricating oils and greases	1,690	7·3
Paint and printing ink	4,959	6·5
Metal manufacture	4,467	0·5
Engineering and electrical goods	48,844	2·0
Domestic electrical appliances	9,706	9·6
Shipbuilding and marine engineering	556	—
Vehicles	13,807	1·2
Metal goods n.e.s.	10,793	1·8
Textiles	11,698	1·4
Leather and leather goods	1,205	2·1
Clothing and footwear	9,181	2·3
Bricks, pottery, glass, cement	5,608	1·3
Timber, furniture	5,869	2·0
Paper, printing, publishing	17,216	2·0
Other manufactures	11,376	2·9
All manufacturing	325,017	3·0

Source: Report on the Census of Production, 1963, Part 131, Table 9.

per cent for soap, detergents and toilet preparations to being negligible for shipbuilding and marine engineering and for many other industries within the Orders.

There are several factors which influence the size of selling costs, such as the nature of the product, the frequency with which new products are introduced, the technical conditions of production, the number of competing firms, the degree of customer knowledge and the susceptibility of customers to persuasive appeals. Some of these factors, such as the degree of knowledge of customers, are the basis of the distinction which is made between producer and consumer goods as far as advertising expenditure is concerned, with consumer goods in general being much more heavily advertised. In some cases the heavy advertising is based on the fact that the products are prestige goods where considerations of price are less important than those of quality and reputation. In other cases the heavily advertised goods are ones where it is difficult for consumers to make accurate evaluations of the relative merits of competing brands because of the complexity of the product and/or the infrequency of purchase. The number of sellers influences matters because it affects the degree of interdependence that is felt between competing firms and also the variety of competitive strategies which is likely to be found in the market, both of which will influence the overall level of advertising in the industry. Finally, the technical conditions of production are important in determining the importance of economies of scale and capital requirements. Where these are important they may offer a sufficient deterrent to new entry to make any further entry-preventing strategies unprofitable. If, however, these entry barriers are unimportant, firms may use advertising and distribution policy in order to raise 'artificial' entry barriers to new competitors.

CHAPTER 4

Market Structure

Economic theory suggests that the structural features of an industry influence the behaviour of firms and the prices, costs, profits, and innovation activity, etc. resulting in its market. In this chapter some of the main features of market structure are examined.

A. CONCENTRATION

Seller concentration refers to the number and size distribution of firms operating in a particular market. In this chapter, however, we will use the term in a more restricted sense; that is, to refer to the percentage share of sales, employment or capacity accounted for by the largest firms in an industry. This measure is usually referred to as absolute concentration.[1] We will first examine the evidence relating to the incidence of high, medium and low concentration industries, secondly examine the determinants of concentration and thirdly comment on the usefulness and limitations of concentration as a structural element which is likely to be useful in predicting market performance.

As far as the incidence of varying degrees of concentration is concerned the information for UK manufacturing industry is very incomplete. Out of 268 industries for which five firm sales concentration ratios were published in the 1963 Census of Production exactly half had a concentration ratio of 60 per cent or more and they accounted for about 70 per cent of sales. Seventy industries had a concentration ratio of 80 per cent ore more and accounted for 45 per cent of sales. However, the published ratios refer to the more clearly definable markets covering about two-thirds of manufacturing sales, and they are very much biased towards the highly concentrated industries. One attempt at estimating the distribution of all UK manufacturing industries by degree of concentration in 1963 finds that industries with a concentration ratio of 60 per cent or more accounted for about 37 per cent of total manufacturing

---

[1] There are several different measures of industry concentration, none of which are ideal. Absolute concentration measures, however, have been the most frequently used in industry studies.

83

sales.[2] Allowing for the various errors which can enter such calcula-
tions there is no doubt that industries with high concentration ratios
account for a sizeable proportions of total sales.

As far as changes in concentration are concerned there is no doubt
that the trend since the 1950s has been in an upward direction.
For 63 comparable industries over the period 1951–63, 40 showed
increases in concentration and 23 showed a decline. A more detailed
picture is available for the period 1958–63. Out of a total of 208
industries which showed a change in concentration 141 (i.e. 68
per cent) showed an increase and 67 (i.e. 32 per cent) a decrease in
concentration. The disparity between the number of increases and

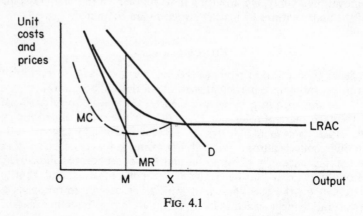

FIG. 4.1

decreases in concentration was particularly great for food and drink,
vehicles, metals, textiles and leather clothing and footwear. For the
first two industry groups the concentration level was already very
high in 1958. In the others, however, the level of concentration in
1958 was generally low.[3]

At the time of writing, the results of the 1968 Census of Production
are still not available, but there is little doubt that the upward trend
in concentration has continued. Indeed it has probably accelerated
largely as a result of the extremely high level of merger activity,
mainly of a horizontal kind, in the second half of the 1960s. This
expectation is supported by the results of a study of public quoted
companies in the manufacturing sector. A comparison of the growth

[2] W. G. Shepherd, 'Structure and Behavior in British Industries, With US
Comparisons', *Journal of Industrial Economics*, November 1972. Shepherd's
estimates incorporate an adjustment to the domestic concentration ratios in
order to allow for imports.

[3] For further details see K. D. George, 'The Changing Structure of Competitive
Industry', *Economic Journal*, March 1972, Supplement.

of the three firm, total net assets, concentration ratio for fourteen industry groups over the periods 1954–59, 1959–64 and 1964–68 revealed that the average rate of increase in concentration was much higher in the latter period than in the two preceding ones.[4]

The factors determining concentration and changes in concentration are, of course, many, and we can mention here only those factors which are of general importance. The first of these is economies of scale. The significant factor is not economies of scale as such, but economies of scale in relation to the size of the market. In other words for the long-run average cost curve (LRAC) shown in Fig. 4.1 the significant relationship is that of OX, the minimum optimal size of firm, to the size of the market in which the firm is operating. This relationship establishes the minimum degree of concentration which is consistent with maximum efficiency. In other words if maximum efficiency is to be obtained all firms in the industry should operate at a minimum size of OX. Where economies of scale are very important in relation to the size of the market this will mean that the market can support relatively few firms of minimum optimal size, so that on this account the level of industry concentration will be high. The actual size of firms, however, depends not only on cost conditions but also on demand and the motivation of management. Thus if a profit-maximizing firm faces a demand curve D, as shown in Fig. 4.1, it will produce an output OM which is less than the minimum optimal size.

The relationship of OX to the size of the market is not the only important factor as far as efficiency and concentration are concerned. Also important are the shape of the cost curve to the left and to the right of OX. The former indicates the extent to which firms of sub-optimal size suffer a cost disadvantage, and is a relevant factor therefore in determining the ease of entry into the industry. We will return to this subject later in the chapter. The shape of the cost curve to the right of OX is relevant in determining to what extent a firm can extend its share of the market without incurring any cost disadvantage. Most empirical work has suggested that, typically, there is at least a fairly wide range of output over which conditions of constant costs apply. There is less agreement, however, as to whether the unit cost curve eventually turns up, thus indicating diseconomies of size. In any case the relevant point is that if there is a range of constant costs then this means that there is no one level of seller concentration which is consistent with maximum efficiency. The degree of concentration consistent with maximum efficiency may in fact be indeterminate over a wide range. Put another way it means

[4] Alan Hughes, *Concentration and Merger Activity in the Quoted Company Sector of UK Manufacturing Industry 1954–69*, mimeo, 1973.

that the actual level of concentration which exists in some industries may be much higher than the minimum degree necessary to secure maximum efficiency. Such cost conditions also offer an explanation as to why firms of different sizes can survive in competition with one another.

The average cost curve drawn in Fig. 4.1 represents the average cost curve of the *firm*. The downward-sloping portion of it reflects the economies of scale, and in the main these are probably technical economies which relate to the plant or establishment. The weight of what evidence is available suggests that multiplant economies are in general slight. In other words most of the important economies of scale relate to the lower unit costs of a large plant as compared to a small one, and there are in most cases, in manufacturing at least, no further substantial cost savings which are due to the operation of several plants by the one firm.[5] If this is so then an analysis of the relationship between the leading companies' share of an industry and the number and size of their plants may give some guide as to the importance of economies of scale in explaining high concentration. The relevant identity in a three-firm concentration analysis is:

$$\frac{\text{Size of three largest firms}}{\text{Size of industry}} \equiv \frac{\text{Number of leading firms' plants}}{\text{Total number of plants}} \times \frac{\text{Average size of leading firms' plants}}{\text{Average size of all plants}}$$

We want to know whether the industry share of the leading firms is due mainly to the operation of larger than average size plants or to the operation of more than a proportionate number of plants. For the US one study based on a sample of 87 industries has come to the following conclusions. First, although the four leading firms typically operate plants of larger than average size, the degree of this inequality in size does not appear to be systematically related to the level of concentration. Secondly, however, multiple plant operation was predominantly carried on by leading firms and the degree of this leading firm dominance was found to be positively related to the level of company concentration. The multiple operations of plants in the same industry by leading companies contributed more to the explanation of concentration differences than did the operation of

---

[5] For some of the evidence relating to the relative importance of economies which relate to large plants and those which relate to multi-plant operation see Joe S. Bain, *Barriers to New Competition* (Harvard University Press, 1956). Of course technical diseconomies within a plant may occur, but there is no need for the firm to incur them, since it can expand by the duplication of plants of optimum size.

larger than average plants.[6] We may tentatively conclude therefore that in the US it is difficult in the majority of cases to explain high concentration by big internal economies of size. Some support for this conclusion is reinforced by Bain's finding based on his study of 20 manufacturing industries. He finds on a national-market basis that in every case but one concentration was greater than that required by single plant economies, and that much of this 'excess' in firm size was due to the multi-plant operations of the four leading firms. Taking sub-markets into account, the degree of concentration was found to be significantly greater than that required for the 4 largest firms to have one optimal plant in 11 out of the 20 industries. These conclusions are based on average data for the 4 largest firms in each industry so that the extent of multi-plant development would be even greater for the largest and second largest firms.

It is of interest to observe that for the UK the average relationships which were found to apply to the US are reversed. Data from both the 1951 and 1958 Censuses of Production show that there is a much closer positive association between the concentration ratio and the plant-size ratio than there is between the concentration ratio and the plant-number ratio, and there is also a strong positive association between the degree of concentration and the average size of plant.[7] In the UK, then, the degree of concentration is more closely associated with the operation by leading firms of plants of larger than average size than with multi-plant operation, which suggests that, *as compared to the US*, economies of scale may be a more important explanation of highly concentrated industries. Or to put it another way, the extent to which concentration is unnecessarily high is less in the UK than in the US. It must be remembered, however, that this finding is only a general tendency and there will be plenty of 'exceptional' cases.

The pursuit of efficiency via economies of scale is only one of the many factors influencing the size of firms and the degree of concentration. Two other factors of general importance are the motivations of management and the desire to restrict competition and gain some degree of monopoly power. The first of these will be discussed in Chapter 5 and so only a brief mention will be made of it here. If,

[6] R. L. Nelson, *Concentration in the Manufacturing Industries of the United States. A Midcentury Report* (Yale University Press, 1962). There is need to look at the absolute size of plants as well as their relative size. Concentration may be unrelated to the latter but related to the former. Nelson finds that concentration was positively related to absolute size but also that the average number of leading firms' plants was also large in industries where the average size was large.

[7] For a detailed analysis see K. D. George, 'Changes in British industrial concentration, 1951–1958'. *The Journal of Industrial Economics*, vol. XV, July 1967.

for instance, the size of the firm is part of the goal structure of management, then the scale of activities will tend to be greater than would result from strictly profit-maximizing behaviour. How important a factor this is in practice is closely related to the organizational efficiency of the firm and its success in adopting new forms of organization which enable a larger size to be obtained without loss of internal efficiency. This does not mean that the entire effect will be for the firm to increase its size in its existing fields of activity, although this is likely to happen to some degree. In addition, the increased-size goal can be pursued by diversification. This form of expansion may well have the effect of increasing the overall level of industry concentration but the effect on concentration in individual industries is less clear.

The desire to restrict competition and gain market power is another important factor influencing concentration which can operate independently of the efficiency factor. The attainment of market power may be the result of internal expansion but often it is the outcome of expansion by acquisition and merger.[8] One of the main reasons for interest in mergers is the role they play in producing high concentration, and this has become a particularly important issue in the UK because of the great merger wave of the 1960s and early 1970s. It was noted in Chapter 2 that the average annual expenditure on acquisitions by non-financial quoted companies during the period 1959–66 was, as a percentage of total capital outlay, nearly twice the level for the years 1953–58. A further very big increase has undoubtedly occurred over the period 1967–72 when the average annual expenditure on acquisitions and mergers was well over twice as much as it was in the period 1959–66.

As was mentioned in Chapter 2, it is impossible to make an accurate assessment of the contribution of mergers to the growth of firms because it is not known how the units which have been brought together would have performed had they remained independent. In particular it is not known what the growth performance of the acquired firm would have been. Estimates of the contribution of mergers to increased concentration must therefore be based on reasonable assumptions concerning the alternative position. One such assumption is that the acquired firm would have grown at the same rate as the industry in which it operates. On the basis of such an assumption Utton estimated the effects of mergers on concentration in UK manufacturing industry over the period 1954–65.[9]

---

[8] For ease of exposition we refer to both of these simply as mergers.

[9] M. A. Utton, 'The Effect of Mergers on Concentration: UK Manufacturing Industry 1954–65', *Journal of Industrial Economics*, November 1971.

He found that for manufacturing as a whole over 40 per cent of the increase in concentration was attributable to mergers.

The importance of mergers in increasing market share is further illustrated by the information shown in Table 4.1, which relates to

TABLE 4.1. *Mergers in UK Manufacturing Industry 1961–68*

Industry group	Number of companies		Net assets of largest companies as % of total net assets in class		
	Beginning 1961	end 1968	No. of Companies	Beginning 1961	end 1968
Food	63	39	2	23	30
Drink	106	51	5	41	68
Tobacco	8	7	1	61	71
Chemicals and allied industries	69	45	4	75	79
Metal manufacture	70	56	1	33	31
Non-electrical engineering	198	138	1	15	10
Electrical engineering	87	63	2	28	46
Shipbuilding and marine	22	17	—	—	—
Vehicles	61	41	3	39	63
Metal goods n.e.s.	98	80	1	37	35
Textiles	192	128	2	30	44
Leather and fur	11	11	—	—	—
Clothing and footwear	63	42	1	28	50
Bricks, pottery, glass, cement	73	44	1	26	24
Timber, furniture	40	34	—	—	—
Paper, printing, publishing	99	72	3	41	49
Other manufacturing	52	40	1	44	50
All manufacturing	1,312	908	28		

Source: Board of Trade, *Mergers, a guide to Board of Trade practice* (HMSO, 1969), Appendix 3 to Annex 4.

quoted companies in the manufacturing sector of the UK with net assets of £500,000 or more at the beginning of 1961. The data are of limited usefulness for concentration studies. For instance, the figures relate to industry groups, they exclude any companies which increased their size in terms of net assets to £500,000 or more after the beginning of 1961, and the percentage of net assets held by the leading companies refers to the net assets of the companies in the sample.

The change in the percentage of net assets in the hands of the largest companies from beginning 1961 to end 1968 is also the combined influence of internal and external growth. However in spite of the limitations of the data the information shown in the table does indicate the marked effect which mergers have on industrial structure. First of all, looking at the first two columns of the table it is apparent that there has been a very marked decline in the number of companies in the survey. For all manufacturing, the reduction in the number of companies was 31 per cent, ranging from no change in the case of leather and fur to a reduction of 52 per cent in the drinks industry.

Over the period an important tendency has been for more large and fewer small companies to be acquired. From 1964 to 1968 the number of non-quoted companies acquired by large quoted companies fell from 868 to 458, whereas the number of quoted companies, which of course tend to be much larger than the non-quoted ones, increased from 71 to 140. The greater importance of the acquisition of large companies is important in so far as it means the development of greater dominance by the largest companies in individual industries. Columns 4 and 5 of the table show the extent to which the net assets of the large quoted companies are concentrated in the hands of the largest companies, and how this concentration has changed from 1961 to 1968. For 10 out of the 12 industry groups for which information is available the concentration of net assets has increased and in some cases, e.g. drink, electrical engineering, vehicles and clothing and footwear, has increased very substantially. This increase in the share of net assets of the largest companies is due both to their internal and external growth, but there is no doubt that the latter has been of major importance.

In so far as a desire to restrict competition is an important motive for acquisitions, and it is a strong motive when the existence or danger of excess capacity is present, the advantages of this method of monopolization are clear. In the first place, attempts to reduce the intensity of competition are likely to be more successful the smaller the number of firms. Secondly, anti-monopoly legislation is far more effective in destroying restrictive agreements between large numbers than it is in breaking monopoly practices in tightly organized oligopolistic industries.

There are two other factors related to market power which influence the concentration of industry. The first is that for certain commodities, especially in the consumer goods field, there may be advantages of large-scale sales promotion. Since the 'pulling power' of a large sales effort is more effective than that of small ones, sales promotion activities tend to benefit the larger firms. It may pay a firm therefore to grow large enough to make effective use of the national advertising media. Similar considerations may lead it to establish links on a national basis with distributive outlets. The latter might range from direct ownership of retail shops to the arrangement of special terms with 'independent' retail outlets.

The second factor is that of 'countervailing power'. In this case the existence of large firms with market power on one side of the market is an incentive to the growth of large firms on the other side, so that the latter can both protect themselves from the market power of their suppliers or buyers, and also share in any monopoly gains. However, the question as to whether countervailing power emerges spontaneously is certainly debatable. In the case of retailing, for example, the emergence of the large national multiple can be largely explained by economies of large-scale distribution. There is little doubt, however, that market power is also important. In other words, it will pay a large retailer, for instance, to expand beyond the size at which economies of size are exhausted if by doing so it can bargain for better terms from its suppliers, and this will usually be the case.

Apart from these general factors other more specific ones have been important in explaining increases in concentration in the UK since the late 1950s.

First, there have been a number of developments which have been important in adding to business uncertainty. These include the attack on restrictive practices, the increasing competition from imports and the question of entry into the EEC. When faced with changed circumstances which threaten its market position management will respond by attempting to change internal or external conditions. One possible response is to change industry structure and the quickest way of achieving this is by acquisition or merger.

Secondly, the years 1965 to 1970 saw a great increase in government intervention in industry with emphasis on rationalizing and standardizing production. The direct efforts of government in this field included the setting up of the Industrial Reorganisation Corporation and financial assistance for rationalization schemes. As far as the government is concerned it may also be said that a high level of concentration is convenient from the point of view of planning, whether this be in the form of indicative planning or of direct government participation in industry.

Thirdly, the emphasis on rationalization and size in order to compete more effectively with large overseas companies has resulted in a favourable government attitude being taken towards mergers, particularly those between firms in the same industry. A favourable attitude of this kind is hardly likely to have other than a positive effect on the number of mergers. This is particularly the case in industries where another powerful inducement to mergers already exists in the form of excess capacity, and where the problems of excess capacity are being intensified by technological change. The importance of government attitudes has been most forcibly put by Walter Adams: 'It seems to me that further investigation may well reveal that mergers are not inevitable either technologically or economically, that they are not merely the product of promoters' dreams and rising stock prices, but rather that their occurrence is intimately connected and inextricably intertwined with the permissive, protective or promotive policies of government toward the monopolization of the economy.'[10]

Finally, government fiscal policy may also have tended to increase concentration. Thus fiscal measures such as Corporation Tax and, in certain sectors, the Selective Employment Tax, are likely to have had a relatively adverse effect on the smaller companies. Furthermore, the encouragement which the tax system has given to the retention of profits may well have the effect of encouraging more mergers than could be justified on efficiency grounds. Merger as a means of using available internal resources may be an important feature of the policy of management which has growth as a goal.[11]

There are then some pretty powerful forces making for higher concentration, although it must not be thought that the factors mentioned above always have this result. In addition there are certain offsetting factors at work as well. Apart from any tightening up of the legal constraints on merger activity the most important of these is the growth of markets and the development of new products.

For 63 industries in the UK for which comparable concentration data were available for 1951 and 1958, there was clearly a tendency for declining or stagnating industries to show increases in concentration, and for expanding industries to show decreases in concentration. Thirty industries showed a decrease or no change in employment and of these 22 (i.e. 73 per cent) had increases in concentration. Thirty-three industries showed an increase in employment and in 20 of these (i.e. 61 per cent) the degree of concentration declined or remained constant. Forty-two out of 63 industries then conformed

[10] See Walter Adam's comments on Markham's survey of mergers in *Business Concentration and Price Policy* (Princeton University Press, 1955).

[11] The financial side of mergers also draws attention to another possibility—the role of the company promoter in actively encouraging mergers. The investment bankers and promoters may play an active role in initiating mergers because of the fees and commissions which they receive for their services. In his survey of mergers in the US, Markham concluded that 'corporate promotion and stock market speculation had a great deal to do with the scope and duration of the first and second merger movements'.

to the hypothesis that there is a negative association between growth and concentration changes. Some of these industries were characterized by big changes in employment associated with big changes of opposite sign in concentration. But, in general, the picture showed big changes in employment associated with *small* changes of opposite sign in concentration.[12] This finding is not unexpected. In expanding industries for example the leading firms themselves will often be able to sustain a rapid growth rate and a very rapid overall growth of the industry will be necessary to reduce concentration or indeed to stop it from rising. By the same token, if over a given period the leading firms in an expanding industry have been active in acquiring other firms then any tendency for concentration to decline as a result of growth may be swamped by the effect of merger activity.

Before leaving this discussion of concentration data a word about its usefulness and limitations. Its usefulness lies in its importance as an element of market structure, and also because it may have an important bearing on market behaviour and performance. The suggestion here is that monopoly practices and outcomes are more likely where a small number of leading firms account for a high percentage of industry output than when a large number of firms is needed to account for a large share of market activity. However, there are important limitations to the usefulness of concentration data. First, there are problems relating to the concentration data itself. The data relate to census trades which, as we saw in Chapter 3, are defined from the supply side on the basis of the principal products produced within establishments. This may lead to a definition of a market which is either over-inclusive or under-inclusive as compared to that which is most appropriate for a study of monopoly and competition. In addition, a business unit is defined as a collection of establishments owned or controlled by the same parent company. The criterion used for defining control is ownership of more than 50 per cent of voting shares, and this underestimates the concentration of control because effective control of a company can be obtained with much less than a half of its shares provided the remaining shares are widely dispersed.

Secondly, even if ideal concentration data were available, it is only one of several important factors which influence market performance. Thus, for instance, we need to know the number and size of the non-leading firms in an industry and the individual shares of the leading firms. Such data could be used to calculate alternative concentration indices, and it will almost certainly be the case that the

[12] This finding is reinforced by more recent US data. See 'Industrial Structure and Competition Policy' in *Studies by the Staff of the Cabinet Committee on Price Stability* (Washington, 1969), p. 62.

ranking order of industries on the basis of a 4-firm concentration ratio will not be exactly the same as that obtained on the basis of, say, an 8-firm concentration ratio. Concentration ratios also say nothing about the *identity* of the leading firms. The persistence of a high concentration ratio will have a very different meaning according to whether the identity of largest firms is the same or is changing over time.

There are several other factors as well, of course, which influence market performance—the nature of competition in an industry, the importance of competition from imports and the products of other industries, the rate of change of demand and the goals of firms. The study of the concentration of trades is, therefore, only a first step in the analysis of monopoly and competition. It is a useful first step because the data are widely available and because one can expect some relationship to exist between concentration and market performance.

B. BARRIERS TO ENTRY AND PRODUCT DIFFERENTIATION

The condition of entry of new firms into an industry, whether such entry is relatively easy or difficult, is another important aspect of market structure. Its significance in terms of business conduct and market performance is that entry conditions influence the extent to which firms can pursue monopoly behaviour without much endangering their share of the market. It is important to note at the outset that it makes a considerable difference to analysis as to whether it is assumed that entry possibilities are confined to entirely new firms or are assumed to apply also to existing firms in other industries. Obviously, when the latter are included the entry possibilities are substantially widened. It may also be argued that as far as the individual firm is concerned, 'entry' may also take place by a firm already in the industry. Thus where product differentiation is important such entry would occur when one firm moves into the production of a closer substitute for another firm's product. It may, however, be more convenient to regard this activity as part of the nature of competition amongst established firms in the industry, but it is important not to lose sight of it.[13]

Having made these preliminary comments, let us now turn to a discussion of the factors which are relevant in assessing the likelihood of the successful entry of new firms.

[13] This point, of course, involves the problem of defining an industry. What we have in mind here is that the degree of substitutability between products may be sufficiently high to justify classifying them to the same industry, and that one of the firms may introduce a new product which is an even closer substitute for the products of some of its competitors.

First, there is the economies-of-scale factor. A barrier to entry will exist in the form of economies of scale where the minimum efficient size of firm is large in relation to the size of the market, and where there is a substantial cost disadvantage in operating firms of a smaller size. The form of the analysis will depend on what assumptions are made about what the potential entrant assumes will be the strategy of existing firms after entry. One assumption that the potential entrant may make is that existing firms will fight to maintain their share of the market and in so doing, allow the price of the commodity to fall. Assuming that all established firms and the potential entrant have the same unit cost curve (excluding normal profit), the important considerations for the potential entrant are the size of entry, the cost disadvantage at various sizes, and the difference between the existing price and the post-entry price. Thus in Fig. 4.2 if entry is planned at size X_0 there will be no cost disadvantage, but price will fall, the extent of the decline being determined by the elasticity of demand. If the existing price exceeds minimum average cost by the amount of the anticipated fall in price then entry will not be effected because the potential entrant will anticipate losses on the investment. At smaller sizes than X_0 the price effect will be less but there will now be a cost disadvantage to consider as well, the size of which is determined by the shape of the unit cost curve at sub-optimal sizes. There will be some scale of entry, however, which will minimize the aggregate disadvantage to the potential entrant. This is shown in Fig. 4.2 by adding the price effect to the unit cost curve to

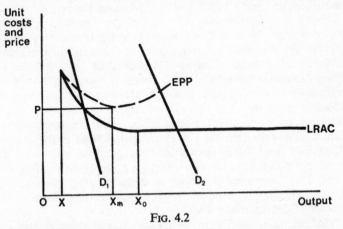

FIG. 4.2

give the curve EPP, which shows the maximum entry preventing price for each scale of output. At size X, entry is on such a small scale that no price-effect is assumed. Entry at larger sizes, however, results in bigger price effects and the aggregate price and cost disadvantages are assumed to be minimized at the entry size of X_m. If the existing price is not greater than P, then entry will not be profitable.

A potential entrant may of course adopt different assumptions; for instance, that existing firms will maintain prices. In this case, if the potential entrant expects a share of the market depicted by demand curve D_1 (drawn on the assumption that all firms charge identical prices), entry will not be profitable so long as price is not greater than P, whereas if the potential entrant expects a share of the market as shown by D_2 there is no economies of scale barrier to entry.

The assumption that existing firms will maintain current prices is less pessimistic than to assume that they will attempt to maintain their market shares. But more pessimistic assumptions are also possible. Thus, for instance, a potential entrant might expect existing firms to react to new entry by increasing output, increasing sales promotion and adopting various predatory tactics in order to prevent the new entrant establishing itself in the market. In this case the maximum entry-preventing price referred to above will lose all meaning, because even if price is above the maximum entry-preventing price there may be no new firms prepared to enter the market if they expect such an aggressive response by established firms.

A second barrier to the entry of new firms may exist because of absolute cost advantages which existing firms may have in the form, for instance, of superior production techniques maintained by continuous technical advance and patent protection, control of essential inputs, and a lower cost of investment funds.

Thirdly, entry barriers may exist in the form of product differentiation advantages of established firms. It is important to note that although differentiation of commodities is necessary for this type of barrier it is the sales promotion activities of firms, particularly through intensive advertising and the development of distributive arrangements, which really give the advantage to existing firms. Indeed in itself the ability to differentiate a product may tend to increase the opportunities for competition. With the introduction of product differentiation, then, the manipulation of both price and selling costs is seen to be part of the strategy which may be adopted by existing firms to restrict new entry, an increase in selling costs taking such forms as intensive advertising allied perhaps with frequent changes in product design, and the development of a network of distributive outlets.

What, in more detail, are the disadvantages which are imposed upon potential entrants and indeed existing small firms in the industry, by intensive sales effort? The existence of heavy selling expenses by existing firms will tend to put potential entrants at a disadvantage for three reasons. First, sales cost per unit of output is likely to be greater for a new firm which is trying to capture a market than for an existing firm which is trying to maintain its share of the market. 'The cost of selling is only in part and in certain conditions a cost of production. At other times and in other conditions it is a cost not of producing but of growing. For once the market has been won it can be retained at a lower selling cost than is necessary to secure it initially. The high cost of selling may be paradoxically at the same time a source of economy ... and a cost of growth which makes it unprofitable for small firms to grow to their most efficient size.[14] A second disadvantage which the smaller firm faces is due to the fact that there are advantages of large-scale advertising, both because the cost per unit of advertising falls as advertising increases, and because there are 'thresholds' in advertising expenditure above which advertising is more effective in influencing consumer decisions. Finally, heavy sales promotion expenditure increases the resources needed by potential entrants to effect successful entry into a market.

This last effect is seen in particular in the case of such products as soap and detergents where there are no substantial problems of entry as far as production is concerned. They are also commodities for which a considerable amount of brand switching occurs so that if the two leading suppliers produced, say, only one brand each then a new entrant could capture a substantial share of the market partly by advertising and partly by capturing a percentage of the 'floating' customers. However the production of several brands backed up by intensive advertising serves to establish substantial entry barriers to new competition. The cost structure shown in Fig. 4.3 illustrates the situation referred to. Because economies of scale in production are unimportant the average production costs give a minimum optimal scale of plant OM, which is small in relation to the size of the market. The heavy advertising costs are shown by the curve AAC, which when added to average production costs gives an average total cost curve ATC which has a minimum point at a much higher level of output. That this picture fairly accurately reflects the position in household detergents is confirmed by several pieces of evidence found in the Monopolies Commission Report, which strongly suggest that the size of the two dominant firms—Unilever, and Procter & Gamble—is very much greater than the minimum size needed to achieve all important economies of scale in production. For instance the Monopolies Commission estimated that in 1964 about 10 per cent of the market was supplied by companies other

[14] E. A. G. Robinson, *The Structure of Competitive Industry* (Cambridge University Press, 1958).

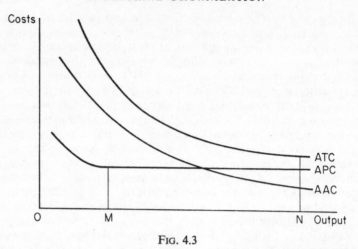

Fig. 4.3

than the two dominant ones. 'These smaller suppliers accounted for about 4 per cent of the total powder and flakes market and about 36 per cent of the liquids market. The total number of suppliers was about sixty of whom fifty supplied liquids and seventeen supplied powders or flakes, some on a very small scale.' The survival of companies of this size hardly points to the existence of important economies of scale in production. Again both the dominant companies have three factories producing detergents, each producing more than one product. In one of Unilever's factories five products are produced, and in Procter & Gamble's case one factory produces five products and another, six. This evidence again shows that the market share of these producers is much higher than that necessary to achieve minimum production costs for one product.[15]

Factors such as economies of scale, absolute cost advantages and selling costs may then, separately or in combination, create important barriers to entry. However, whether or not a dominant firm or group of firms in a highly concentrated industry will in fact attempt to set an entry-preventing price depends on circumstances. If the firms are long-run profit maximizers it may not be beneficial to adopt such a policy even if it would be effective. That is, the firms might judge their long-run profit position to be more favourable by charging a price higher than the maximum entry-preventing one, because the higher profits earned now are more than enough to offset the lower profits attainable after entry has occurred. For an entry barrier of given height, judgment on the relative profitability of the two

[15] See The Monopolies Commission, *Household Detergents: A Report on the Supply of Household Detergents* (HMSO, 1966).

courses of action will depend on the firms' assessments of such factors as the speed of response of potential entrants to an entry-inducing price, and the extent to which new entry would result in increased price competition within the industry and a fall in their market share. The faster the response of potential entrants and the greater the increase in competition within the industry after entry has occurred the more likely it is that existing firms will adopt a price policy designed to prevent entry. The height of entry barriers themselves of course has an important bearing on the likelihood of entry-preventing price policies being adopted, for the greater the excess of price over unit costs which can be maintained by existing firms without inducing entry, the less likely are they to do anything that threatens to spoil their market position.

It is important, however, not to overstate the importance of barriers to new competition. In particular it is worth while to emphasize again the importance of entry by firms established in other industries and to remind ourselves of the importance of growth and technological change in explaining diversification. In a rapidly expanding market or in one where there is a rapid rate of technological change, entry conditions are not likely to be much affected by the price and profit levels of established firms. Such conditions are likely to attract large firms in other industries not only because of the obvious opportunities for further expansion but also because of the prospects of future profits. Given the importance of economies of scale, the more rapid the rate of expansion of market demand the less likely it is that the entry of a new firm will result in excess capacity. Where technological know-how is an important factor the more likely it is that a firm will be able to enter an industry with an advantage in terms of a superior process or product. Furthermore, for the firm which is considering whether to diversify into another industry what is important is not so much the profit performance of existing firms but its own prospective profits. Of course, the former may be used as a guide to the latter, but where market demand is increasing rapidly or where there is a rapid rate of technological advance, entry-preventing price policies on the part of existing firms, if attempted, are not likely to stand much chance of being successful.

So far, product differentiation has been looked at as an entry barrier or, more accurately, as the basis on which established firms will be able to build up a marketing advantage of varying degrees of strength over potential entrants. But product differentiation is also an important feature of the structure of markets in its own right, and it has an important influence on the nature of competition between existing firms and on market performance.

Product differentiation may be based on a number of different factors such as differences in product design, differences in the amount of service offered to customers, persuasive advertising coupled with consumer ignorance about the true qualities of the product, the ownership of a large distribution network, and differences in location which result in differences in prices (including transport costs) faced by the consumer. The importance of product differentiation varies greatly from industry to industry, but it tends to be a far more important factor in consumer-good industries than in those supplying producer goods. The various sources of product differentiation also vary a great deal in importance. Thus in the case of goods like detergents, persuasive advertising is important; in the sale of motor vehicles the emphasis is on product designs and dealer networks; in retailing it is on differences in location and in the amount of service supplied with the goods, and so on.

The existence of product differentiation has important implications for the behaviour of firms because it opens up a variety of new competitive strategies of the 'non-price competition' variety. There are also important implications for market structure and performance. A range of outcomes is possible, from large numbers of firms competing on the basis of a wide range of variables—prices, advertising, product quality and design, to the dominance of a few sellers competing mainly by means of advertising and other non-price variables. In the case of consumer goods there is a strong likelihood in fact that a few firms will get into an advantageous position. This is because it is in this sector that market shares are most likely to be affected by heavy advertising and frequent style changes. The greater variability in the growth rates of firms which this implies may itself mean more rapid increases in concentration if firm growth is a matter of mere chance.[16] In addition, the advantages of large-scale sales promotion, especially through the medium of television, will be a strong force resulting in increases in concentration. In an analysis of 33 consumer goods industries in the US, in which television network advertising exceeded a quarter of a million dollars in 1963, J. M. Blair found that 25 recorded significant increases in concentration while only 8 registered declines. This was over a period when in US manufacturing as a whole increases in concentration were roughly matched by decreases.[17]

[16] See P. E. Hart and S. J. Prais, 'The Analysis of Business Concentration', *Journal of the Royal Statistical Society*, 1956.

[17] J. M. Blair, *Economic Concentration: Structure, Behavior and Public Policy* (Harcourt, Brace, Jovanovich, 1972), pp. 322–3.

CHAPTER 5

Business Behaviour

The conventional theory of the firm examines the determination of price and output under conditions of given tastes and a given technology. That is, the demand and cost conditions for a given product produced by the firm are assumed to be determined by factors external to the firm. Much of the literature also assumes a single-product firm and that the sole objective of the firm is to maximize profits. We saw in Chapter 2 that, at least from the point of view of understanding the process of growth of the firm, the assumptions of a given technology, a given pattern of consumer demand and the production of a given commodity have to be abandoned. An analysis of the growth of firms has in short to recognize that progressive managements are continually attempting to change demand and the techniques of production to their own advantage and are also on the look-out for profitable opportunities to diversify into new lines of activity. This chapter is concerned with two other important aspects of the firm—the firm's objectives, and some issues relating to the determination of price and output.

A. BUSINESS GOALS

Most of the literature dealing with business goals has been concerned with the question of whether these goals can be accurately described as profit maximization. The debate has focussed attention on such issues as decision-making under conditions of uncertainty, the divorce between the ownership and control of large companies, and the nature of competition in product markets and in the capital market. This section attempts to summarize some of these basic issues.

Firms do of course operate under conditions of uncertainty. One important implication which we have already had occasion to refer to is that under such conditions profit maximization has no unique meaning. The consequences of alternative courses of action to the firm's profit position are not perfectly known. Rather, each course of action is associated with a range of outcomes of varying degrees of probability. By devoting resources to the collection of information the firm can reduce uncertainty, but there is a limit to the usefulness of this course of action both because of the limited resources which the firm has for collecting information and of the cost of acquiring it.

The problem of having to make decisions under conditions of uncertainty is likely to result in the adoption of profit goals which can best be described as 'satisfactory profits'. This is applicable to all firms regardless of their organizational form. Particular attention has been paid however to firms where there is a divorce between ownership and control; that is, where control is in the hands of a management team which has no equity stake, or only a very small one, in the firm. Such firms may display two important tendencies. First, as far as profit performance is concerned there may be a strong tendency to play safe and to avoid risky ventures. When management has little equity stake in the firm it will gain relatively little when the firm makes exceptionally high profits, but stands to lose a great deal from exceptionally low ones. As compared to owner-controlled firms there may, therefore, be a tendency to undertake projects which offer a very high probability of a reasonable return and to avoid devoting much time to the search for projects which might yield an exceptionally high return but which also carry a high risk of failure. Secondly, management may have a preference for goals other than profit maximization. Thus, for instance, managerial salaries and prestige are more closely related to the size of firm than its profitability, and when promotion takes place largely within the firm the size and remuneration of the management team are likely to be important aspects of the goal structure.

A divorce between ownership and control may, then, have important repercussions on the working of the private enterprise sector of the economy, and it is clearly important to have some idea of the extent to which the resources of the private sector are concentrated in this form of organization. The task of estimating the extent of the divorce between ownership and control is not an easy one. There are some cases, for instance, where the single largest shareholder owns more than 50 per cent of the voting shares, where the distinction is clear. The problem is where to draw the line in the case of minority holdings. How many shareholders holding what percentage of shares is necessary to secure control over policy? Clearly there is no one answer to this question, the outcome depending on the degree of cohesiveness of a small group of shareholders who control a significant minority of shares and the degree of indifference of the remainder. In some cases a minority shareholding of as little as 20 per cent may be sufficient to secure control. But other factors are also important. These include the number of shares held by the board of directors, the number of directors to be found amongst the top, say, 20 shareholders, and the type of major shareholders; that is, whether the major shareholders are persons, other commercial and industrial companies or financial institutions.

Using yardsticks such as these Professor Sargent Florence attempted to estimate the extent of the divorce between ownership and control in the UK industrial and commercial sector in 1951.[1] His data were taken from a sample of companies with assets of over £200,000, and it was estimated that about 30 per cent of the companies were owner-controlled and that the remaining 70 per cent were characterized by divorce between ownership and control. This was almost certainly an overestimate of the extent of divorce even within the population of large companies because the criteria used to establish the existence of owner control were rather stringent. It is certainly, of course, an overestimate of the extent of management control for the whole economy because it excludes the smaller firms in both the goods and service sectors of the economy, where divorce between ownership and control is not normally found. It must be remembered, however, that the importance of the large companies is out of all proportion to their numbers. For instance, in 1968 there were just over 1,200 public quoted companies operating in UK manufacturing industry with net assets of £½ million or over. The 100 largest companies (or 8 per cent of the total) accounted for about 70 per cent of the total net assets of this sector of manufacturing.

It has to be concluded, therefore, that a very important part of the private enterprise sector of the economy is characterized by management control and that the goal of these firms may not be accurately described as profit maximization. It has been argued, however, that even though some firms may want to pursue goals other than profit maximization the struggle for survival will result in their elimination from the market. In other words, in a highly competitive world only the profit maximizers will survive. But such an outcome need necessarily occur only under very restrictive assumptions. Thus where there are many firms producing a homogeneous product under conditions of constant costs, where a large proportion of existing firms are profit maximizers and where these firms are not at any financial disadvantage as compared to the non-profit maximizers, then indeed only the profit maximizers will tend to survive. But in the oligopolistic industries which characterize the manufacturing sector there will be a wide range of situations where non-profit-maximizing firms will be able to survive just as easily, or indeed be

[1] P. Sargent Florence, *Ownership, Control and Success of Large Companies, An Analysis of English Industrial Structure and Policy 1936–1951* (Sweet and Maxwell, 1961).

more likely to survive than the profit maximizing ones. For instance, where important economies of scale can be gained at larger outputs, or where entry barriers such as the ownership of distribution outlets can be erected against new competitors, then firms pursuing growth-maximization policies may drive the maximizers out of business.[2]

There is another major aspect of competition however, which may see to it that the profit maximizers are in a favoured position. This is the competition for investment funds. It has been argued that '... competition in the capital market will allocate monopoly rights to those who can use them most profitably. Therefore so long as free capital markets are available the absence of competition in product markets does not imply a different quality of management in monopolistic as compared with competitive enterprise.'[3] The basic issues have been set out by Professor Baumol.[4] First, if it is to serve as an efficient allocator of funds in the sense of supplying funds more readily to those firms with the highest prospective earnings per unit of assets, the market would have to value stocks on the basis of the capitalized value of the company's expected future earnings flow. Of any two firms, therefore, the one with the highest earnings prospects will have the highest share prices and therefore will be able to raise additional funds more easily. Secondly, there is the question not only of the efficient allocation of new funds but also of the efficient use of existing assets. If all firms had to go into the market from time to time for new funds, and if share prices did reflect future earnings prospects, then management would be forced to be efficient because of anticipated future capital requirements. Both the efficient use of existing assets and the efficient allocation of new funds would thus tend to be assured. There are, however, two major difficulties.

First, actual share prices seem to be only tenuously related to future earnings prospects. They are affected by many other factors including speculation and the amount of information available to shareholders. Typically, the information available to shareholders is such that a range of profit outcomes will be compatible with reasonable or satisfactory performance from the shareholder's point of view. Given the fact that the firm operates under conditions of uncertainty and that investment has to be planned for several years ahead it will not be possible to compare the actual profit performance

[2] For a detailed critique of the proposition that the struggle for survival eliminates the non-profit maximizers see Sidney G. Winter, Jr., 'Economic "Natural Selection" and the Theory of the Firm', *Yale Economic Essays*, vol. 4, No. 1, Spring 1964.

[3] A. A. Alchian and R. A. Kessel, 'Competition, Monopoly and the Pursuit of Pecuniary Gain', in *Aspects of Labour Economics* (Princeton, 1962).

[4] William J. Baumol, *The Stock Market and Economic Efficiency*, The Millar Lectures, Number Six (New York, Fordham University Press, 1965).

with what could have been achieved by more efficient and 'profit-conscious' management except under rather extreme circumstances—such as where the firm makes losses which are not easily attributable to circumstances outside the control of management.[5]

Secondly, many large companies escape the direct discipline of the market for investment funds by financing expansion out of retained earnings. Thus, for instance, in a study of the financing of twenty large US corporations over the period 1939–58, Professor Gordon Donaldson found that in seven of the corporations the retained earnings amounted to more than 100 per cent of total long-term capital requirements, in ten it was 80–100 per cent and in only three did it fall below 80 per cent.[6]

There is, however, an indirect way in which the stock market may impose a strict discipline on companies, and that is by the threat of a take-over bid. The remaining question of importance, therefore, is whether there is any systematic tendency for less profitable companies to be acquired by the more profitable ones. Again there is very little evidence to suggest that this is so. Indeed one study which examined forty-six acquisitions in the UK in the period March–May 1967 found that the evidence did 'not support the thesis that it is a distinct characteristic of the majority of companies being acquired to have a rate of return that is relatively low for the industry concerned'.[7] The reasons for mergers are indeed so diverse that it would not be difficult to think of as many reasons why one should expect the acquired company to be more profitable than the acquiring one as it is to expect that the reverse would be the case.

Monopoly power in product markets and the imperfect functioning of capital markets are such, therefore, as to enable firms to survive and prosper without rigidly pursuing profit-maximizing behaviour. In addition to the *opportunity* for pursuing non-profit goals, however, there must be the *desire* to pursue them. In the managerial theories of the firm the desire for large size is invariably

[5] There are two types of shareholder, however, who may have both the information and interest in reducing the importance of non-profit-maximizing goals. These are the manager–shareholder and the institutional shareholder. In the case of the former there may be a conflict between profit and non-profit-maximizing activities, the net effect on the preference function of management depending on the number of important shareholders in the management team and the size of their holdings. The growing importance of the institutional shareholder may have a significant effect but there is as yet little evidence as to whether they impose important constraints on the management of the industrial and commercial corporations.

[6] G. Donaldson, *Corporate Debt Capacity* (Boston, Harvard Business School, 1961).

[7] H. B. Rose and G. D. Newbould, 'The 1967 take-over boom', *Moorgate and Wall Street*, Autumn 1967.

regarded as an important part of the managerial preference-function.
Thus in Baumol's theory the firm is assumed to maximize sales
subject to a profit constraint, in Marris's they are assumed to maximize the growth rate subject to a security constraint, and in Williamson's, managers derive satisfaction from increasing expenditure on
staff and emoluments.[8] In all three, the size of firm tends to be
greater than that which would evolve under strict profit-maximizing
behaviour. As an example we can take Baumol's theory of sales
maximization. Fig. 5.1 illustrates the single-product case with no

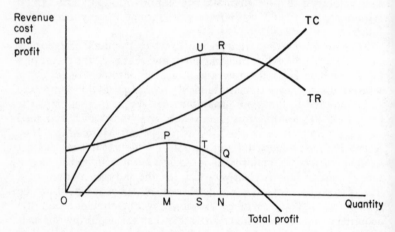

FIG. 5.1. *A Model of Sales-Revenue Maximization subject to a Profit Constraint*

advertising. For the profit-maximizing firm output will be OM. For
the firm which maximizes sales-revenue, output will be greater than
OM so long as the minimum profit constraint is less than the maximum profit level MP. If the minimum profit constraint is NQ or
less, then the firm will succeed in maximizing sales revenue, so that
sales-revenue maximization will be unconstrained. For minimum
profit levels between MP and NQ the profit constraint will be
effective and the firm will not be able to attain the highest point on
the total revenue curve. The position will therefore be one of constrained sales-revenue maximization. Thus with a profit constraint of
say ST, the best that the firm can achieve is a sales-revenue of SU
which is less than the maximum sales-revenue NR. When advertising

[8] See William J. Baumol, *Business Behavior, Value and Growth* (Harcourt,
Brace & Co., 1967); R. L. Marris, *The Economic Theory of Managerial Capitalism*
(Macmillan, 1967); O. E. Williamson, *The Economics of Discretionary Behavior:
Managerial Objectives in a Theory of the Firm* (Prentice-Hall Inc., 1964).

expenditure is introduced the likelihood of a constrained sales maximum solution is increased. For if it is assumed that increased advertising expenditure always increases physical output though with diminishing returns, then with price constant, total revenue always increases as advertising expenditure increases and, since the marginal revenue of advertising expenditure is always positive, increased advertising can be undertaken until profits are reduced to the minimum level. Whether the outcome is a constrained or an unconstrained sales maximum, however, the size of the firm will be greater than the profit-maximizing firm so long as the minimum profit constraint is less than MP.

B. BUSINESS BEHAVIOUR

The above discussion may be summarized by saying that over a wide range of market situations there is no compulsion on the firm to pursue continuous profit-maximizing behaviour. It is not possible to give here a comprehensive view of the literature on business behaviour, and indeed in terms of our prime interest which is in the assessment of market performance much of it would be rather unrewarding. However, some discussion is necessary in order to develop an understanding of some of the factors which are likely to influence the responses of firms to changes in their environment including those changes resulting from government policy.

1. *Managerial Decision-making*

One aspect of business behaviour which is of interest from this point of view is managerial decision-making, and in particular the work done in this field by the behavioural theorists.[9] The following outline is illustrative of the approach adopted in this field.

First, it is recognized that because of uncertainty the firm has only incomplete knowledge of its cost and revenue functions and must make decisions on the basis of the best estimates it can get from its internal and external information systems. This includes obtaining information on the likely reaction of competitors to any changes in, for instance, price and advertising policy which the firm might introduce.

Secondly, the management of the firm establishes a number of different goals it wishes to achieve in any decision-period. These goals represent two major elements. The goals are the outcome of the best judgement of each of the members of the management team as to the achievement necessary in sales, production and profit, for the

[9] See, for instance, R. M. Cyert and J. C. March, *A Behavioral Theory of the Firm* (Prentice-Hall, 1963).

firm to survive and grow. In addition the goals represent the desires of the individual members for the survival and growth of the individual sub-units they represent within the firm.

Thirdly, these goals are acceptable-level goals, in the sense of setting the minimum performance which decisions made on price, output, investment, etc. are expected to achieve. When available decision alternatives are not capable of achieving the set of goals, a search process is instituted by the firm. This is aimed at changing the internal or external conditions (or both) to enable a set of decisions to be found that will achieve the goals. The goals are also a function of the level of achievement in the market. The achievement of the goals in one period will lead to increasing the appropriate goals in the next period. If on the other hand the firm is unsuccessful in achieving its goals, it will institute a search process that will enable it, in prospect at least, to achieve them.

The firm is seen, therefore, as an adaptive organization; an organization which adapts its behaviour as it learns more about its environment, and as its position within the environment changes. Thus, for instance, in a young or immature oligopolistic industry where each individual firm has little knowledge about its competitors there may be a general disinclination to change the price of a product because of the fear of an adverse response—an expectation that price rises will not be followed whereas price reductions will be, with the possibility of an outbreak of intensive price competition. This sort of situation is the one depicted by the kinked demand curve; that is, where the elasticity of demand is high for a price increase but low for a price reduction. Prices, therefore, tend to be sticky at the prevailing level. Although this may approximate the situation in some situations it is unrealistic to assume that it will continue indefinitely. The longer firms survive in competition with one another the more they will learn about each other's behaviour and the more likely it is that overall behaviour will be guided by some form of tacit collusion. In this situation firms will be much better informed about such factors as the motives underlying a price change by one member of the group. They are much less likely, for instance, to mistake a price change which is intended as a signal to alter the overall price level in the industry for one intended as an aggressive move designed to affect market shares.

Again, the firm's behaviour will vary according to its position in relation to the goals of management which in turn are affected by market conditions. Thus for a firm with market power which has continually been attaining its goals, there may be some relaxation of the pressure for increased efficiency. This may be reinforced to the extent that some of the goals which the firm aims for may be set lower than would have been the case in a more competitive situation. If, however, there is a change in the market situation of the firm due, say, to a major technical advance by a competitor which threatens the firm's position, then the drive to be as efficient as possible is likely to be revived.

2. *Price and Output Policy*

In the manufacturing sector, markets are typically of the oligopolistic type. That is, they are characterized by some degree of interdependence between competitors. In addition to uncertainties concerning general demand and cost conditions, therefore, there is also the problem facing each firm of anticipating the reaction of competitors to any important policy moves which it makes.

The problem of dealing with uncertainty cannot be over-emphasized, and under conditions of uncertainty it is important to understand the behavioural rules of the firm and how these rules are modified as a result of learning. The way in which behaviour may be modified as the firm learns more about its environment has already been illustrated. Here we are concerned with a closer examination of behavioural rules—or rules of thumb—and in particular with full-cost pricing.

Full-cost pricing policy is a method by which price is arrived at by adding a 'normal' or 'desired' profit margin to unit costs. Several different formulae exist. One is to calculate unit cost at the standard volume of output—the output which would be produced at normal capacity working. To this estimate of unit cost the profit margin is then added. There are of course problems associated with the use of full-cost formulae, but it can be readily appreciated that so long as the leading firms in an industry use the same formula and have similar costs, or so long as there exists an accepted price-leader using a full-cost formula, then a fair measure of co-ordination between the firms is assured as far as price policy is concerned.

The use of a standard volume formula would, for given cost conditions, leave prices unchanged over the business cycle. A formula whereby price is arrived at by adding a given margin to the unit costs of the output actually produced would call for price increases during a recession—so as to cover higher unit fixed costs, but for little or no increase during an upswing in activity unless costs have increased because of heavy pressure on capacity. The policy of maintaining price stability during an upswing may have the advantage of reducing the strength of the long-run forces of substitution and the entry of new competitors thus enhancing long-term growth prospects and the firms' long-term competitive position.

The use of any full-cost rule will mean that manufacturers' prices will tend to be much more influenced by changes in costs than by short-run changes in demand. From the point of view of maintaining industry discipline this makes sense because prices are changed only in response to clear-cut changes in the environment which will have a fairly uniform effect on competing firms. Such changes include an increase in wages arising from a new industry-wide wage bargain, and an increase in the price of raw materials.

But if prices are not very sensitive to short-run demand changes there must be some other mechanism for clearing markets. This mechanism is found in changes in stocks and in the length of order books. These supply adjustments are essential in maintainining orderly pricing behaviour in oligopolistic markets. When a set of prices has been established it is likely that, because of the difficulties of accurate forecasting, output will be greater or less than the demand forthcoming at those prices. Given that production plans cannot be instantaneously adjusted the difference between demand and current production must be met by changes in stocks or in the length of order books. Such changes enable prices to be maintained and to make frequent price adjustments unnecessary. Of course there are limits to the extent to which it is worth making such changes rather than adjusting prices. There are capital costs involved in holding stocks, and customers may be alienated as order books lengthen. However, as a general tendency, we should expect to find supply changes more important and short-term price adjustments less important in oligopolistic than in atomistic markets.

Although full-cost pricing may be a good account of the method by which firms arrive at prices it does not throw much light on the factors that determine the profit margin. An understanding of these factors is obviously crucial and here we draw attention to two interesting possibilities.

First, firms may attempt to set entry-preventing prices. In this case the profit margin will be determined by the importance of the various barriers to entry outlined in the previous chapter and by the accuracy of the firms' estimates of the limit price. Given that a successful price policy of this kind is in operation then it can be seen to be consistent with the basic elements of the full-cost approach. Thus if prices are changed only in response to industry-wide cost changes this makes sense in terms of maintaining the entry-preventing price level because the cost changes will tend to affect both existing and potential competitors to the same extent. Furthermore the emphasis on changes in stocks and length of order books is important in maintaining entry-preventing prices in the face of fluctuations in demand. This is particularly important where the price policy is being operated by a group of oligopolists because the price–

output combination which is established relates to the group as a whole. It does not establish rules for the division of the total output between members of the group. The market shares have to be determined by some other means. But having been determined it will still be the case that only by chance will the combined output of the group correspond exactly to that required to maintain the entry-preventing prices. Stock changes and order book adjustments are thus important in dealing with unforeseen imbalances between current production and demand and so allow agreed prices to be maintained over longer periods of time.

The second method by which profit margins may be determined is particularly relevant in industries where there is a dominant firm which has growth as an important goal. In such industries the margin may be determined by the dominant firm acting as a price leader and arriving at the desired price by relating its short-run pricing policy both to the needs of finance for expansion and to the effects on future demand. The availability of finance, whether internal or external, depends on past profitability and future prospects as seen by the capital market. The firm, therefore, can increase the availability of finance by earning abnormal profits achieved both by cost reduction and price increase, with the extent of the latter depending upon the inelasticity of the demand curve in the relevant range. Price increases will, however, tend to decrease the rate of growth of the firm, and if growth is a major objective of the firm it will have to strike a balance between the effect of higher prices on the short-run availability of finance, and the effect on the rate of growth of demand for the firm's products.

It is not possible to predict the precise path the growth firm will take but it is interesting to speculate on the comparative behaviour of an oligopolistic industry where growth is the main motivation of the firm, an oligopolistic industry with short-run profit as a goal and a competitive industry, assuming for each one that there is a rightward shift of the demand curve.

For both the profit-maximizing industries, price policy will be based on current demand conditions, so that in Fig. 5.2 the price for the competitive industry will be near to OC_1 in period 1, and the immediate response to the increase in demand to D_2 will be a price increase to OC_2, with the long-run adjustment resulting in a price of OC_1, assuming constant costs. For the profit-maximizing oligopolist the price in period 1 is OP_1 and in period 2 it is OP_2.

In the case of the oligopolistic industry with growth as the main motivating force, the firm will be concerned with the effect of the price charged in period 1 on the demand in period 2, so that price adjustments are likely to be a much less important short-run response to increases in demand. The price has to be consistent with the firm's growth aim. The firm may be assumed to have some idea as to the increase in market demand, its own goal in terms of market share, and what this implies in terms of growth, or it may simply have a goal of maximizing growth. At price OP* the increase in demand will be AB and this will require a certain amount of finance. This price will also be associated with a given profitability which in turn, assuming a given dividend policy, is associated with the ability to raise finance. If profitability at price P* is such as to enable the firm to raise the finance required to expand capacity to meet the extra demand, then this price will be consistent with both the firm's dividend requirements and its requirements of finance for growth.

Another interesting case arises where the combined need for

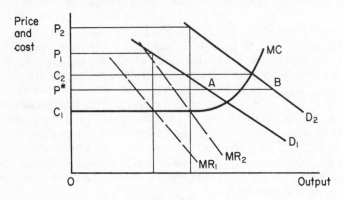

FIG. 5.2

finance to expand and low prices to foster growth can be met by intertemporal price discrimination. Thus if, to simplify matters, we think in terms of a two-period analysis only, units of the commodity which are produced in the first period may be sold at a much higher margin above marginal cost than those produced in the second, a pricing strategy which may be particularly relevant to the introduction of a new commodity. The market position of the firm allows such a strategy to be followed because in the first period there will be less competition from close substitutes than in the second, so that a higher price can be charged for a given volume of output. This behaviour is thus consistent with profit maximization, but it is also consistent with other goals such as growth maximization. By charging a higher margin initially the firm is able to generate more finance for further expansion which is induced by allowing prices to fall more rapidly than costs over time. In this respect the sequence of events is also similar to highly competitive conditions with high profits in the short run followed by low profits in the long run.

So far no account has been taken of advertising and other sales promotion expenditure of firms. Competition through advertising is, of course, a well-known method of competing among oligopolists. In most cases it departs quite quickly from being merely a form of imparting information to a method of trying to convince prospective customers of product differences that are either trivial or non-existing. Advertising is of course only one method of differentiating a product. Other factors such as research and development expenditure are also important. Their relative importance will depend on such factors as the nature of the product and of the market—by the opportunities for technical advance, the susceptibility of consumers to persuasive advertising and the likely response of competitors. In practice it will often be difficult to separate the importance of advertising and research and development as a means of differentiating a product, and indeed the two often go together. In Chapter 2 we referred to the trivial nature of much research and development work in large firms—the sort that leads to minor improvements or just changes in such products as vehicles, and household appliances. Product changes of this kind whether based on technical improvements or changes in style are a particularly attractive form of competition in oligopolistic markets. Whereas price reductions can be matched almost immediately, the response to a product change can take place only after a lag, the length of which depends on such factors as the importance of the change, whether it is protected by patents, and on the ability of competitors to produce a close substitute.[10] Whether the product change is trivial or important, however, it is often associated with heavy advertising expenditure.

An important aspect of advertising and other sales promotion activities emerges when they are viewed as an attempt to separate the joint considerations of the firm's need for finance and future growth of demand. If the policy weapons of the firm are restricted to price competition then every proposed price change must be viewed with respect to its effect on short-run profitability and long-run growth of demand. Advertising can be used to help separate the two goals of profits and growth from their dependence on one policy weapon, with pricing oriented primarily towards the finance factor and advertising expenditure aimed at maintaining the growth of

[10] It is an oversimplification to say that price changes can be matched immediately. It is important to distinguish between a firm's 'list prices' and the ones which are actually paid by customers. The difference between the two is found in the various discounts available to customers in the form of bulk-purchase discounts, discounts for prompt payment, etc. A firm may, by varying the size of such discounts, engage for some time in secret price cutting.

demand. This behaviour reduces the degree of uncertainty involved in attempting to increase demand by price reductions. Distributive arrangements can also be very important in this respect. To give just two examples. Kodak has a 'policy of confining distribution to certain appointed outlets. It is implicit in this attitude that Kodak is dependent upon the good will of the retail chemists [who] . . . have remained the principal outlets for black and white and colour film and the principal retail intermediaries between the public and the processors. The policies pursued by Kodak and other suppliers have played a large part in bringing this situation about'.[11] There is little doubt that this policy has been aimed at preventing price competition. In the case of the distribution of flat glass, Pilkington confines 'the supply of stock sizes (for which prices are lowest) to specialist glass merchants who invest in the necessary premises, stocks and equipment to handle and cut glass in all sizes and provide the full range of services which the glaziers and smaller merchants, as well as the general public require. To allow non-merchant customers such as builders . . . to buy from the manufacturers at merchant's terms when it suited them to do so would, in the company's view "undermine the whole structure of the trade" and so reduce the volume of the merchant's business as to impair his efficiency.'[12]

Firms can and do go further than the type of behaviour described above in order to reduce the likelihood of price competition, by entering into restrictive agreements with their competitors. Direct agreements of this kind were particularly widespread before 1959 when the early adverse reports of the Restrictive Practices Court started to result in the cancellation of large numbers of registered agreements. Agreements to restrict competition are still prevalent, however, although often in a form which does not require them to be registered in the Court. A detailed description and discussion of these agreements can be obtained by a reading of the various Restrictive Practices Court cases and the Monopolies Commission reports. I wish only to make the following general points.

First, agreements are usually, or need to be, more formal in industries with low concentration than in substantial and highly concentrated oligopolistic industries. They can therefore be more readily identified in such industries.

Secondly, if an existing agreement is declared illegal the possibilities of finding an alternative collusive behaviour pattern which attains the same results is much greater in the more concentrated

[11] The Monopolies Commission, *A Report on the Supply and Processing of Colour Film*, HMSO, 1966, p. 108.
[12] See The Monopolies Commission, *A Report on the Supply of Flat Glass*, HMSO, 1968.

industries, where, for instance, the close interdependence of sellers without any formal agreement may be sufficient to secure uniformity of action.

Thirdly, and as noted above, restrictive agreements relating to the distribution of goods are also found in industries dominated by one firm. Furthermore, the agreements may involve foreign suppliers. Thus Courtaulds, for instance, has regulated the imports of cellulosic fibres into the UK by means of arrangements with producers in the European Free Trade Association countries.[13] Again in the case of flat glass there are a number of informal arrangements between Pilkington and Continental suppliers. For instance, there are annual discussions to decide what discounts should be allowed to individual merchants in the UK, and Pilkington gives a week's notice to the Continental producers of intended price changes. Furthermore Pilkington's exclusive rights to the float process of making flat glass must also, through its licensing policy, enable it to have a substantial influence on international competition.[14]

Finally it should be noted that the mere existence of collusive agreements does not necessarily imply that they are effective in achieving their aims. Secret price cutting by members to the agreement, competition from firms outside the agreement, and competition from substitutes, for instance, may mean that the agreement is ineffective in attempting to cause departures from a highly competitive position. Much will depend of course on the dispersion of efficiency in the industry, whether or not low-cost firms also have the bargaining power associated with size, the state of trade, and so on. Thus although price leadership, for instance, may seem to be well established in an industry, the prices of the leader may nevertheless vary with the threat of independent action by competitors or with the emergence of secret price cutting. On the other hand the absence of any outward manifestation of collusive behaviour does not mean that monopolistic pricing policies are not present. In highly concentrated industries a very entrenched agreement on prices may exist as a result of interdependence together with the fact that firms have co-existed long enough to have learnt a great deal about the behaviour of rivals.

[13] See The Monopolies Commission, *A Report on Man-made Cellulosic Fibres*, HMSO, 1968.
[14] See The Monopolies Commission, *A Report on the Supply of Flat Glass*.

CHAPTER 6

Structure–Behaviour–Performance Relationships

The main elements of market structure, business behaviour and market performance have now been reviewed. It remains to look at some of the relationships which are likely to exist between the main variables and in particular to examine some of the results of empirical work in this field. Before turning to this, however, a reminder is needed. In dealing with empirical work we are never dealing with data which are perfect from the point of view of what is ideally needed to test a hypothesis. For instance, concentration ratios refer to census trades and not to theoretical industries. Again, figures of the profitability of firms are not ideal for the purpose of testing the degree of allocative efficiency, and the profitability of different firms may not be strictly comparable because of different accounting conventions, the frequency of revaluations and so on. In the case of variables such as entry barriers no 'ready-made' set of data exists, and the research worker can only arrive at estimates of such barriers after a great deal of detailed research in individual industries. The research worker has to get as close to the ideal figures as possible, but he can never achieve perfection so that there are always shortcomings attached to the data which have to be borne in mind when interpreting the evidence.

It would be tedious to attempt a comprehensive review of all the empirical work which has been carried out. We will, therefore, select some of the more interesting relationships in order not only to present some of the results of empirical work but also to illustrate the difficulties involved in interpreting these results.

A. PROFITABILITY AND MARKET STRUCTURE

By far the greatest amount of empirical work has been in the testing of structure–performance relationships, and particularly with the relationship between market structure and profitability. There are of course a large number of factors influencing profitability and an attempt to take account of all of them would entail detailed

116

studies of individual industries. Such an approach would obviously lack generalization and the alternative is to carry out a cross-sectional analysis of a limited number of basic dimensions for which data are available. We are concerned, therefore, with any systematic relationships that might exist between profitability and the major aspects of market structure: concentration, barriers to entry and growth. It follows that we have to look at the average profitability performance over a fairly long period of time, for otherwise any systematic influences that do exist may well be hidden by a variety of short-run influences.

It is convenient to begin by reporting the results of a study which examined the relationship between seller concentration, barriers to entry and rates of return of leading companies in thirty industries in the United States from 1950 to 1960. The main conclusions of this study were first that there was 'a distinct cleavage between the average profit rates of two groups of industries, divided according to whether the concentration ratio for the top eight firms is greater or less than 70 per cent'; secondly that 'the average profit rates of industries with very high entry barriers are distinctly higher than those with low-substantial barriers to entry'; and thirdly that 'industries with high concentration ratios and high barriers to entry appear to be at the core of any resource misallocation due to monopolistic pricing'.[1]

In view of our discussion in Chapter 4 these results are entirely plausible. Some degree of positive association between concentration and profitability and between barriers to entry and profitability is to be expected. The nature and strength of these relationships, however, deserve further consideration. First, the nature of the relationship is in the form of a distinct difference in the average profitability of groups of industries rather than in the form of a continuous relationship between profitability and the structural factors. Thus, for instance, in the case of concentration the main result is the higher average profitability performance of industries with high concentration ratios. There is a suggestion then that the relationship between concentration and profitability may be in the form of a distinct difference in the average profitability of one or two groups of industries divided according to the degree of concentration, with little systematic association between concentration and profitability within the groups. This again is quite plausible on grounds of theory. It may be for instance that above a certain level of concentration collusive behaviour predominates whereas below it the tendency is for independent conduct patterns to be pursued resulting in more effective competition.

[1] H. M. Mann, 'Seller concentration barriers to entry and rates of return in thirty industries, 1950–1960', *Review of Economics and Statistics*, vol. 48, 1966.

In another study by Collins and Preston, however, which examines the relationship between concentration and price–cost margins in US manufacturing industries in 1958 the conclusion is that the statistical association is better described as a continuous one.[2] This study also demonstrates that the relationship between concentration and price–cost margins varies greatly between the ten industry groups which were examined. For industries in the 'food and kindred products' group the square of the correlation coefficient was +0·40 indicating that 40 per cent of the inter-industry variation in price–cost margins could be explained statistically by the variation in concentration. And the regression coefficient was +0·31 indicating that a concentration ratio 10 per cent above average was associated with a price–cost margin 3 per cent above average. For 'apparel and related products', however, the correlation coefficient was virtually zero, and the relationship between concentration and price–cost margins was a slight *negative* one.

In a similar study relating to 1963 the authors again found a picture of diversity. Two interesting findings in this later study were, first, that the relationship between concentration and price–cost margins in 1963 tended to be strongest for the group of industries in which concentration increased between 1958 and 1963, and second, that the relationship was stronger for the consumer goods sector than for producer goods.[3]

These two studies relate concentration to price–cost margins in the same year and so are a test of concentration on short-run profit margins. As mentioned earlier a stronger relationship between concentration and longer-run profitability may thus be hidden by special short-term influences. However, a comparison of other studies in this field which have looked at average profitability over a run of years shows similar diversity of results, although it is fair to say that they differ widely in such respects as the periods covered and the industry classification used.[4] In any case there are other grounds for believing that the true relationship between concentration and profitability is likely to show considerable diversity across industry groups. These reasons can be summed up by saying that concentration is only one of several factors influencing profitability and that as between industries the other important factors vary in strength and in the nature of their relationship with profitability. It also

[2] N. R. Collins and L. E. Preston, *Concentration and Price–Cost Margins in Manufacturing Industries* (University of California Press, 1968).

[3] N. R. Collins and L. E. Preston, 'Price–Cost Margins and Industry Structure', *Review of Economics and Statistics*, 1969.

[4] For a recent survey see B. S. Yamey, 'Do Monopoly and Near Monopoly Matter? A Survey of Empirical Studies', in M. Preston and B. Corry (eds) *Essays in Honour of Lord Robbins* (Weidenfeld & Nicolson, 1972).

appears that the relationship between concentration and profitability is weaker in UK industry than in the US. Monopolies Commission reports have certainly shown instances where high concentration is associated with high profitability, but the very few more general statistical studies suggest a much weaker association than that found in the US. In so far as this is true it may be because of such factors as the greater competition which UK industry faces from imports, and the fact that UK monopolies tend to have been less long established than their US counterparts. We can summarize then by saying that, in general, empirical work has found a positive association between concentration and profitability although, as one would entirely expect, the relationship is not equally strong for all the industry groups studied.

On barriers to entry there is much less evidence available because of the need for very detailed field work before a judgment on the height of entry barriers can be made. The attempts which have been made do suggest, however, that very high entry barriers do at least have an important positive effect on profitability and one which is exercised independently of the level of concentration.

Although profitability is related to the degree of seller concentration and to the height of entry barriers this does not of course rule out the possibility that profitability is also related to some other factors which might indeed be more important than the ones so far mentioned. One such factor which may well be of particular importance is the growth rate of firms and of industries. We would like, therefore, to have answers to the following questions. First, does the degree of concentration and height of entry barriers have an appreciable effect on profitability which is independent of the growth factor? Secondly, what can be said about the relative importance of concentration, barriers to entry and growth as determinants of profitability? To examine these questions we return to Professor Mann's data, adding to it the average annual growth of net assets of firms in the sample as a measure of growth.

A crude method of testing whether concentration and barriers to entry exert an influence on profitability which is independent of the growth rate of firms is to examine the relationship between concentration, barriers to entry and profitability for fast- and slow-growing industries separately. This is done in Tables 6.1 and 6.2. In Table 6.1 both industries and firms are classified according to the rate of growth of net assets. Within each growth class there is a marked difference in profitability according to whether the 8-firm concentration ratio is 70 per cent and over, or less than 70 per cent. On an industry basis, for example, the fast growing industries with high concentration have an average profitability of 14·6 per cent, com-

TABLE 6.1. *Profitability of Industries and Firms classified according to Industry Concentration Ratio and Rate of Growth, 28 US Industries, 1950–60*

8-firm con-centration ratio	Annual compound rate of growth of industries, %		Annual compound rate of growth of firms, %		
	Fast 7 and over	Slow < 7	Fast 9 and over	Medium 6 and < 9	Slow < 6
'High' 70% and over	14·6	11·1	15·2	13·2	10·5
Low < 70%	9·5	8·0	12·2	9·7	6·4

TABLE 6.2. *Profitability of Industries and Firms classified according to Barriers to Entry and Rate of Growth*

Barriers to entry	Annual compound rate of growth of industries, %		Annual compound rate of growth of firms, %		
	Fast 7 and over	Slow < 7	Fast 9 and over	Medium 6 and < 9	Slow < 6
Very high	18·5	12·7	19·6	15·3	11·3
Substantial	11·8	10·6	13·3	10·8	10·6
Moderate–low	10·6	8·1	11·8	11·1	7·0

pared to 9·5 per cent for fast-growing industries with low concentration. The table also shows clearly (looking along the rows) that profitability is positively related to growth. For firms in high concentration industries, for example, the fast growers have an average profitability of 15·2 per cent while the slow growers have a profitability of 10·5 per cent. For industries with low concentration on the other hand the fast- and slow-growing firms have an average profitability of 12·2 per cent and 6·4 per cent respectively.

Table 6.2 shows the profitability of industries and firms classified according to rates of growth and barriers to entry. Looking first at the columns there is a clear relationship within each growth-class between profitability and barriers to entry. Secondly, looking along the rows there is within each barrier-to-entry class a positive association between average profitability and rate of growth, a particularly striking feature being the high profitability of firms which combine high entry barriers and fast growth.

The results summarized in Tables 6.1 and 6.2 then seem to strengthen the conclusion that barriers to entry and concentration ratios are important factors in explaining profitability. These factors seem to exert a significant influence which is independent of the rate of growth. It is also clear, however, that there is an important relationship between profitability and growth. Further it is of interest to note that the above relationships are also found *within* the broad categories so far used. For instance, within the group of industries with an 8-firm concentration ratio of 70 per cent and over, the average profitability of industries with very high concentration ratios (i.e. 4-firm concentration ratios of 75 per cent and over) is 14·1 per cent, compared to 11·9 per cent for the rest. Within this group there is also a close association between profitability and growth.

TABLE 6.3. *Regression Analysis, Profitability and Explanatory Variables 28 US Industries, 1950–60*

Equa-tion	Con-stant	Regression coefficients of explanatory variables						R^2
		G	C	R_1	R_2	CR_1	CR_2	
1	5·55	+0·86 (0·22)						0·37
2	5·56		+0·11 (0·03)					0·40
3	1·86	+0·65 (0·18)	+0·09 (0·02)					0·56
4	3·00	+0·63 (0·15)	+0·04 (0·02)	+4·39 (1·20)	+1·69 (1·08)			0·70
5	4·70	+0·67 (0·14)				+0·07 (0·01)	+0·04 (0·01)	0·62
6	3·93	+0·63 (0·06)	+0·02 (0·03)	−5·00 (4·30)	+1·97 (3·10)	+0·12 (0·06)	−0·00 (0·04)	0·73

Figures in parentheses are the standard errors of the regression coefficients.

To take the analysis any further resort has to be made to regression analysis. The results of the analysis are given in Table 6.3, the variables used being as follows:

P = profitability (ratio of pre-tax net income to average net worth)

G = average annual growth of net assets

C = 4-firm concentration ratio

R_1 and R_2 = dummy variables relating to barriers to entry.

Equations 1 and 2 show the average relationship between profit-ability and growth and profitability and concentration respectively. Equation 1 tells us that a rate of growth 10 percentage points above average tends to be associated with profitability 8·6 per cent above average, whereas equation 2 says that a concentration ratio 10 percentage points above average tends to be associated with a profit-ability 1·1 per cent above average. The degree of 'explanation' of profitability is 37 per cent for the growth variable and 40 per cent for the concentration variable. Equation 3 includes both growth and concentration as explanatory variables. The coefficients of both variables are highly significant and the overall degree of 'explanation' is 56 per cent.

Since barriers to entry cannot be measured in quantitative terms in the same way as the other variables, they have to be included by using two dummy variables—R_1 and R_2. $R_1 = 1$ for 'very high' entry barriers and 0 for other classes, and $R_2 = 1$ for 'substantial' entry barriers and 0 for other classes. When these two variables are included with growth and concentration (equation 4), the degree of 'explanation' is 70 per cent. Both the growth and the very high barriers-to-entry variables are clearly highly significant. The concentration ratio is also just significant at the 5 per cent level, but the value of the partial regression coefficient has been greatly reduced.

Finally, it was decided to combine the concentration and barriers-to-entry variables so that in the partial regression coefficient CR_1 all concentration ratios are eliminated except where they are combined with 'very high' entry barriers, and in the coefficient CR_2 all concentration ratios are eliminated except where they are combined with 'substantial' entry barriers. The results of using these variables are shown in equations 5 and 6. In the former they are included with the growth variable and together they 'explain' 62 per cent of the variability in profits, all the partial regression coefficients being highly significant. The degree of explanation therefore is rather better than for growth and concentration alone. In equation 6, which includes all the explanatory variables, the only variables which are highly significant statistically are growth and concentration combined with 'very high' entry barriers.

The interpretation of these statistical results is highly complex and the following must be regarded as a tentative set of conclusions. All of them of course are qualified by the fact that the data refer to one group of firms over a specific time period.

First, the highly significant relationship between growth and profitability is a well-established one, and any monopoly policy which is based on realized profitability should at least distinguish between fast- and slow-growing industries or (ideally) firms.

Secondly, the evidence suggests that difference in concentration as such may not add a great deal to the explanation of differences in profitability, but that differences in concentration do exert an important influence *within* groups of industries with substantial or high entry barriers. This result must on the one hand be treated cautiously because the simple correlation between concentration and profitability (equation 2) does show the former to be an important variable. In any case, for practical purposes concentration data will remain useful in identifying industries where monopoly power is most likely to be abused. For this purpose it is reassuring to note that there is a close association between the height of entry barriers and the degree of concentration. In Mann's data, for instance, for the 'very high', 'substantial' and 'moderate–low' barriers to entry industries, the average 4-firm concentration ratios are 81 per cent, 65 per cent and 47 per cent respectively. But the suggestion that in a more complete analysis concentration may be seen to play a less important role is not surprising, for although a highly concentrated industry *may* be associated with high profitability a large number of situations are possible depending amongst other things on whether the industry is expanding or contracting, and on the degree of internal, intra-industry and potential competition. From the point of view of internal competition for instance, one factor of importance, given the 4-firm concentration ratio, is the number and size-distribution of the remaining firms. Thus if the 4-firm concentration ratio is, say, 60 per cent, industry profits might vary widely depending on whether the remaining 40 per cent of output is produced by another four firms of roughly equal size or by a much larger number of very small firms.

Thirdly, the analysis suggests the importance of high entry barriers arising for instance from patent protection, heavy advertising expenditure and economies of scale. In these cases the means exist whereby firms can maintain excess profitability over a long run of years. Similar results to these have also been arrived at in another study of US data. The authors conclude that 'for industries where products are differentiable investment in advertising is a highly profitable activity. It is likely that much of the differential in profits is accounted for by the entry barriers created by advertising expenditures and by the resulting achievement of market power'. Furthermore 'the role of concentration appears closely linked to that of technical entry barriers and there is little remaining influence which is evident'.[5]

[5] William S. Comanor and Thomas A. Wilson, 'Advertising market structure and performance', *The Review of Economics and Statistics*, vol. 49, No. 4, November 1967.

Fourthly, there remains the possibility of an inter-relationship between growth and barriers to entry, in so far as high profitability due to high entry barriers will enable firms, as far as the supply of finance is concerned, to grow faster than would be possible had they to face more competition. Indeed a two-way relationship between growth and barriers to entry may exist, because not only does the high profitability emanating from high entry barriers enable faster growth to be achieved, but the rapid expansion of the assets of leading firms may also have some effect in repelling would-be competitors. Here of course we have to take the demand side into account because too rapid a rate of expansion will lead to a fall in profitability, but up to a point at least this will be consistent with the goals of management. These problems would not be too difficult if firms were restricted to one industry but they become much more intractable in the case of the diversified company where profits based on high entry barriers in one area of the firm's activities may be used to finance growth in other areas. Thus it is possible to envisage a situation where the high profitability of a company is apparently 'justified' by the need to finance a high overall growth rate but that this might conceal important areas of monopoly which should receive the attention of the authorities.

B. ADVERTISING, MARKET STRUCTURE AND BUSINESS BEHAVIOUR

Advertising has already been mentioned as an important factor in relation to entry barriers and thus in helping to explain high profitability in certain industries. It is worth while taking our examination of advertising a little further with the emphasis on advertising intensity as the factor to be explained.

Clearly the type of product and particularly the extent to which it is differentiable is an important determinant of advertising expenditure. For this reason empirical work has concentrated on the consumer goods sector and has sought to explain variations in the level of advertising expenditure within this sector.

One important general tendency has been the part played by advertising in the development of a method of distribution dominated by the manufacturer rather than the wholesaler. By producing his own branded goods, advertising them at a uniform national price, and very often developing his own channels of distribution with direct sales to retailers, the manufacturer was able to build up consumer allegiance to his goods, and expand his sales on a scale which would have been extremely difficult and perhaps impossible under a method of distribution where the wholesaler has the initiative in determining the range of products which is produced. Advertising, then, was an important factor which contributed towards the growth of large manufacturing firms and thus to the development of more highly concentrated industries. This aspect of advertising has been emphasized in particular by Nicholas Kaldor. 'It is probably no exaggeration to say that without the support of large-scale advertising this attempt of manufacturers to release themselves from dependence on wholesalers' goodwill by building up consumers' goodwill could not have succeeded.'[6] Advertising was not of course the only weapon available to manufacturers in their efforts to dominate distribution. In addition distribution policy itself was directed so as to increase or maintain dominance. This could occur by forward integration so as to acquire retail outlets, and also by the use of such weapons as exclusive dealing and special discounts. Thus, for example, the Monopolies Commission's Report on Wallpaper (1964) found that the largest group in the trade was reducing competition by its use of exclusive dealing, loyalty discounts and restriction of supply. Again in the Commission's Report on the Distribution of Petrol (1965) the ownership of petrol stations, restrictions on the disposal of premises, and the exclusion of competitors' lubricating oils were some of the factors by which the major producing companies were attempting to maintain their positions of dominance.

One major consideration, then, is the association between large-scale advertising and other selling expenses, and products where manufacturers' branded goods predominate. Although the move towards manufacturer domination was also accompanied by a general tendency for industries to become more highly concentrated, it does not follow that the developments which have been outlined mean that advertising is justified by economies of scale or that a strong positive association would be observed between advertising intensity, as measured by the advertising–sales ratio, and the degree of concentration.

It is frequently argued that advertising enables economies of scale to be achieved and thus that it results in lower prices to consumers. For this to be *possible*, advertising must result in increased output. In addition, a larger volume of output must be associated with lower unit production costs or with a lower profit per unit of output. Such an outcome is most likely perhaps when starting from a position where there are many firms in an industry and where the increased output of successful firms is achieved by the elimination of the unsuccessful ones. But in more concentrated industries advertising may be a substitute for price competition and the advertising

<hr />

[6] Nicholas Kaldor, 'The economic aspects of advertising', *Review of Economic Studies*, vol. XVIII, No. 45, 1949–50.

campaigns of individual firms may largely offset one another. Furthermore, advertising is often aimed at *differentiating* a product, and is also often associated with frequent changes in style. In these cases advertising is an activity which *prevents* the attainment of economies of scale.

There are several reasons why a strong positive association between advertising-intensity and the degree of concentration should not be expected. The advertising–sales ratio is an imperfect measure of the degree of large-scale sales promotion activities. The ratio may be small but the absolute amount spent on advertising may be large, as for instance, in the case of motor vehicles. In addition the importance of the non-advertising elements in sales promotion activities will vary between industries. Furthermore, advertising and other selling costs are only one of many factors influencing the degree of concentration so that again we would not expect to find any strong systematic relationship between the two. In an analysis of forty-two broadly defined consumer goods industries in the US in 1947, 1954 and 1958, Telser found only a low correlation between advertising intensity and the level of seller concentration and therefore concluded that there was little support for an inverse association between advertising and the degree of competition.[7] A more recent study, however, based on a more appropriate industry breakdown and which attempted to select firms which appeared to use advertising as the principal means of sales promotion, found a marked relationship between concentration and advertising intensity.[8]

A positive association between concentration and advertising intensity says nothing about the *causal* relationship. This in fact may run either way. We have argued previously that when sales promotion activities are pursued by firms, then even if initially they are all of much the same size, the end-result is likely to be the emergence of a few dominant firms. Here the causal relationship runs from advertising expenditure to high concentration. In addition, however, the degree of seller concentration may in turn affect the intensity of advertising as the development of more highly concentrated oligopolistic markets makes sales promotion expenditure a safer form of rivalry than price competition. Thus the *behaviour* of firms in concentrated industries is also important in determining the intensity of non-price competition. The extreme case is found in the detergents market where the Monopolies Commission found a situation

[7] Lester Telser, 'Advertising and competition', *The Journal of Political Economy*, December 1964.

[8] H. M. Mann, J. A. Henning and J. W. Meehan, Jr., 'Advertising and concentration. An empirical investigation', *The Journal of Industrial Economics*, November 1967.

of 'exceptionally high competitive advertising campaigns which tended to cancel one another out'. Such behaviour on the part of firms also results, as argued in Chapter 4, in additional entry barriers to new competition and therefore to the strengthening of market power.

So far then we have seen that heavy advertising and other sales promotion expenditure is associated with manufacturers' brand domination, and that such expenditure is particularly large in a number of highly concentrated oligopolistic industries where it forms an important part of the competitive behaviour of existing firms, including the creation of barriers to new competition. There is one other point of great importance as far as advertising and market structure is concerned. Whereas large-scale advertising is associated with manufacturers' brand control, the more recent development of retailers' domination is characterized by the absence of heavy sales promotion expenditure. The successful supermarket chains, variety stores and department stores in fact do very little advertising and what they do is almost entirely informative. Furthermore, the large orders of the multiple retailers are important in increasing the efficiency of producers, particularly the smaller ones, and thus in increasing competition amongst manufacturers. The low advertising costs and the discounts which large retailers can obtain from manufacturers as a result of large standardized orders and buying power, means that the retailer's own branded goods offer the consumer a very close substitute to the manufacturer's brand, at a lower price. The growth of market organizations which contain large retailers is a development which seems more likely to cater for the demands of consumer than is the case with manufacturer's domination. The large retailer can take the initiative in deciding what products to make available to consumers and, since unlike the manufacturers, the retailers are in close daily contact with the customer, they are much more likely to be aware of and responsive to his needs. It is quite possible of course for a situation to develop in which the consumer does not gain, and where monopoly profits are shared between the manufacturer and retailer. The likelihood of this happening, however, depends on the strength of competition at the retail end. Certainly at the moment there is no reason to doubt the importance of the growth of large-scale retailing in promoting the interests of the consumer by eliminating wasteful advertising expenditure and increasing the efficiency with which goods are distributed.

C. OTHER STRUCTURE–BEHAVIOUR–PERFORMANCE RELATIONSHIPS

1. *Innovation*

Very little empirical work has been undertaken to test for any systematic relationship between other structure, behaviour and performance relationships because of the difficulties of compiling suitable data.

One important set of hypotheses concerns the association between innovation and market structure. There are two conflicting views. On the one hand, it is argued that market power favours innovative activity. Firms with market power, it is claimed, will have several advantages over those that have to face many competitors. These include, greater financial resources, the ability to take a longer view and to employ more research personnel on long-term projects, and the fact that they are able to appropriate for themselves a greater share of the benefits of an innovation. On the other hand, it is argued that monopoly power is likely to slow down the rate of innovation because of a weakening of the competitive stimulus. This could occur as the result of one firm dominating the market or alternatively because of restrictive agreements between firms in an oligopolistic market. Leaving aside the problem of restrictive agreements for the moment, where does the optimal balance lie between these various factors?

In industries dominated by one firm it might be expected that the dominant firm would have little inducement to show much urgency in innovation because there is little that it can take away from its competitors. However, because it has a lot to lose, such a firm may be expected to react quickly if an innovation made by a small competitor threatens its market position. Although there are cases—such as the introduction of the stainless steel razor blade—which fit these expectations, it does not mean that dominant firms never display great initiative. Pilkingtons, for instance, has a long record of innovative success in the making of glass.

In general, however, a better balance between safety and competition is likely to be found where there are several fairly equally matched firms. Each one then has a big incentive to be first with an innovation because there is a lot to be gained—the market share of the others. This situation also has the advantage of having several centres of initiative so that there is less danger of development on a narrow front.

Beyond some point, however, it might be expected that larger numbers would have an adverse effect on the rate of innovations, because of less price discipline and the expectation of more rapid imitation and the consequent fear of losses. Similar considerations may apply with regard to entry conditions. In general, the possibility of entry might be expected to have a favourable impact on innovation but *very* easy entry conditions may have an adverse effect.

The strength of these various forces, however, depends on several other factors which are of greater or less importance in any given situation—these include the importance of product differentiation, the size and rate of growth of markets and the importance of economies of scale in research and development.

The empirical evidence on all this is at the moment very limited but the findings may be summarized as follows.[9] First, differences in the opportunity to innovate are more important than market structure in explaining inter-industry differences in innovative performance. Where opportunities are abundant and where product differentiation based on research and development is an important aspect of competition, differences in market structure seem to have little effect. Second, the strongest correlations between market structure and rate of innovation seem to occur in industries where other conditions, especially opportunities to innovate and the rate of growth of demand, are unfavourable. Third, for such industries, moderate levels of concentration—four or five-firm concentration ratios of about 50 to 60 per cent—seem to give the best results. Finally, relatively easy entry seems to be important not only in the process of invention and innovation but also in the rate of *diffusion* of new technology. The entry of new competitors not committed to the established technologies of an industry has perhaps been the single most important force leading to rapid innovation.

It has already been mentioned that part of the argument against market power was that firms may attempt to reduce the uncertainties associated with competition by means of restrictive agreements and that this would tend to reduce the pressure to innovate. Here again there are advantages and disadvantages of restrictive agreements which have to be considered in order to arrive at a balance of probabilities with regard to the likely net effect. The basic argument in favour of restrictive agreements is that, where they are effective, they reduce the uncertainty about the yield of an investment. This is achieved by increasing the amount of information which a firm has on the planned increase in supply of its rivals, and therefore reduces the likelihood of a much bigger increase in capacity than in demand. On the other hand, although restrictive agreements may allow capacity to be adjusted more smoothly to changes in demand, they may also have undesirable effects, such as monopolistic restriction of supply, impediments to the growth of the most efficient firms,

[9] See, for example, O. E. Williamson, 'Innovation and Market Structure', *Journal of Political Economy*, February 1965; F. M. Scherer, 'Market Structure and the Employment of Scientists and Engineers', *American Economic Review*, June 1967; W. S. Comanor, 'Market Structure, Product Differentiation and Industrial Structure', *Quarterly Journal of Economics*, November 1967; J. Tilton, *International Diffusion of Technology: The Case of Semi-Conductors* (Allen & Unwin, 1972).

and exclusion of new entry. Clearly the likely net outcome will vary according to circumstances. Thus, for instance, the type of uncertainty which restrictive agreements might usefully reduce by the provision of more information is least important in industries where demand is expanding rapidly and where each individual extension to capacity is small in relation to the increase in demand.

There are two general types of market situation where a case may be made for restrictive agreements. The first is during the price competition that may occur during a recession. During the initial stage of a recession, prices are likely to be governed by the firms' idea of a normal price which will be sufficient to cover the average total costs of production. The longer the recession lasts, however, the more likely it is that price-cutting will occur as firms attempt to win new orders. The severity of the price-cutting will be related to the importance of overhead costs in the total costs of the firm. The more important they are, and the greater therefore the difference between average total costs and average variable costs, the more severe price-cutting is likely to be. The lower is the elasticity of demand for the industry's product the less effective price-cutting will be in stimulating demand. From the point of view of innovation such a state of affairs would not cause concern if it resulted in the speedy elimination of the most inefficient firms, but this is unlikely. During a recession all firms are likely to suffer to a greater or lesser extent, and sometimes the most efficient firms will be damaged most. These firms may have small financial reserves due to heavy investment during the preceding boom whereas the firm with large financial resources even though technically backward will be in the best position to weather the crisis. In any case, long-term investment plans and research projects are likely to be dropped as firms concentrate on the more urgent short-term problem of survival. In situations of this kind it has been argued that a restrictive agreement, by reducing the amount of price-cutting and maintaining profit margins, will have a favourable effect on technical change.

The second market situation where restrictive agreements may have a net beneficial effect is illustrated by the heavy electrical industry. The characteristics of the industry have been outlined by G. B. Richardson.[10] These include firstly, a demand for the product which is governed largely by the investment programme of a monopoly buyer (the Central Electricity Generating Board), and which is liable to big fluctuations. Thus if the industry is to supply peak demand requirements this means the periodic emergence of excess capacity. Furthermore the problem of excess capacity is

[10] G. B. Richardson, 'The pricing of heavy electrical equipment: competition or agreement?' *Bulletin of the Oxford Institute of Statistics*, vol. 28, February 1966.

likely to be accentuated as a result of competitive investment programmes in the preceding boom. Secondly, the individual orders
which firms receive from the buyer are very large and it is important
to each firm that it gets a share of them, not only from the point of
view of short-run profitability, but also so as to have the necessary
experience to keep abreast of research and development work which
is also very important in this field. Richardson argues that free
competition is not likely to yield a satisfactory adjustment of supply
to demand. The losses incurred as a result of price-cutting in lean
years, which tends to be severe because of the importance of overhead costs and the importance of winning at least one large order,
are not likely to be adequately compensated for by excess profits in
good years. Over a run of years, therefore, it may not be possible to
earn a normal rate of return on capital, so that research and development work is likely to suffer. Accordingly Richardson argues that a
restrictive agreement which secured greater co-ordination of investment plans would give a more satisfactory performance than the
free market. Both the Monopolies Commission and the Restrictive
Practices Court, however, have condemned agreements between
manufacturers in this field.[11] An alternative solution of course is the
merger of the competing firms and this is what in fact has happened.
The structure of the market has been greatly changed by the mergers
which have brought together the General Electric Company,
Associated Electrical Industries and English Electric.

In both cases outlined above the basic argument is that the free
operation of the market mechanism creates so much uncertainty
that firms are unwilling to invest adequately in research and development work. A useful purpose of restrictive agreements, therefore, is
that they increase the safety of the firm's operations sufficiently to
maintain research and development work on a profitable basis. It is
interesting to note that such arguments have featured more promin-
ently in the later cases brought before the Restrictive Practices Court
than in the earlier ones. Restrictive practices will be looked at in
more detail in Chapter 9 and at this stage I wish only to make the
following remarks.

First, the effectiveness of restrictive agreements is often very
limited and especially in those situations where, it is argued, they
would be most likely to result in a net gain to society. Thus, for
instance, during a recession there are very strong pressures making
for price-cutting activity, particularly when the number of firms is

[11] See The Monopolies Commission, *Report on the Supply and Export of
Electrical and Allied Machinery and Plant*, HMSO, 1957; and the Restrictive
Practices Court, *Associated Transformer Manufacturers' Agreement*, LR, 2RP,
295.

large and when there are ample opportunities for secret price-cutting in the form of discounts and rebates.

Secondly, restrictive agreements formed during a slump often turn out to have a more or less permanent existence, and to the extent that they are effective in protecting the less efficient firms they will retard structural change in the industry and the greater concentration of the industry's resources in the hands of a smaller number of the more efficient firms, which is likely to be a far more effective and efficient solution to the industry's problems.

Thirdly, the most effective agreements are generally found where the number of firms is small. In these more highly concentrated industries restrictive agreements are more effective in restricting competition between existing firms and in preventing new entry.

2. *Technical Efficiency*

Very little information is available on the relationship between market structure, business behaviour and technical efficiency, i.e. the extent to which output is produced at the lowest possible cost. As a guide to policy we have to be content therefore with a few guidelines based in part on empirical work on cost curves and in part on the experience of the working of actual markets.

Much of the evidence on cost curves suggests that the most typical shape of the long-run average cost curve is one that has a wide range of constant unit cost above the minimum optimal size of firm, and in many cases there are no indications that the largest firms suffer from any diseconomies of size. If this is so then in high concentration industries a large proportion of output is likely to be produced in plants and firms of efficient size, unless of course large firms are made up of several establishments each one producing at a low level of specialization and standardization. With cost conditions of this kind it also follows, however, that in a number of cases technical efficiency would be unimpaired at lower levels of concentration than those that actually exist. We should also remind ourselves of three other important considerations. First, the size of the market may be such that lower production costs could be achieved with greater standardization but will not be so long as consumers show a preference for the existing degree of variety. Secondly, policy relating to efficiency must take into account technical progressiveness as well as costs of production based on existing techniques, and the optimal industry structure may not be the same on both accounts. Thirdly, discussion of the typical shape of the unit cost curve must not blind us to the fact that there are considerable variations in internal efficiency even between firms of the same size. In his survey of economies of scale Caleb Smith concluded that 'Examination of the data that are available and that conceivably might be available shows that we cannot hope to make very satisfactory empirical studies of the long-run cost function. I believe that if we asked the student of the data to tell us in detail just what cost differences exist between different types and sizes of plant and firm and what causes, if any, he could discover for those differences the information would go farther to clarify the practical questions to which we seek answers than would studies of the relation of cost to size'.[12]

The incidence of firms of less than the minimum optimal size will vary from one industry to another, but two types of market situations in particular are likely to be associated with a high proportion of inefficiently small firms. First, there are the declining industries with low concentration. Here the market mechanism works very slowly in eliminating firms and even slower in eliminating capacity so that conditions of excess capacity will be widespread. Also, as argued in the previous section, the excessive price competition in these industries is likely to hinder the adoption of the latest techniques so that the industry becomes less competitive in world markets, and if the latest techniques favour larger units the size distribution of firms will become increasingly inappropriate to efficient market organization. Secondly, restrictive practices combined with easy entry conditions and a large supply of new entrants may also result in a large number of inefficiently small units. Conditions of this kind together with the ability of firms to employ cheap labour, often in the form of self-employment, have characterized the distributive trades sector. The growth of multiples, the abolition of resale price maintenance and in some cases the Selective Employment Tax have, however, increased the difficulties of survival for small firms in this field. Of course by no means all small firms are inefficient, and what appears to be an inefficiently small firm from the point of view of the supply of a standardized product or service may in fact involve no inefficiency when it is recognized that a specialized commodity or service is being supplied.

D. CONCLUSIONS

It is evident from the discussion in this and some of the earlier chapters that there is no simple set of conclusions to be drawn which would enable us to identify market structures and patterns of behaviour which are inevitably associated with bad market performance. Theory and empirical work does, however, suggest some

[12] C. A. Smith, 'Survey of the empirical evidence on economies of scale, in *Business Concentration and Price Policy*' (Princeton University Press, 1955), p. 229.

tentative conclusions which form a useful background to policy considerations.

First, there is a general tendency for high profits to be associated with high concentration and high entry barriers which is independent of the growth factor. The most important factors are probably the entry barriers which firms in high-concentration industries can erect in the form of restrictive arrangements in the distribution of goods, and intensive advertising. The association of intensive advertising with the development of manufacturer's brand dominance also fits into this picture. There are situations of course where very high concentration is justified by economies of scale. In situations of this kind, however, especially in the extreme case where there is only one dominant supplier, the efficiency advantages of size have to be weighed against the dangers of market power. Where the efficiency gains seem to outweigh the dangers of monopolization it must still be realized that, unless competition from imports is important, there is no effective competitive control on the behaviour of the firms and for policy purposes some alternative control has to be sought. It is in highly concentrated industries also that restrictive agreements are most likely to become firmly established and most difficult to remove. The performance of highly concentrated industries may be improved by the emergence of large buyers. In these cases, control on the monopoly power of big business has emerged in the form of counter-vailing power on the other side of the market. There is no guarantee, however, that this situation inevitably works to the advantage of the consumer.

Secondly, low concentration in itself does not appear to result in bad performance, but when associated with a secular decline in demand or fluctuations in demand it may result in poor performance in terms of subnormal profits, low wages and an inefficient organization of production, which the market mechanism is slow to rectify. Such industries will also tend to have a bad performance in the field of technical change. Low concentration may also combine with easy entry conditions, restrictive agreements and a weakly organized labour market to result in bad market performance in terms of efficiency.

Thirdly, it is important in considering monopoly situations to examine the process by which, and the time period over which firms have attained dominant positions, and in particular to examine the importance of vertical integration and mergers. Both may be desirable on grounds of efficiency, but there are also dangers of monopolization; one because of control over sources of supply or outlets, and in the other because of the rapid emergence of a firm to a position of dominance in an industry.

Finally, moderate degrees of concentration, say where the four or five leading firms control about 50 or 60 per cent of the market, seem to give favourable performances in several dimensions. Concentration levels of this order are in most cases sufficient for the most important economies of scale to be realized, and they do not appear to be associated with excessive profitability. Furthermore, market structures of this kind appear to have a positive impact on the rate of innovation especially under conditions of slow growth and where there are few opportunities for technical advance.

oligopoly.

CHAPTER 7

Problems of Public Policy

The preceding chapter examined some of the empirical evidence concerning the relationship between market structure, business behaviour and market performance. Such evidence is clearly relevant to issues of policy, but before turning to these it will be useful to examine some of the theoretical background. This will serve to pinpoint the main issues and also to indicate both the usefulness and limitations of individual policy weapons, such as monopoly legislation, in their ability to contribute towards the improvement of economic performance. We look first at the theory of resource allocation and then at some wider issues of public policy.

A. THE ALLOCATION OF RESOURCES

The body of economic theory which has been most closely related to monopoly policy is that which deals with the allocation of resources. The basis of such theory is the concept of an optimal allocation of resources, the optimum being defined as a position where it is impossible to reallocate resources in such a way as to make some people better off without making at least one person worse off. In standard textbook treatment it is demonstrated that an optimum position will, assuming the absence of external economies and diseconomies, be attained in long-run equilibrium under a regime of universal perfect competition.[1] As an aid to policy-making such a concept is clearly subject to very severe limitations. The following points in particular need to be emphasized.

First, the optimum situation is defined with respect to a given distribution of income. Unless the pattern of demand remains unaltered in response to changes in income distribution, changes in the latter will affect relative prices and so change the optimum position. There is in general, therefore, a different optimum position for each pattern of income distribution. It follows that even if we

[1] For an explanation of how the various 'marginal conditions' for optimal resource allocation are satisfied in long-run equilibrium with perfectly competitive markets, see W. J. Baumol, *Economic Theory and Operations Analysis* (Prentice-Hall, 1961), Chapter 13.

knew the economic system to be efficiently organized in the 'Pareto optimal' sense, such a situation would not be satisfactory unless the pattern of income distribution were socially desired. From the point of view of individual policy decisions it has to be recognized therefore that both the efficiency and the equity aspects of a policy have to be taken into account by the policy maker.

Second, the ideal allocation of resources relates to a long-period equilibrium, and the question has been asked how are we to know that, given the existence of perfectly competitive markets, such a position will in fact be *attained*. The type of problem involved here can be illustrated by the following simple example. The curves D_1

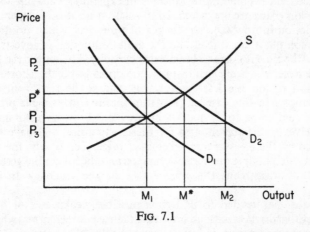

FIG. 7.1

and S represent the demand and supply conditions in a perfectly competitive market with an initial equilibrium price–output combination of P_1 and M_1. Assume an increase in demand to D_2. The new long-period equilibrium is one with a price of OP^* and output of OM^*. But it takes time to expand output so that the short-run effect is for price to increase to P_2. Demand price is thus much higher than supply price and it is this which gives producers the incentive to expand output. However, they all plan expansions of capacity and all these expansions are based initially on the price P_2. The result may then be an increase in supply from M_1 to M_2. The adjustment of capacity has been much greater than that required to achieve the equilibrium position and the industry is therefore left with a great deal of excess capacity. In this case, therefore, the failure to adjust smoothly to the equilibrium position is due to the fact that many sellers independently plan their expansion of capacity on the basis of incomplete information.

Of course, this simple picture needs to be modified in many ways. Thus, if fluctuations in demand can be foreseen, then capacity can be adjusted to the average demand over the cycle so that taking the good years with the bad, normal profits are made. This implies periods when capacity will be less than demand, so that the issue is fundamentally a question of what is the socially most desirable level of capacity in relation to demand? Should capacity at all times be sufficient to meet demand, including peak demand, without the need for sharp increases in price, or should it be so adjusted to demand as to minimize the unit costs of the industry over the cycle? Again, it is likely that producers will learn from experience. Some, for instance, will become more cautious in expanding capacity so that expansion plans are staggered. In this case a great deal depends on the relationship between the length of time over which producers' expansion plans are spread and the gestation period of investment; that is, the time it takes to build extra capacity. The longer the time-period over which expansion plans are spread and the shorter the gestation period the less serious will tend to be the problem of over-supply. In this case output from the first investment projects will be coming on to the market before some firms have committed themselves to expansion, and for these, expansion will have to be planned on the basis of a lower market price. Conversely, the more concentrated in time are expansion plans and the longer the gestation period of investment the greater will be the tendency to over-supply.

All this has tended to underline possible weaknesses of highly competitive markets with no interdependence between firms, whereas in fact manufacturing industries are typically oligopolistic. Studies of behaviour in such industries have tended to show that prices are not in fact perfectly flexible in response to short-run changes in demand; that prices are in fact rather sticky, and that the short-run response to, say, an increase in demand, is often to allow stocks to fall and order books to lengthen. This gives existing firms several advantages, the main ones relating to the adjustment of capacity to demand. Stock movements and lengthening order books give the firm some concrete evidence about how much extra capacity is needed, whereas an immediate increase in price to shake off excess demand does not. Furthermore, a 'moderate' price policy may result in existing firms forestalling the entry of newcomers, thus reducing the likelihood of excess capacity emerging as the result of new entry. On the other hand, where customer loyalty is important a major aspect of competition between oligopolists may be the competitive expansion of capacity. No one firm will want to be caught for long with insufficient capacity and thus be unable to supply customers, because a proportion of these customers may then be lost permanently to competitors. Competitive expansions of capacity during periods of rising demand may, therefore, lead to the emergence of substantial excess capacity. At this point the firms will cut back sharply on their investment programmes.[2]

The foregoing discussion is clearly a very oversimplified account of investment decisions in actual markets, but it does serve to emphasize that markets with a wide variety of structural features may fail to bring about a smooth adjustment of capacity to demand. The seriousness of the situation depends upon circumstances—upon the rate of increase of market demand, the importance of fixed costs and the size and indivisibility of capital units, and the extent to which investment decisions are bunched. The efficient adjustment of capacity to demand is an important practical problem which is swept under the carpet in the static analysis of optimal resource allocation.

A third problem associated with resource allocation is the existence of external economies and diseconomies. The equality of marginal cost and price, which results in perfectly competitive markets under profit-maximizing rules of behaviour, reflects only private costs and benefits. But if in the process of production certain costs are imposed on others and no compensation is paid, or certain benefits are conferred but no payment received, then market price will no longer be an accurate index of the marginal value of goods to society. From society's point of view what is required for ideal allocation is not the equality of price with marginal private cost but the equality of price with marginal *social* cost. For industries where external economies are unusually important the scale of activity will not be large enough from the point of view of society because some of the benefits associated with it are not reflected in the price which firms receive for their goods. An example is labour retraining schemes undertaken by a group of firms some of the benefits of which accrue, as a result of labour mobility, to others. For industries where external diseconomies are unusually important the scale of activity will be over-expanded from society's point of view because some of the costs involved are not taken into account by the firms involved. The classical examples are those of air and water pollution and traffic congestion.

In addition to externalities in production there are also externalities in consumption due to the interdependencies in the welfare of individual households. Thus the purchase by one household of a new model car or household appliance may excite the envy of

[2] For a discussion of the importance of consumer loyalty and its effect on oligopolistic price and investment policy see James S. Duesenberry, *Business Cycles and Economic Growth* (McGraw-Hill, 1958), Chapter 6.

neighbours and 'compel' them to increase their consumption expenditure in order to maintain a given level of satisfaction. It is on such interdependence of consumer welfare that much of the success of large-scale advertising rests.

The last two problems—of the process of adjustment by means of the market mechanism, and of externalities—apply not only to individual industries. They are also basic factors which underlie the regional problem. If regional allocation of resources took place quickly and smoothly, and on the basis of costs and benefits which were those borne by *society* there would be no economic basis for a regional policy. The latter is made necessary by various weaknesses in the market mechanism. Thus even if the adjustment process was based on adequate long-run information which reflected the costs and benefits imposed on society, government intervention might be justified on the grounds that the adjustment worked too slowly and caused too much hardship. The case for intervention is greatly strengthened when, because of divergences between social and private costs and benefits and insufficient information, a socially efficient allocation of resources would not be achieved.

The problem of 'externalities' leads to the general problem of the choice of goods. It is of course what the theory of optimal resource allocation is all about, but the problem is that, apart from the difficulties already mentioned, the free play of the competitive system may do a rather bad job of things. In the first place there are certain essential demands which cannot be effectively realized by individual purchases in the market but which have to be supplied on a communal basis and financed by taxation. In the United Kingdom the provision of services in this way has gone beyond the point where everyone is agreed that this is the best way of providing them. The health and education services are cases in point. But two important points need to be made. First, a person's idea of how many goods and services should be supplied communally, which could in fact be organized on the basis of individual purchases in the market, will be related to the degree of inequality of income distribution. Thus although a person might argue for the public supply of certain services in a system where the distribution of income and wealth is very unequal, he may be quite prepared to see the same services purchased in the market in a regime where the distribution of income and wealth was more equitable. The only satisfactory solution is first to attain a pattern of distribution which was generally regarded as fair and then to decide what proportion of goods and services it was more efficient to produce 'outside' the market.

Secondly, however, given the fact that a certain proportion of activity takes place in the public sector there is the problem of deciding on the allocation of resources between this sector and the private one. This is the problem of 'social balance'. The problem is a very great one especially in a system where every increase in public expenditure is condemned as a further encroachment on the sovereignty of the consumer. Consumer sovereignty, however, is not the sovereignty of completely informed individuals acting independently, but of individuals whose knowledge is imperfect, whose desires are to some extent interdependent, and who are subject to much persuasive sales promotion activity. The interaction of these factors results in a tendency for too large a proportion of the nation's resources to get absorbed by the private sector. The argument has been presented most forcefully by Professor Galbraith. 'Advertising operates exclusively, and emulation mainly, on behalf of privately produced goods and services. Since management and emulative effects operate on behalf of private production, public services will have an inherent tendency to lag behind. . . . The engines of mass communication, in their highest state of development, assail the eyes and ears of the community on behalf of more beer but not of more schools. Even in the conventional wisdom it will scarcely be contended that this leads to an equal choice between the two.'[3]

But the problem of the choice of goods involves more than the choice of goods and services which can or cannot be purchased in the market and the problem of the relative size of these two sectors. It also exists within the market sector itself. To give just two examples. A problem which has already been mentioned in Chapter 3 is the possible conflict between variety and standardization. In some cases there is a clear advantage in favour of standardization as in the case of electric fittings and bicycle spare parts. In others, economies of scale are relatively unimportant and efficient production of a 'product' is consistent with a large variety. But there are other instances where economies of scale are extremely important and where consumers can either have a very restricted choice of products at a low price or a greater variety of products each at a higher price. Such a situation exists in the case of the production of motor vehicles where a reduction in product differentiation would result in economies of production and distribution. The varied tastes of consumers, however, cannot be fully met because some will prefer the more standardized system while others will prefer variety. The market does not generate a satisfactory solution to this problem. In other markets consumers will not be given an adequate choice of products even where economies of scale are not important. This will occur for instance where firms compete in terms of heavy promotional expenditures and quality improvements or 'model

[3] J. K. Galbraith, *The Affluent Society* (Hamish Hamilton), 2nd edn, p. 230.

changes', but do not offer consumers the choice of a lower price–
lower quality alternative. In many instances the true choice is not
even one between quality and cheapness but one between a high-
priced product backed by heavy advertising and an identical product
which is not heavily advertised.

The final set of problems I wish to discuss in relation to resource
allocation relates to the theory of second best. The basic argument is
that if there are sectors of the economy within which the marginal
conditions are not satisfied and for some reason these constraints
cannot be removed, then it does not follow that a policy of pursuing
optimizing behaviour in the free sectors will lead to a more efficient
allocation of resources. The relevance of this analysis to the subject
matter of this book is clear. Given the fact that the private manufacturing sector, for instance, is composed of industries with varying
degrees of monopoly which are unlikely to be completely removed,
should the state pursue marginal cost pricing policies in the nationalized sector? Again, given the fact that monopoly and restrictive
practices legislation is inevitably uneven in its effectiveness, what
general validity does policy in this field have from the point of view
of improving resource allocation? The situation is further complicated because firms may pursue different objectives in different
market situations. The analysis of optimal resource allocation
assumes that profit maximization is the goal of all firms. Whereas,
however, in highly competitive markets firms may be forced to
behave as profit maximizers, in oligopolistic markets they may have
sufficient freedom to pursue other objectives such as revenue
maximization subject to a minimum profit constraint. The revenue
maximizer will produce a larger output in any period than a profit
maximizer as long as the profit constraint is less than the maximum
profits attainable. In this situation, therefore, resource allocation
may be nearer to the ideal than would be indicated on the basis of
universal profit-maximizing behaviour.

More generally the basic practical question is whether a piecemeal
approach to economic policy is feasible in view of the complex
interdependencies of the economic system. The answer is that it
depends on circumstances. In practice this means that to be reasonably confident of improving matters policy has to concentrate on
the most obvious cases of deviation from efficiency—that is, for
example, on the most blatant examples of external diseconomies and
the exploitation of market power. Furthermore there may be sectors
of the economy within which there are large discrepancies between
relative prices and relative costs and where it is fairly safe to assume
that the gains to be achieved by a more rational price structure
within the sector are likely far to outweigh any possible repercussions

on the rest of the economy. If, for instance, in the transport sector or the fuel and power sector, relative prices are greatly out of line with relative costs, a policy of optimizing within these sectors while largely ignoring the effects on the rest of the economy may well result in a net improvement in resource allocation.

B. OTHER POLICY ISSUES

All of the preceding discussion has been focussed on the problems associated with resource allocation. There are two other problems which need to be mentioned.

First, the analysis of the previous chapters makes it clear that, even when attention is restricted to matters of efficiency, resource allocation may not be the only concern of the policy-maker, and in particular that internal efficiency and growth may also be important. The fact that more than one goal is involved in policy-making means that additional complexities appear. Thus, for instance, the difficulty of ensuring internal efficiency is a particularly important problem which has to be faced if marginal-cost pricing is adopted in decreasing cost industries, because such industries would then have to be run at a loss. Indeed even though there may be some good reasons why a decreasing cost industry should adopt marginal cost pricing, considerations of internal efficiency may be sufficiently powerful to outweigh them and to point to the greater desirability of a pricing policy which at least allowed the industry to break even. In other words, there may be more to be gained from increased internal efficiency than from improved allocative efficiency. Again, the fact that policy-makers are interested in growth and the process of innovation complicates the treatment of the monopoly problem; because if innovative activity is positively associated with size and market power, then a policy which might be appropriate from the point of view of static resource allocation analysis might not be appropriate from the point of view of the innovation process.

Secondly, the goals of government policy comprise more than efficiency and progressiveness. They also include full employment and a reasonable degree of price stability; goals which are also related to constraints imposed by the balance of payments. The basic question is whether issues such as the level of employment, the rate of inflation and the balance of payments should be the concern of the government agencies whose task it is to implement monopoly legislation. In the United Kingdom the answer seems to be that it should. Thus, for instance, in the 1956 Restrictive Trade Practices Act, the maintenance of employment opportunities in development areas and the promotion of exports are two of the permitted defences of a restrictive agreement. Again in the evaluation of mergers, the balance of payments and regional policy are relevant considerations as well as efficiency and competition.

The need to consider several policy goals certainly makes the application of monopoly policy much more complicated and the outcome of individual investigations more uncertain. Should a merger be permitted, for example, because of the likelihood of favourable balance of payments effects even though there is no reason to expect significant benefits in any other direction? Should a merger which is likely to result in substantial gains in efficiency be prohibited because of redundancy problems? If so how much redundancy is required to offset any given expected gain in efficiency? Should restrictive agreements be allowed where they form the basis of a plan for import substitution? And so on.

When confronted with problems such as these there is much to be said for restricting monopoly legislation to the pursuit of increasing efficiency. It is not a question of one policy weapon being completely unrelated to all except one policy objective. Neither is it necessary to restrict the use of one policy weapon to the attainment of one goal. Fiscal policy, for instance, may be used as a means of controlling the overall level of demand, and in its discriminatory role it may also be a powerful weapon for the purpose of effecting a reallocation of resources. Rather, it is the fact that a particular policy weapon is more appropriate for dealing with some objectives than others, and that the possibility of *conflict* in attempting to attain several goals simultaneously is reduced by a judicious selection of weapons and their 'allocation' to different objectives. It is a question, therefore, of how many policy weapons the government is able or willing to use and for what purpose. Monopoly policy has a small and uncertain effect on employment, income distribution and the balance of payments. In any case policy goals in these areas are more appropriately dealt with by means of fiscal policy and exchange-rate adjustments. If these goals have to be considered in the implementation of monopoly policy they will, however, certainly complicate matters and very likely lead to a substantial weakening of monopoly policy as a weapon for dealing with industrial efficiency and progressiveness.

A good example of this is the extent to which recent merger policy has been concerned with the balance of payments. In the British Insulated Callender's Cables/Pyrotenax merger, for instance, the Monopolies Commission thought that the more rapid increase in exports 'may turn out' to be 'the most valuable result of the merger for the public interest'. Again in the Unilever/Allied Breweries report the Commission saw the importance to 'the public interest in present circumstances of securing a substantial improvement in the United Kingdom balance of payments'. In both cases the Commission found in favour of the proposed merger.[4] It is interesting to speculate what the outcome would have been had the Commission investigated these cases at a time when the country had a large balance of payments surplus.

The government, then, has a number of basic goals and also several policy weapons which it can use to attain them. We are interested in the goals of efficiency and progressiveness. The discussion in this chapter has been important in indicating the range of problems involved in dealing with these goals, and also in putting into perspective the areas where particular policy weapons are likely to make some contributions towards improving performance. The goals of efficiency and progressiveness involve considerations of such problems as dynamic adjustment, externalities, the choice of goods, and the relationship of progressiveness to the degree of monopoly power. The available policy weapons include monopoly and restrictive practices legislation, discriminatory fiscal policy and direct government intervention in industry. Monopoly policy is most relevant to considerations relating to allocative efficiency and progressiveness within the private sector. There are other important aspects of efficiency, however, which it leaves largely untouched. These include the allocation of resources between the public and private sectors and external diseconomies, problems which are best dealt with by means of fiscal policy and direct government intervention. The remaining chapters are concerned with some of these basic policy issues.

[4] By the time the Commission reported on the Unilever/Allied Breweries proposed merger, however, there had been a sharp fall in Unilever's share prices and the merger was shelved.

CHAPTER 8

Monopoly and Merger Policy

A. INTRODUCTION

A major aspect of government policy in the field of industry is legislation relating to monopoly and restrictive practices. No attempt is made here to examine in detail the operation of this legislation. This has been very adequately dealt with in more than one book. Rather, what we are concerned with is to obtain a general view and an appraisal of some of the major aspects of policy in so far as they affect the processes of competition, growth and structural change.

The purpose of monopoly and restrictive practices legislation is to improve, according to some criterion or set of criteria, the economic performance of industries. The approach may take two main forms, one designed to control business behaviour, and the other to control market structures. The latter may in turn take the form of measures designed to *remedy* existing market structures which are associated with poor market performance, or of *preventing* the emergence of market structures which are expected to lead to adverse market performance.

The emphasis in Britain has been on attempting to improve market performance by influencing business behaviour. An important part of the policy has been the legislation relating to restrictive agreements amongst producers and to resale price maintenance. Responsibility for this aspect of policy has rested with the Restrictive Practices Court and the various issues relating to it are examined in the next chapter. In addition the Monopolies Commission has the responsibility for investigating monopoly situations and certain mergers, and of making recommendations to the government where it is found that a monopoly or merger is operating or may be expected to operate against the public interest. It is to this monopoly and merger policy that we now turn.

B. MONOPOLY AND MERGER LEGISLATION

British monopoly policy dates from the Monopolies and Restrictive Practices Act 1948. The passing of this Act owed much to the fact that the economic climate had changed so drastically as compared to the inter-war years. During this period of severe depression the Government encouraged the cartelization of private industry in an attempt to increase price stability and the profitability of investment. The acceptance by the Government of a full-employment policy in the 1944 White Paper on Employment Policy was probably a necessary forerunner to the passing of the 1948 Act.

The Act, however, did not mark the beginning of an all out attack on monopoly and restrictive practices. The Government's position was very much one of having an open mind on the merits and disadvantages of monopoly, and of emphasizing the need for more information to get a better picture both of the extent of monopolies and restrictive practices and also of their economic effects.

The Act set up a Monopolies and Restrictive Practices Commission which was to institute inquiries into monopoly situation referred to it by the Board of Trade (now the Department of Trade and Industry). Monopoly was defined as a condition where at least one-third of a class of goods was supplied in the UK by a firm or group of firms acting together so as to restrict competition. The first task of the Commission was to investigate whether the suppliers of the goods covered were indeed monopolists as defined by the Act. Next came the gathering of information from firms and their suppliers, customers, competitors, etc., on past and present behaviour resulting from or engaged in to preserve the monopoly position. This included an investigation of the costs, prices and profits of the monopolists. The Commission then had to decide whether the evidence relating to business behaviour and performance was contrary to the public interest and if so to consider what recommendations to make for the removal or modification of the offending practices.

There was no presumption then that monopoly was bad as such and necessarily inferior to more competitive market structures. Indeed in 'defining' the public interest the Commission was instructed to take into account, among other things, the need to achieve efficient production and distribution, a more efficient organization of industry and trade, the fullest use and best distribution of men, materials and industrial capacity, and the development of technical improvements. But there was no suggestion that the best way of achieving these goals would be through maintaining competitive markets, and indeed there was no mention of the word competition in defining the public interest.

The Commission was enlarged in 1953 in order to speed up its work but was reduced in size again in 1956 with the passing of the Restrictive Trade Practices Act. The job of investigating restrictive practices was transferred to the Restrictive Practices Court, and the

Commission's work was restricted to that of investigating 'unitary' monopolies.

The Monopoly and Mergers Act 1965 restored the size and organization of the Commission more or less to what they were between 1953 and 1956, and greatly strengthened the anti-monopoly legislation. The Commission was now able, after a reference had been made to it by the Board of Trade, to inquire into the supply of monopolized services as well as goods, and also to undertake general inquiries into practices likely to restrict competition but which were not registrable under the 1956 Act. The Board of Trade was also empowered to refer a merger or proposed merger to the Commission. Such a reference could be made where the merger would lead to or strengthen a monopoly position as defined by the 1948 Act, or where the value of the assets taken over would exceed £5 million. A proposed merger which qualified under one or other of these criteria could be held up until the Commission had reported. If it was decided that the merger operated or could be expected to operate against the public interest the Board of Trade had the power to stop the merger, to break up the merger if it had already taken place, or to allow the merger to proceed but subject to conditions. The Act also gave the Board of Trade new powers for taking action on the basis of the Commission's reports on monopoly situations. It could require the publication of price lists, regulate prices, prohibit acquisitions and order the division of companies.

In July 1973 the Fair Trading Act was passed to replace, with revised provisions, the Acts of 1948 and 1965.

The Act created a new office, that of Director General of Fair Trading, and conferred upon the office a number of important duties. First, the Director is to supervise and control consumer trade practices such as the terms and conditions of sale of goods and services, advertising and labelling of goods, etc. Second, the Director took over from the Department of Trade and Industry responsibility for keeping under review the carrying on of commercial activities in the United Kingdom with a view to becoming aware of, and ascertaining the circumstances relating to, monopoly situations or uncompetitive practices. The Director also took over the functions of the Registrar of Restrictive Trading Agreements in registering restrictive agreements and referring them to the Restrictive Practices Court.

The Monopolies Commission is renamed the Monopolies and Mergers Commission. Monopoly references to the Commission may be made by the Director General of Fair Trading or by the responsible Minister. For merger investigations, references may be made only by the Minister. The office of the Director, however, has the duty to keep informed about actual or prospective mergers which may qualify for investigation and to give the Minister advice about what action to take in connection with them.

The definition of a monopoly situation is changed from a minimum of a one-third market share to a one-quarter share, and for mergers a reference may be made either on the basis of this new monopoly criterion or, as before, if the value of the acquired assets exceeds £5 million. Monopoly and merger reference may be made which require the Commission to restrict its investigation to whether specified acts or omissions (e.g. concerning prices) may be expected to operate against the public interest. In the main, however, the important changes introduced by the Bill are in the administrative machinery of monopoly policy. There is little in the way of a change of approach in dealing with monopolies and mergers.

One point is perhaps worth mentioning, however, and that is the change, as compared to the 1948 Act, in the definition of the public interest. It has been pointed out that in the 1948 Act the public interest guideline did not mention the word competition but simply stressed the need for greater efficiency. In the 1973 Act, however, the Commission 'among other things shall have regard to the desirability of maintaining and promoting effective competition between persons supplying goods and services in the United Kingdom; . . . of promoting, through competition the reduction of costs and the development and use of new techniques and new products and of facilitating the entry of new competitors into existing markets; . . . and of maintaining and promoting competitive activity in markets outside the United Kingdom'. However, although there is clearly an emphasis on competition, the Commission is still instructed to take into account 'all matters which appear to them in the particular circumstances to be relevant' and specific mention is made of the desirability 'of maintaining and promoting the balanced distribution of industry and employment in the United Kingdom'. Whether there will be any fundamental change in the conduct of monopoly and merger policy as a result of the new Act remains to be seen.

So much for the legislation. We now turn to the basic analytical and practical problems of public policy, dealing first with monopoly and then with mergers.

C. PROBLEMS OF PUBLIC POLICY—MONOPOLY[1]

The basis of monopoly policy rests on the theoretical analysis of market structures which suggests that the effectiveness of the competitive control mechanism is related to market structure. Thus in

[1] This section deals not only with markets which are dominated by one firm, but also with those where a small number of firms dominate the market.

highly concentrated industries with substantial entry barriers, the dominant firms will, for instance, have greater discretion in fixing prices so that high concentration will be associated with monopoly profits. This tendency will be reinforced if there is collusion amongst firms, a practice which is most feasible and most entrenched where numbers are few. The positive association between the degree of concentration and profitability is of course a general *tendency* and not one which is invariably found. Nor should it be taken to imply that, where high profitability is found in a highly concentrated industry, this is *necessarily* a reflection of adverse market performance from the public interest point of view. Other factors have to be taken into account including the persistency of the high level of profits, the growth performance of the firm, its record of technological advance and the degree of risk involved.

1. *Normal Profits*

The evaluation of the profit performance of a firm invariably involves a reference to the concept of a 'normal' rate of profit, so much so that it can be said that such a concept is essential to the sensible implementation of an anti-monopoly policy. In static analysis normal profits are thought of as the minimum level necessary in the long term to attract or maintain capital in an industry. This minimum is not the same for all firms and industries but varies so as to reflect varying degrees of risk to investors. However, monopoly policy has to be conducted within a dynamic setting in which firms and industries show different rates of growth and in which profits provide finance for expansion, either as retentions by the firms or as the means by which outsiders are persuaded to invest in the company. It has been suggested, therefore, that a normal rate of profit for a firm should be defined by reference to the rate of growth of the firm, so that the higher the growth rate the higher the normal or 'necessary' rate of profit, again with an allowance, for any one firm or industry, for an abnormally high or low degree of risk.[2]

Let us suppose that for a number of firms, say the 100 largest manufacturing companies, a distinct positive association between profitability and growth is observed over a given time period. Diagrammatically we can, as in Fig. 8.1, draw a line PP showing the *average* relationship between the two variables, the actual scatter of observations lying on either side of the line. What now can be said in assessing the profitability of a firm such as A which is located well above PP?

[2] This suggestion was put forward as an application to incomes policy but the idea is equally applicable to monopoly policy. See R. L. Marris, *Incomes Policy and the Rate of Profit in Industry* (University of Cambridge, Department of Applied Economics, Reprint Series No. 238).

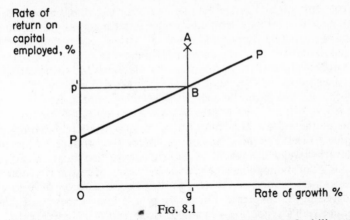

FIG. 8.1

On the basis of the average relationship between profitability and growth over the period concerned the profitability of A appears to be excessive. For a rate of growth of g' the PP curve suggests a 'normal' rate of return of p' so that 'abnormal' profitability amounts to AB. Before concluding that this is undesirable, however, the high profitability of firm A relative to its growth rate has to be explained. Three factors need to be distinguished and their relative importance assessed. First, the high profitability may be due entirely or in part to abnormally high risks which the firm has to face. In this case, although firm A has been successful over the period concerned its field of operation is one where the risks of failure are greater than the average for all manufacturing activity. Since this is a frequent argument made in defence of exceptionally high profitability, but also one which is not always valid, it is important that the strength of the argument should be assessed. In such an assessment it would certainly be relevant to see if, for individual investment projects, there is evidence of substantial losses as well as substantial profits both for other firms in the same line of activity and for periods in the history of the firm under examination. This was done for instance in the case of the Monopolies Commission report on the supply and processing of colour film. The opinion of the majority of the Commissioners who investigated this case was that 'photographic manufacturing is not a particularly high risk activity, and that, so far as colour film is concerned, a monopoly position founded upon Kodak's reputation with the public is not likely to be suddenly eroded. So far as we are aware the Eastman Kodak organisation has suffered no serious setback throughout its history.'[3]

[3] The Monopolies Commission, *Colour Film, A Report on the Supply and Processing of Colour Film* (HMSO, 1966), p. 106.

Secondly, high profitability may be due to monopoly power. The firm may, for instance, maintain a high profit margin by such practices as restricting output and creating barriers to new competition by exercising a restrictive control over sources of supply or distributive outlets and by heavy promotional outlays. Several such practices are revealed in the reports of the Monopolies Commission. Thus in the case of the supply of man-made cellulosic fibres, for instance, the Commission found that the behaviour of Courtaulds exemplified 'one of the classic disadvantages of monopoly, the limitation of supply to the level most advantageous for the producer, which is below the level which would be met in a competitive situation'. Some examples of monopolistic behaviour by means of restrictive control over outlets have already been given in the discussion of vertical integration in Chapter 2. On heavy promotional expenditure, the Commission's report on household detergents concluded that the price policies and the policies on advertising and promotion operate against the public interest by restricting entry, inflating advertising and sales promotion to the detriment of direct price competition, and raising prices.

Thirdly, high profitability may be the result of exceptionally able management, not only in terms of the day-to-day task of the efficient organization of production and distribution but also in 'getting in first' with new developments, or in being prompt in adopting successful innovations made elsewhere. The management factor also draws attention to the importance of managerial attitudes and in particular the extent to which management is willing to exploit a favourable market situation. Recognition of the wide variation in internal efficiency and in managerial attitudes also leads to the conclusion that monopoly power is not necessarily reflected in high profits. The potentialities for high profits may be foregone in favour of a quiet life.

The definition of normal profits in terms of the growth rate of the firm does not, therefore, offer a ready made prescription for policy decisions. It provides a starting point for analysis but does not eliminate the need for a careful assessment of the relative importance of a number of factors which influence profitability. How powerful a starting point the average relationship between growth and profitability turns out to be depends on the persistency of this relationship over time and also on the persistency with which a firm shows an abnormally high level of profits. Thus if the position and slope of the curve PP in Fig. 8.1 remain roughly constant over a long period of time the greater the claims of the curve in establishing a *desired* relationship between profitability and growth. The greater the persistency with which firm A earns exceptionally high profits the less likely it is that much of the excess profits can be legitimately explained by abnormal risk factors and exceptionally efficient management. As far as the management factor is concerned, this implies that the position of firms may be expected to change over time in the efficiency ranking of their managements. However, this is by no means inevitable, and a firm may be able to maintain a position of superiority over its rivals by, for instance, continually 'getting in first' with technical and organizational advances. In such a situation, however, the firm is likely to achieve a dominant position so that the risks it has to face compared to those faced by firms in other industries may dictate a *less* than average return on capital.

2. *Assessment of Market Performance*

Profitability is of course only one aspect of market performance. Although the above discussion has shown that other aspects of performance, such as the efficient organization of resources, the degree of progressiveness, and the height of selling costs, do have to be examined when evaluating profitability, in practice it will be desirable in the first instance to examine the important aspects of performance separately. Where profitability is high it will then be necessary to introduce some of the other dimensions of performance along with structural and behavioural factors as possible explanatory variables. The degree of emphasis on any one aspect will vary according to the circumstances of the industry. Thus selling costs will be an important factor for some firms but not for all, technical advance for some but not for others, and so on. In some instances the emphasis may not be on explaining a high overall profitability but on elements of inefficiency such as a misallocation of resources within the firm and a failure to exploit technical advances.

The task of undertaking anything like a complete assessment of the market performance of a firm is clearly a very formidable one. But certain basic questions should lie at the heart of any enquiry.

First, where high profits are involved, to what extent can they be justified by the growth and innovative performance of the firm, due regard being paid to the degree of risk facing the firm?

Secondly, how far is an existing position of market dominance being buttressed by behaviour which is designed to restrict competition? Such behaviour includes restrictive agreements with domestic and foreign producers, and restrictions placed on the distribution of goods.

Thirdly, to what extent is the present size of a firm based on considerations of efficiency? In attempting to establish the answer to this question the firm should be required to demonstrate the importance of economies of scale—both the technical economies relating to the size of plant and the non-technical economies relating to the size of the firm. Further, in evaluating problems of efficiency it will usually be instructive to examine the process by which the firm has attained large size or a position of market dominance. In particular, attention should be paid to the extent to which it has been associated with exclusionary and other restrictive behaviour, and to the relative importance of internal growth and growth by merger. Positive evidence relating to the first of these factors certainly makes the efficiency basis of existing size rather suspect. Also size is less likely to be associated with efficiency if it has been achieved mainly by mergers rather than by internal growth. In this case, however, attention would have to be devoted to the pattern of merger activity, and to any evidence of gains in efficiency following mergers as a result of rationalization schemes.

These questions vary of course in the extent to which they are capable of being answered in quantitative terms. A quantifiable answer is most feasible in the case of economies of scale, but one should not underestimate the problems of estimation especially in view of the fact that economy of size is a multi-dimensional factor. The most blatant types of exclusionary tactics can be unearthed without much difficulty, although the more subtle methods may go unnoticed even after a detailed enquiry. Even so it is easier to discover elements of restrictive behaviour than to estimate their aggregate effect on market performance. Fortunately, however, this is of no great consequence since a general presumption can certainly be made that exclusionary and predatory behaviour which increases or reinforces positions of market power should be prohibited. The problems are greater in the case of innovation. It is agreed that successful innovation should be rewarded by excess profits, but it is not at all obvious just *how much* of a reward is required, and thus to what extent excess profits are justified on the grounds of providing the necessary incentive to innovative activity.

Nevertheless, in spite of the difficulties involved, the basic questions which have been outlined should be asked and, whenever possible, answered in quantitative terms. The Monopolies Commission has, with varying degrees of forcefulness, pursued these basic issues in its investigations of monopoly situations. Its investigations, however, have been least satisfactory in dealing with economies of scale and in particular with failing to examine systematically and to quantify the claimed cost savings associated with size.[4] Since the economies of scale argument forms a vital part of the defence of large companies it is reasonable to suggest that in all monopoly

[4] See Alister Sutherland, *The Monopolies Commission in Action* (University of Cambridge, Department of Applied Economics, Occasional Papers, No. 21.)

enquiries a quantification of cost savings at both plant and firm level should be made. Indeed, there is much to be said for giving explicit instructions to the Commission, always to ask certain basic questions such as the ones outlined, and wherever possible to answer them in quantitative terms.

3. *Remedies*

It is much easier to say all this than it is to devise an appropriate set of remedies for monopoly situations. These remedies may be divided into three broad categories—indirect measures designed to change business behaviour, direct 'intervention' in the running of a business by means of an efficiency audit, and measures aimed at changing market structure. However, before turning to a consideration of these remedies it will be useful to distinguish between three different types of monopoly situation. First, there are the markets where a dominant firm position or a high level of concentration is justified by important economies of scale and where there may or may not be offsetting disadvantages relating to the monopoly power of firms. Secondly, there are situations where the existing degree of concentration cannot be justified by efficiency considerations in the sense that an organization of production in a larger number of units would not result in any loss of efficiency, but where there is no evidence of monopolistic restrictions. Thirdly, there are the markets where the existing degree of concentration is not justified by efficiency considerations and which also show marked evidence of undesirable performance due to monopolistic behaviour.

There are some remedies which would not be applicable to all three situations. For instance, a recommendation to enforce a division of a company into two or more separate units might be sensible in relation to the third situation but not to the first. On the other hand there are a number of useful remedies, particularly those indirect ones which impinge upon the behaviour of firms, which may be applicable to all three situations.

First, a very aggressive approach towards agreements designed to restrict competition, and particularly against those which increase the height of entry barriers, may succeed at least in eliminating the grosser forms of monopolistic abuse. This attitude has in fact been fairly consistently maintained by the Monopolies Commission.

Secondly, the degree of monopoly power in the home market may be reduced by more international competition brought about by a reduction in tariffs. The rapid post-war growth of international trade in industrial goods has greatly increased the importance of this form of competition, so that the competitive control mechanism is not always as diluted as it appears to be on the basis of the structure of the domestic market. There are a number of monopoly situations, however, where substantial tariff protection exists, and where it would be possible, therefore, to increase the degree of international competition. The Monopolies Commission reports on wallpaper, flat glass, colour film and cellulosic fibres show a substantial amount of tariff protection and in the two cases—colour film and cellulosic fibres—the Commission recommended that the tariff be reduced.

International competition may, therefore, play a useful role in reinforcing the competitive constraint. However, it is also important to note that apart from tariff protection international competition can also be weakened by agreements between firms. We have already noted the arrangements which Courtaulds and Pilkington made with continental producers.[5] More recently the Justice Department of the United States has filed a suit against Westinghouse Electric and the Japanese firms of Mitsubishi Electric and Mitsubishi Heavy Industries for violating the Sherman Anti-trust Act. The suit alleges that the companies maintain agreements for the exchange of patent and technology licences which prevent sales of a number of electrical goods by the Japanese companies in the US and by Westinghouse in Japan.[6]

Thirdly, there is one aspect of adverse market performance—excessive selling costs—which can be attacked directly. We have already noted some of the disadvantages of heavy promotional expenditure—the 'artificial' stimulation of desires, excessive product differentiation, less price competition and higher entry barriers. Furthermore it is important to note that expenditure on advertising and other promotional efforts is increasing rapidly. In Britain, advertising expenditure alone increased from £121 million in 1948 to £590 million in 1965.[7] The time has surely come to discourage this type of activity. The basis of a general policy could be to disallow advertising and other promotional expenditures as deductible items for tax purposes. Such a tax could be progressive but with exemption up to a certain limit so as not to penalize the small firm, particularly one which is attempting to enter a market. Beyond this exemption limit the higher the marketing expenditure the higher would be the rate of tax, with really penal rates applicable to those few cases where the levels of promotion are extremely high. At the same time there could be some direct control in the form, for instance, of a limitation on repetitive television advertising.

There would of course be difficulties in a fiscal approach of this kind. In particular there is no clear division between production and selling costs. There would be some difficulty, for instance, in

<hr/>

[5] See Chapter 5. [6] See *The Times*, Wednesday, May 13, 1970.
[7] See P. Doyle, 'Economic aspects of advertising: a survey', *The Economic Journal*, September 1968.

determining the allocation of expenditure on activities such as packaging. Similarly, problems would arise in distinguishing between transport and sales staff. Again, since it would be desirable to exempt marketing expenditure aimed at overseas markets, there would be further problems in determining the amount of marketing expenditure incurred on account of domestic sales. If a general fiscal approach is not acceptable to the government, the Monopolies Commission could be instructed always to examine the selling expenses of firms and to recommend what action to take in those cases where the expenses are regarded as being substantially in excess of what is required for efficient marketing.

Any scheme to control promotional expenditure would involve anomalies and attempts at evasion. However, there is no reason to believe that substantial net advantages would not be achieved. These would be in the form of immediate price reductions to consumers and the longer-term advantages of more effective competition, and a lessening of the pressures exercised by businesses to manipulate consumer demand.

Measures of this kind, designed to improve market performance by changing business behaviour would have a significant effect if rigorously pursued. There is the further question of the applicability of more radical remedies in the form of general direct 'intervention' in the running of a business by means of an efficiency audit, and by enforcing structural change.

In situations where high concentration is justified by economies of scale, or where enforced structural change of an industry is not feasible, and where the forces of competition are too weak to act as an effective control mechanism, a substitute control in the form of an efficiency audit can be used. This would amount to an examination of the internal efficiency of a firm, and would also examine and control aspects of performance such as the level and rate of increase in prices. The National Board for Prices and Incomes gave great prominence to this method of control and indeed seems to have greatly exaggerated its useful role. 'The traditional policy towards the problem of monopoly has been to try to restore competition. The fact has to be faced that this can rarely be done. A fully competitive situation requires that the market should not be dominated by any single firm or a small number of firms, that there should be no restrictive trading agreements . . . that other firms are free to enter the market and compete. . . . The answer to this kind of situation is then an efficiency audit.'[8] If the Board was suggesting that

8 National Board for Prices and Incomes, *Fourth General Report*, July 1968 to July 1969 (HMSO, 1969), p. 18. The Board was abolished in 1970.

there is need for an efficiency audit whenever there is competition amongst the few this is a great exaggeration. There will certainly be cases where unworkable performance associated with high concentration will not be readily cured by attempts to modify behaviour, and where structural change is also ruled out. Here the efficiency audit may be 'the only answer'. However, unworkable performance in terms of long-run price competition, product improvements and innovation is not always found whenever there is high concentration. Furthermore, where firms are showing a steady rate of internal growth this in itself may have salutary effects on performance. In those cases where an efficiency audit is justified, however, the benefits may be substantial. For, as we have seen, where the competitive stimulus is weak the firm is not forced to operate at maximum efficiency. The most valuable contribution which was made made by the National Board for Prices and Incomes was to emphasize the possibilities of improving internal efficiency and it is in this way also that an efficiency audit scheme would contribute to an improvement in industrial performance.

The structural approach to the monopoly problem is applicable in principle when the size of the firm is substantially greater than the minimum size which is regarded as necessary to achieve all the important economies of production, marketing and research and development. In arguing the case against the enforced division of companies it is not enough to establish that there will be a loss of some economies, because this has to be set against the likely benefits arising out of a greater degree of competition—benefits which, if the initial position is one of great security, may be particularly important in terms of the amount and direction of research and development work. The case for enforced division depends, therefore, on the extent to which existing performance is unsatisfactory. Where, as in the second situation mentioned above, a firm of much greater than minimum optimal size shows no significant signs of unworkable performance there is no strong case for enforced division. The case is most compelling where the failure to justify large size by economies of scale is allied with important aspects of unworkable performance.

The *feasibility* of enforced division, however, depends on the structure of the firm, the availability of new management and the degree of prosperity of the industry, the second and third of these factors being closely related. The division of companies has on occasion been considered by the Monopolies Commission. In one of the early reports, on matches, the solution was mentioned but considered unfeasible, mention being made of the difficulty of ensuring that the separate companies would obtain supplies of raw materials on equal terms, and of the relative smallness of the industry and the poor prospects of expansion. In its report on Cellulosic Fibres, the Commission considered that splitting Courtaulds' interests would lose some of the benefits arising from Courtaulds' size. It is not at all clear, however, from the report, that the losses would be important. However, had the Commission devoted more thought to the subject it may well have concluded that the relatively slow-growing and fluctuating demand and the difficulties under such circumstances of attracting good management were good enough reasons for regarding enforced division as too risky a solution.

In some of the other reports it is surprising that enforced division was not considered. This is particularly so, for instance, in the case of wallpaper and detergents. In the case of wallpaper, the Commission was very critical of the way in which Wall Paper Manufacturers Ltd had used acquisitions to maintain its command over the market, and it did not find that the monopoly position so established had resulted in significant gains in efficiency. In the case of detergents, production is again carried on in several separate establishments and although economies of scale are not systematically studied by the Commission there is a lot of evidence which suggests that they are relatively unimportant and certainly nowhere near important enough to justify the domination of the market by two firms.

It should not be thought that advocating enforced division of companies is unrealistic. Occasionally, firms divest themselves of branches or acquisitions that have not been successful. It is appropriate that this action should be extended to areas where divestiture would be in the public interest. In a few cases the purpose of enforced division will be to increase the number of competitors. There will be more frequent cases perhaps of companies which are excessively diversified and where outside pressure is needed to enforce some lateral disintegration in order to increase the degree of specialization. Of course such a policy is only one aspect of the overall strategy of curbing monopoly power, and it should be used only when conditions are clearly such as to make it feasible.

There is one less drastic aspect of the structural approach to remedies which the Monopolies Commission has been prepared to advocate, and that is the control of further acquisitions by dominant companies. Such a recommendation was made, for instance, in the case of wallpaper and cellulosic fibres. Here there is a means by which the government *could* exercise an effective control via the structural approach.

D. MERGERS AND ACQUISITIONS[9]

After the Monopolies and Mergers Act of 1965, however, the

[9] For brevity, mergers and acquisitions will hereafter be referred to as mergers.

Labour government adopted a very permissive attitude towards mergers, and indeed in the previous year it set up a special body, the Industrial Reorganisation Corporation (IRC) whose job it was to encourage mergers—presumably those in the national interest which would not have come about, or not come about quickly enough, without some official prodding and public money.

By June 30, 1969 the Board of Trade had assessed the likely effects of 430 actual or prospective mergers. Only twelve were referred to the Monopolies Commission and in three cases the Commission concluded that the mergers would operate against the public interest and recommended that they should not be allowed to proceed. The favourable attitude of the government was reflected in a speech made by the President of the Board of Trade in February 1969. 'In general, mergers are desirable if they lead to better management or genuine economies of scale without eliminating workable competition. In my view more often than not in Britain mergers will fulfil this condition.'[10] It is interesting to compare this view with that expressed by the Prices and Incomes Board and quoted above, which saw an efficiency audit as the substitute for competition where the latter 'is lacking or insufficiently effective or cannot be restored', some combination of these being seen as the usual state of affairs. And after four years of feverish merger activity the Monopolies Commission was able to conclude that there 'is no reason to think that this merger activity has so far led to the growth of companies whose absolute size is such as to raise important questions for the public interest. It is, however, leading to the continued absorption of medium-sized companies not necessarily accompanied by gains in efficiency.'[11] Surely the absorption of medium-sized companies is a matter which raises extremely important questions for the public interest since they offer the main challenge to established positions.

A further cause for concern is that it is not necessary to demonstrate that a merger will result in positive benefits to the public interest. 'In the great majority of cases, as was always envisaged, the Board have decided that even though the mergers could not be classified as positively desirable in the national interest and so to be actively encouraged, there were not sufficient grounds to refer them to the Commission for a full scale examination with all that would entail.'[12] When a merger has been referred, the Commission still

[10] See Board of Trade, *Mergers: A Guide to Board of Trade Practice* (HMSO, 1969), Annex 5.

[11] The Monopolies Commission, *Unilever Limited and Allied Breweries, a report on the proposed Merger, and General Observations on Mergers* (HMSO, 1969), p. 41.

[12] Board of Trade, op. cit., p. 1,

does not have to decide whether it is positively in the public interest, and the enquiry has to proceed at such high speed that it is not possible to undertake a full-scale examination with all that *should* entail.

The government's attitude was influenced by a number of factors including an uncritical association of efficiency with size and the unfavourable comparison of the size of many British companies with their US counterparts, and an emphasis on structural change with an encouragement to mergers as being the quickest way of seeing things happen. As for the dangers associated with the behaviour of the merged companies the government was comforted with the thought that the 'behaviour of the merged company can be examined at a later date to see that it does not conflict with the public interest'.[13] But surely since the government recognized that the large majority of mergers assessed since 1965 could not be classified as positively desirable in the public interest, it would have been far more satisfactory to preserve competition and thus avoid the inevitable, and probably very costly, series of reports and efficiency audits at a later date.

Of course, all this is not to say that there are no good reasons for mergers or even that the majority of the mergers that have occurred since 1965 have not been justified. No information is available on which to make a judgment on this issue. It remains, however, to bring out some broad points which may be of use in developing a framework of analysis for dealing with mergers.

The central issue is that a merger may have importance in terms both of *potential* gains in efficiency and a reduction in competition. Where this is the case a proper evaluation of the situation can only be made by an attempt to estimate the likely net gain or loss to the consumer and the public interest. From this point of view the following points are relevant.

First, there is need to distinguish between size and the process of attaining large size. We have argued that the most important elements of increased efficiency are associated with the process of growth rather than with size as such, so that the efficiency gains obtained simply by merging firms into larger units may be small. This, however, is an empirical question, which points to the need to quantify the gains from economies of scale. Firms should be required to estimate the extent to which costs will be reduced, to explain how the reductions will be achieved and over what period of time. Such evidence could then be scrutinized by the relevant government agency. It should be the responsibility of the firms, therefore, to 'prove' the benefits of a proposed merger. Consideration of what is

13 Board of Trade, op. cit., p. 1.

practical also suggests two other points. First, policy would have to concentrate on mergers involving large companies. It would not be practical, and anyway not especially desirable, to apply it to mergers between small companies. It should, however, apply to the case where a large company proposes to acquire a small one. Secondly, since a detailed enquiry is costly, it should not be enough for the firms to prove some benefit, however small. The benefits should be substantial. Insistence on this point would save the trouble of investigating a large number of 'doubtful' cases.

Secondly, even if a merger is likely to lead to substantial efficiency gains account has to be taken of the time-lag between the merger and the realization of the gains. If the time-lag is of the order of, say, two or three years it must be recognized that a great deal could have been accomplished in the same period by internal growth. In this connection the nature of the market, and in particular the rate of growth of demand, is important. Thus in a rapidly expanding industry internal growth will be effective in increasing the size of the firm, and in particular the expansion of demand will provide the safety element which is necessary to induce firms to undertake investment in increased capacity and in research and development. In a declining industry, on the other hand, and particularly one with a highly competitive market structure, there may be serious obstacles to the internal growth of firms and the case for mergers can be quite strong. Such an industry may be characterized by chronic excess capacity because of the slow adjustment of capacity to the lower level of demand, a capital stock biased towards old equipment, and a declining quality of management. In such a situation the major benefits from a merger are to encourage the scrapping of old machines and investment in new ones by reducing the degree of uncertainty associated with excess capacity, and to increase the proportion of the industry's assets under the control of efficient managers. The point to emphasize, therefore, is that a merger should be seen to promise substantial benefits which could not easily be achieved by means of internal growth.

Thirdly, the previous point draws attention to the importance of management, and in particular to the fact that the loss of efficiency due to internal or managerial weaknesses can be large. The contention that mergers may increase efficiency as a result of a change in management attitudes is a general point which in principle is applicable to all industries.[14] However the degree of urgency with

[14] This point is particularly applicable to an acquisition made by an American company. In general US subsidiaries in Britain have a higher rate of return on capital than their British-owned competitors. See J. H. Dunning, *The Role of American Investment in the British Economy*, PEP Broadsheet 507, February 1969.

which structural change is needed and the availability of feasible alternatives does vary according to the nature of the industry under consideration. Thus in a highly competitive market with little or no growth there may be strong arguments in favour of mergers which increased the concentration of resources controlled by the more efficient management teams, because the alternative of internal growth is likely to be slow and uncertain. Furthermore, internal growth in the growth-motivated firms may well take the form of diversification into the newer growth sectors of the economy and while this in itself is to be desired it does little to increase efficiency in the declining industry.

In expanding industries there will again be managements of differing degrees of efficiency, but in these cases the need to concentrate resources in firms which currently have the most efficient management is much less. The fundamental point is that in expanding sectors it is more likely that the firms which fall behind will be able to find ways, often by the infusion of new management, of increasing their efficiency and thereby re-creating favourable growth conditions. The search behaviour described in Chapter 5 and, for instance, Downie's analysis of the competitive process, are consistent with the expectation that in expanding firms a setback to growth will be followed by remedial measures. But more important perhaps is that in expanding industries competition is more likely to be enhanced by new entry. The encouragement of mergers in order to concentrate resources in the hands of the management team which is currently the most efficient and growth-motivated is a short-sighted policy which does not recognize the fact that the most efficient firm of today may in the future be superseded by another, and also that the creation of a much more highly concentrated industry may increase the barriers to the entry of new firms. Of course, a firm may be slow in improving its efficiency, but this may indicate not so much the desirability of an acquisition as the need to put pressure on management to improve performance. The same point can be made to qualify the argument that the capital market and in particular the threat of a take-over bid is an effective sanction against the inefficiency of management. Because in so far as a firm which currently has inefficient management is taken over this in the long run may not in all cases be the change which results in the biggest gain in efficiency. Furthermore we have already drawn attention to the fact that there is little evidence to support the hypothesis that there is a strong tendency for acquired firms to have a lower profitability than the acquiring ones.[15] An important feature of a large proportion of acquisitions is not that there is a consistent

[15] See Chapter 5.

relationship between the profitability of the acquired and the acquiring company but the fact that the acquiring company is larger and in particular has, in absolute terms, greater liquidity.

Fourthly, the greater financial power of the large companies means that the smaller companies are particularly susceptible to take-over bids. Many small and medium-sized companies have vigorous growth records and have clear prospects for the continuance of such growth. They thus pose an important competitive threat to larger companies which provides a very powerful incentive to the larger companies to acquire them and so to protect or to enhance their monopoly position. This also draws attention to the problem of the best re-grouping of productive capacity in industries where a clear gain is likely to be achieved as a result of rapid structural change which concentrated production in fewer units. It is not at all obvious that this should be done in such a way as to enhance the power of the dominant firm. Rather, careful consideration should be given to the possibility of creating an industrial structure in which competition takes place between a smaller number of firms of more similar size.

It remains to say a few words about conglomerate mergers. The basic questions to be asked about conglomerate mergers are the same as those relating to horizontal and vertical ones. What are the prospects of gains in efficiency being realized, and what are the dangers in terms of loss of competition. As far as efficiency is concerned a conglomerate merger may result in gains arising from the more efficient management of existing assets. Further gains may be realized as a result of scale advantages in finance, management, marketing and research and development. How important in quantitative terms these economies are likely to be clearly depends on the size of the firm being acquired and also, apart from the first economy mentioned, on how closely related the new activity is to the conglomerate existing activities, either in terms of production or marketing. The more tenuous the links between a company's various interests the less likely it is that any important economies of scale exist.

There are several ways in which competition may be affected by conglomerate mergers, the outcome depending on such factors as the structure of the industry being entered, the feasibility of entry by internal expansion rather than by acquisition, the particular firm acquired, and the behaviour of the conglomerate after entry. Thus, for instance, where a conglomerate moves into a highly concentrated industry by acquiring one of the smaller existing firms which is unable to expand its market share, competition in the industry is likely to be increased. A net gain in terms of the strength of competition is less likely if the firm acquired is a fast-growing one which is already providing an actual or potential threat to larger firms. A crucial question then is whether such a progressive firm would be acquired by one of the existing large firms in the industry, or whether this threat would be avoided or prevented by merger legislation.

Where, on the other hand, a large conglomerate company enters an industry where the typical firm is much smaller than the conglomerate, there is certainly a danger that competition will be weakened. This may result because other firms in the industry fear retaliation and thus refrain from price competition, or because the conglomerate uses its overall financial strength to build up a monopoly position in the industry by engaging in a predatory short-run pricing strategy designed to drive competitors out of the market.

However, subject to certain safeguards, the growth of conglomerate companies may result in important gains in efficiency and in the strength of competition. Such safeguards may take the form of a restriction on the type of firm which the conglomerate is allowed to acquire. Thus, for instance, it may be prevented from acquiring one of the largest five or six firms, say, in an industry, and also any medium-sized firm which has a good profitability and growth performance. In this way conglomerate mergers would be more likely to result in efficiency gains and to strengthen competition. Similarly where it became evident that a conglomerate had used its financial power to gain a monopoly advantage in an industry the government should make it clear that it would use its powers of enforcing a division of the company's assets. A further important safeguard to abuse would be to require firms with a diversity of interests to publish separate accounts for their main activities. 'Light is the sovereign antiseptic and the best of all policeman.'

It would certainly be dangerous to take the view that the growth of conglomerate companies is somehow undesirable, and that efficiency is maximized by a neat or 'logical' division of companies on the basis of existing industry boundaries. The past history of the sources of invention and innovation for instance are too diverse to justify such a policy. This is part of a more general point that emerges from this discussion of merger activity, which is the danger of emphasizing the present to the neglect of the future. Just as the theory of the firm is now concerned with inter-temporal problems, so should the government consider these in dealing with problems of industrial structure.

CHAPTER 9

Restrictive Practices

The second main aspect of policy towards monopoly and competition is legislation to control restrictive trade practices. The legislation has been concerned with two main types of restrictive practice: agreements among producers, and resale price maintenance—a practice whereby manufacturers determine the resale prices of their goods. We look at these two main aspects of policy in turn.

A. RESTRICTIVE AGREEMENTS

1. *The 1956 Act*

The first major attack on restrictive trade practices in the United Kingdom came with the passing of the Restrictive Trade Practices Act, 1956. This Act was the response to increasing concern about the widespread and very entrenched nature of restrictive agreements which emerged from special enquiries into individual industries such as building materials, cement, and textile machinery; the reports of the Monopolies and Restrictive Trade Practices Commission which was established in 1948, and especially from the general report of that Commission on collective discrimination.[1]

Part I of the 1956 Act provided for the registration of agreements with the Registrar of the Restrictive Practices Court.[2] All agreements between two or more persons carrying on business in the production or supply of goods under which restrictions are accepted by the parties in respect of the prices to be charged, the terms or conditions of sale, quantities or types to be produced, the process of manufacture, the persons or areas to be supplied or the persons or areas from which goods are to be acquired, had to be registered. Such agreements are deemed contrary to the public interest unless the Court is satisfied of one or more of the following circumstances:

[1] Monopolies and Restrictive Practices Commission, *Collective Discrimination: a Report on exclusive dealing, collective boycotts, aggregated rebates and other discriminatory trade practices*, HMSO, June 1955.

[2] Part II deals with resale price maintenance which we examine in the next section and Part III restricts the activities of the Monopolies Commission to the investigation of monopoly situations. The functions of the Registrar were transferred to the Director General of Fair Trading in the Fair Trading Act, 1973.

(a) That the restriction is reasonably necessary to protect the public against injury;
(b) that the removal of the restriction would deny to the public as purchasers, consumers or users of any goods, specific and substantial benefits;
(c) that the restriction is reasonably necessary to counteract measures taken by a person not party to the agreement with a view to restricting competition;
(d) that the restriction is reasonably necessary to enable fair terms to be negotiated with a large supplier or purchaser;
(e) that the removal of the restriction would be likely to have a serious and persistent adverse effect on unemployment in an area;
(f) that the removal of the restriction would be likely to cause a reduction in export business;
(g) that the restriction is reasonably required for the purposes of supporting other restrictions in the agreement which are in the public interest.

In addition to successfully negotiating one or more of these seven 'gateways', the parties defending a registrable agreement have to further satisfy the Court that the restriction is 'not unreasonable having regard to the balance between those circumstances and any detriment to the public or to persons not parties to the agreement'.

It is clear from the above that the structure of the 1956 Act is such as to present the Court with great difficulty.

First, there is not, as in the United States, a clear commitment to competition and an outright prohibition of certain restrictive agreements. Rather, although there is a general presumption in favour of competition, it is clear that there may be a number of situations in which the public interest would be best served by maintaining a restrictive agreement.

Secondly, the definition of public interest is very widely drawn, embracing several objectives such as the maintenance of employment and the promotion of exports, which are specifically mentioned in the gateways, as well as others such as the level of prices and the rate of technological advance which can be introduced as a defence of an agreement via gateway (b). Furthermore, the Court has to balance any benefits of a restriction against any detriment to the public or to persons not parties to the agreement.

This very general approach means inevitably the need to decide on the relative importance of different objectives and of different group interests. The Court, however, is given little guidance on this and is forced to make its own policy decisions. Thus for instance it has had to balance the possible gains from increased efficiency against an increase in local unemployment, and the possible advantages resulting from an agreement in the form of increased exports against possible disadvantages to domestic consumers in the form of higher prices. The Court has also had to involve itself in economic prediction. It has had to reach a decision, for instance, on whether technological change is likely to be promoted by a restrictive agreement as compared to the likely outcome under free competition, and on whether prices are likely to be lower with a restrictive agreement than with free competition because of the reduction in risk facing individual manufacturers. The requirements of the Act, therefore, 'forced the Court not only to make economic predictions and forecasts but also to evaluate the economic effects of agreements in the light of the interests of different groups and of competing policy objectives'.[3]

Finally the case-by-case approach, together with the wide range of possible grounds for exemption, has meant that the decisions of the Court have not been entirely predictable and of a kind which gives a clear guide to businessmen. This indeed was foreseen by the majority in the report on Collective Discrimination, who argued that a 'general prohibition would give industry clear and unequivocal guidance as to the Government's policy and would avoid the uncertainty and waste involved in detailed inquiries in each individual case'.[4]

2. *Effects of Legislation against Restrictive Agreements*

In spite of these difficulties, however, the 1956 legislation has resulted in the disappearance of the majority of registrable agreements, and indeed the degree of success achieved has been great enough to suggest that the result would not have been much different had the United States approach been adopted. The most important question, however, is what has been achieved.

The abandonment of restrictive agreement was certainly not, in general, followed by widespread short-run price competition. An early enquiry into the effects of the disappearance of agreements found that in two-thirds of the cases manufacturers reported no change in prices or in the intensity of competition.[5] This finding was not surprising for a number of reasons. First, the period in which the enquiry was conducted was one of a generally high level of

[3] R. B. Stevens and B. S. Yamey, *The Restrictive Practices Court, A Study of the Judicial Process and Economic Policy* (Weidenfeld & Nicolson, 1965), p. 142.

[4] Monopolies and Restrictive Practices Commission, op. cit., p. 86.

[5] J. B. Heath, 'Restrictive practices legislation: some economic consequences', *Economic Journal*, vol. LXX, September 1960.

demand so that there was no general downward pressure on prices as a result of a shortage of orders. Secondly, the abandonment of an agreement does not mean that the 'understanding' which firms have developed dissolves overnight. Collusion based on past learning will often ensure uniformity of behaviour after a formal agreement has disappeared. Thus, for instance, firms may have developed a particular mark-up formula in order to calculate the effects on prices of changes in wages and raw material costs. Thirdly, in oligopolistic industries, the abandonment of a restrictive agreement is frequently replaced by a system of price leadership which again may result in a great deal of uniformity as far as prices are concerned. Finally, simple interdependence between a small number of sellers may also be sufficient to ensure a high degree of uniformity of behaviour. The effectiveness of legislation against collusive behaviour is clearly dependent then on the structure of industries. In the United States Bain has argued that the uneven incidence of the enforcement of the law against collusive agreements is in large part due to the difficulty of dealing with the more highly concentrated industries where several alternative methods are available for achieving a given end. Economic theory certainly supports this view.

In predicting the areas where short-run price competition is likely, however, it is not enough to classify industries according to certain structural dimensions such as the degree of concentration. The nature of the business activity is also extremely important. A particularly important distinction is between firms whose production consists of products made to the producer's own design, and which are marketed on a more or less 'continuous flow' basis, and firms whose sales consist of products made to specification, and where orders come at relatively infrequent intervals. We may call the former type of firm marketers and the latter jobbers. This of course is a very oversimplified classification. Firms often combine 'jobbing' and 'marketing' work, and the nature of jobbing work in terms for instance of the size and frequency of orders varies a great deal. Nevertheless it is a fundamental distinction for understanding many aspects of industrial behaviour.[6] It is in jobbing work, particularly where the size of an individual order is large and infrequent, that short-run price competition, following the abandonment of a restrictive agreement, is likely to be greatest. If order books are long this tendency will be postponed, but it is almost certain to occur with the appearance of excess capacity. The *opportunity* to cut prices without the knowledge of close competitors exists because firms are not aware of the bids being submitted by their rivals. The *incentive*

[6] See for instance H. F. Lydall, 'Aspects of competition in manufacturing industry', *Bulletin of the Oxford Institute of Statistics*, November 1958.

to cut prices is also great during periods of excess capacity because of high overheads and the need to keep specialized equipment and personnel occupied, and the importance, therefore, of winning orders especially where these are large and infrequent. In the case of firms producing goods to their own design which are marketed in large quantities, short-run price competition amongst oligopolists after the abandonment of an agreement is likely to be less widespread and certainly less severe, although there will be greater freedom to offer better terms to important customers.

It is not enough, however, to judge the impact of restrictive practices legislation by its effect on short-run price competition. From the point of view of efficiency the more important effect of the elimination of restrictive agreements is the general tendency for competition 'as a dynamic process' to be strengthened. In other words the emphasis should be on the beneficial effects which the greater exposure of firms to competition has on facilitating long-run structural changes by removing obstacles to the expansion of the more efficient firms. One aspect of this change will be differential price changes based on differences in efficiency gains over time, so that the firms which achieve the biggest gains in efficiency will be able to establish a price advantage over their competitors.

The remaining question is how are these beneficial long-run changes related to short-run price competition, and is the gain in efficiency over the longer period always positively associated with the degree of short-run price competition? We saw in Chapter 6 that there may be circumstances where the encouragement of short-run competition will not lead to a satisfactory outcome in terms of the longer-term development of an industry so that there may be something to be said in favour of restrictive agreements. But to allow firms to operate a restrictive agreement which could be used to improve market performance always carries the danger that it will actually result in monopolistic exploitation. Thus a potential benefit of an agreement may be to reduce an excessive degree of risk, but the actual outcome may be a monopolistic restriction of supply. Quite apart from this there is also the question of alternative courses of action which might be open to firms when restrictions on competition are removed.

One such possibility is of course merger and acquisition which, as we have seen, has been a major feature of industrial change in the United Kingdom in the post-war years. It is impossible to say how important a part restrictive practices legislation has played in accounting for them, but undoubtedly it has been one of the underlying causes. Although an increase in concentration may be an alternative way of restricting competition when restrictive agreements have to be abandoned, there is no reason to believe that all or even the majority of mergers and acquisitions were motivated by this consideration or that they have had this result. Here again, it is impossible to attach precise quantitative significance to any one causal factor because of the several influences at work.

Apart from mergers and acquisitions, other developments have served to temper the effects of the restrictive practices legislation in the manufacturing sector.

The first of these is the growth of 'information agreements'. This is an arrangement whereby firms notify each other, usually via a trade association, of prices charged, and sometimes about other factors, such as costs, as well.[7] There may well be good reason to distinguish between different types of information agreement. Certainly the Board of Trade seems to do so. 'In a number of industries schemes of inter-firm cost comparisons have been adopted . . . with the objective of raising the general level of efficiency in an industry by showing firms taking part in the scheme what operational results their competitors are managing to achieve. The typical scheme of this kind involves a comparison not of prices but of costs expressed in terms of cost-ratios.'[8] Information agreements, however, are in the main a post-1956 development and are, therefore, and particularly as far as prices are concerned, very suspect as being a direct replacement for the registrable agreements listed in the 1956 Act. Certainly, economic analysis would lead us to expect that a systematic exchange of information by firms in oligopolistic markets would tend to increase interdependence and thus lead to a more monopolistic outcome by increasing the likelihood of collusive behaviour or effective price leadership. This possible outcome has been recognized by the authorities, and the Restrictive Trade Practices Act, 1968 gives the Board of Trade the power to call up certain specified types of information agreement for registration. How rigorously the matter will be pursued remains to be seen.

What is certain, however, is that the 1968 Act has weakened restrictive practices legislation in two important respects. First an additional 'gateway' (h) has been added to the 1956 Act, so that a restriction can now be defended on the grounds that it 'does not directly or indirectly restrict or discourage competition to any material degree in any relevant trade or industry and is not likely to do so'. This applies to all agreements although it was probably added mainly as a defence of information agreements. Secondly, the 1968

---

[7] For a detailed account of different types of information agreement see D. P. O'Brien and D. Swann, *Information Agreements, Competition and Efficiency* (Macmillan, 1968).

[8] *Board of Trade Journal*, February 28, 1969.

Act also provides for the exemption from registration of certain agreements of importance to the national economy, where the object is to promote efficiency or create or improve productive capacity, and where that object cannot be achieved within a reasonable time except by means of an agreement. This appears to be the result of the growing embarrassment resulting from the work of the Economic Development Committees (EDCs), some of which has involved inter-firm co-operation which is registrable under the 1956 Act. In view of this it will be worth while looking at the role of the EDCs in more detail.

3. *The Economic Development Committees*[9]

The formation of the EDCs was a reflection of a growing dissatisfaction with competition as a means of promoting structural change, or at least to effect the necessary changes quickly enough. The aspect of structural change which has particularly drawn the attention of the EDCs is the switch of resources into investment and exports. 'It is not enough to switch resources into investment and exports. We have to shift resources into the right investments and the right exports. All twenty-one of the Little Neddies are working at this moment to identify where this shift of resources can be achieved, what are the right investments and which are the profitable exports.[10] Firms, therefore, are not to be relied upon to discover and to take advantage of profitable investment opportunities, and it is assumed that some forms of co-operative or planned system will work more effectively than the competitive one. We saw earlier how this increasing emphasis on co-operation associated with the work of the EDCs resulted in 1968 in an amendment which is likely to substantially weaken the 1956 Restrictive Trade Practices Act.

In addition to their activities relating to studies of exports and imports the EDCs have devoted much attention to efficiency, and

[9] The first Economic Development Committee was set up in 1964 following the early work of the National Economic Development Council (NEDC). The NEDC, consisting of representatives of industry, trade unions and the government, was established in 1962 as an instrument for planning the growth of the economy. Its role was to examine the performance and plans of industry, to consider obstacles to faster growth and to seek agreement on ways to improve national competitiveness and efficiency. One of its first actions was to produce a report on the growth of the economy from 1961 to 1966. In the course of this study a number of industries were consulted to discover what their plans for investment and output were over the period. Following this it was agreed that it would be desirable to establish consultation on a more permanent basis. Thus the EDCs were formed. There were nine in 1965 and the number has now grown to twenty-one.

[10] H. F. R. Catherwood, Director-General of the NEDC, 'The planning dialogue', *National Westminster Bank Review*, May 1969.

there have been several studies of international and inter-firm productivity comparisons, manpower requirements, production planning and control, and management training, all intended to contribute something to improving performance. There is certainly plenty of scope for action to increase efficiency given a willingness on the part of both management and trade unionists to accept changes. However, it is easy to recognize that a lot can be done to improve matters. It is much more difficult to turn words into deeds. The EDCs are advisory bodies and have no powers of compulsion over the individual firms in the industry.

Apart from their specific attempts to increase efficiency and to promote exports and import substitution, the main argument for the EDCs is that they increase the amount of information available to firms. The efficiency of the market mechanism depends on the information available to decision-makers. If the EDCs then can improve the information on the future state of demand, on existing capacity in the industry and on the capacity of firms which supply inputs, this should help the investment decisions of firms to result in a smoother adjustment of capacity to demand. Of particular importance is the argument that the EDCs by increasing information and thus reducing uncertainty will result in an increase in investment while at the same time ensuring that the new investment will not be so great as to lead to excess capacity and a failure to earn a normal return on capital. This claim assumes that the degree of uncertainty associated with 'free' competition is such as to lead to an unfavourable balance between safety and competition. As a result firms are reluctant to invest in new capacity and in research and development.

Clearly, circumstances will vary a great deal from one industry to another. They are likely to be most unfavourable where equipment is highly specific, economies of scale are very important in relation to the size of the domestic market, and where there is strong competition either from domestic or overseas producers. These are circumstances where, because of the heavy penalties resulting from excessive investment, no firm may be prepared to undertake an investment without assurances that it will not be followed by a domestic competitor.

The difficulties and dangers of the task of planning investment on the basis of this kind of co-operation, however, should not be underestimated.

First, there is the tremendous difficulty of arriving at a consistent *and* a credible set of predictions about the levels of output in different sectors of the economy. Even where the economy is divided into broad sectors the problems are great, but the less disaggregated the attempt is the less useful it will be for individual firms.

Secondly, even if a credible prediction can be arrived at for the output of an industry this still leaves undetermined the market shares of individual firms, and from the firm's point of view what matters is its expected share of the market. Where businessmen have divergent views about their relative market shares an agreed overall prediction about the state of demand will not suffice to establish a nice adjustment of capacity to demand. Indeed without some form of market-sharing agreement it is difficult to see how, except by chance, a good adjustment will come about. More important is the fact that forecasts of the overall level of demand are likely to be of limited use in industries where innovation and new entry are important. Under such circumstances an 'effective procedure' for adjusting capacity to demand is likely to have adverse consequences on both innovation and new entry and thus to severely weaken the competitive process. The more effective the power to adjust capacity to demand the more effective also it is to adjust capacity in such a way as to earn monopoly profits and restrict competition.

Thirdly, it is important to recognize that in a dynamic competitive economy some waste of resources is inevitable. Investment and innovation are risky so that the natural reaction is to delay decisions while more information is gathered. The counterbalance to this is the fear that someone else will get in first and gain a lead in the industry. There will be mistakes as well as successes, and it is by the associated system of penalties and rewards that the competitive process operates. Co-operation between firms removes 'unnecessary' duplication in research and reduces the danger of excessive investment but also reduces the vigour of competition. It is a question, therefore, of which one, competition or co-operation, gives the best results, or rather, a question of how much co-operation should be allowed to intrude upon the competitive process. Because of the marked differences that exist between industries with regard to such factors as the specificity and indivisibility of equipment, the size and rate of growth of the market, and the extent of international competition, it is not likely that a single answer to such questions will be found to apply to all cases. It is hard to avoid the conclusion, however, that developments in recent years suggest that a policy of co-operation has to some extent superseded that of competition as the main regulator of economic activity.

B. RESALE PRICE MAINTENANCE

1. *Legislation*

Until the Restrictive Trade Practices Act of 1956 and the Resale Prices Act of 1964, manufacturers in Britain were free to maintain resale prices either by individual or collective action. In the case of individual r.p.m. the manufacturer stipulated the resale prices of his own goods, and could enforce these prices by withholding supplies from retailers who were not adhering to his terms, or by taking legal action. Resale prices could also be set by associations of manufacturers who could take collective action, such as the withholding of supplies, to enforce resale terms.

The 1956 Act prohibited the collective enforcement of r.p.m. but increased the powers of manufacturers in enforcing individual r.p.m. This legislation did not have much effect, although it did perhaps do something to increase the degree of flexibility in the relationship between manufacturer and retailer, and made individual manufacturers more susceptible to the pressures of multiple retailers.

The 1964 Act was a much more powerful piece of legislation and provided for the prohibition of individual r.p.m. except for 'exempted' goods. A class of goods could be declared to be exempted by the Restrictive Practices Court if as a result of the abandonment of r.p.m.:

(a) the quality or the variety of goods would be substantially reduced to the detriment of consumers; or

(b) the number of retail outlets would be substantially reduced to the detriment of consumers; or

(c) the retail prices would in general and in the long run be increased to the detriment of consumers; or

(d) the goods would be sold by retailers under conditions likely to cause danger to the health of consumers; or

(e) any necessary services actually provided with or after the sale of the goods would be substantially reduced to the detriment of consumers.

It is clear from this that in deciding on the balance of advantages and disadvantages of the practice of individual r.p.m. the 1964 Act requires the Restrictive Practices Court to have exclusive regard to the interests of consumers. Furthermore in restricting the 'escape routes' to five specific benefits the Act made it difficult for manufacturers to make a successful defence of their case. Indeed, the manufacturers of confectionery, footwear and pharmaceuticals are the only ones to have defended their resale practices before the Courts and only pharmaceuticals was successful. Pharmaceuticals and books [the publishing industry successfully defended the Net Book Agreement in 1962], are therefore the only products on which manufacturers can now enforce r.p.m.

To understand the likely effects of prohibiting r.p.m., however, it is necessary first of all to examine the likely consequences of the practice itself.

2. *Consequences of r.p.m.*

The basic point is that r.p.m. restricts competition by imposing a uniform price on a commodity, and that, typically, it raises distributors' margins above the competitive level. From this basic proposition a number of consequences follow.

First, whereas the preferences of consumers vary in terms of the desired price/service combination, the practice of r.p.m. does not give him a choice. Thus the consumer is not able to choose between a shop which sells a commodity at a relatively high price but also offers a lot of service, and one which sells at a lower price but which offers very little service.

Secondly, r.p.m. means that the price charged by different distributive outlets is the same regardless of differences in their location, efficiency, and the amount of service actually supplied with the sale of goods. The more efficient firms are unable to attract more customers by offering lower prices so that the growth of the efficient at the expense of the less efficient is retarded. This does not mean of course that the more efficient firms will be unable to increase their share of the market. Their greater efficiency will enable them to attract more customers by offering a better service, and/or to earn higher profits with which to finance a faster growth rate. However, r.p.m. does remove price competition which is the most powerful force affecting market shares.

Thirdly, r.p.m. is an obstacle to the development of new forms of distribution based on lower prices and less service. Again this is not to say that it is *impossible* for new methods of distribution to develop. Thus new retail firms based on self-service developed rapidly in the grocery field, although it should be added that r.p.m. was never as firmly established in this field as in the case of other consumer goods. Pressure on r.p.m. can also come about by the diversification of large retail firms as occurred in the case of the sale of cigarettes and alcoholic drink in supermarket stores. The development by large retailers of their own branded goods also exerts pressure in the same direction.

Fourthly, because r.p.m. prevents price competition it tends to increase the amount of competition in service. The amount of service offered tends to be greater than is demanded by consumers in the sense that, if given the choice, a substantial proportion would prefer to have lower prices and less service in the form, for instance, of elaborate packaging and attention from sales staff.

One particular aspect of competition in service which has received much attention is the argument that r.p.m. results in a larger number of shops than would exist under a more competitive situation and thus is the creator of excess capacity. Even where r.p.m. does not exist the theory of monopolistic competition leads us to expect some degree of excess capacity because of the structure of the distributive trades. That is, where there are many close competitors each with downward-sloping demand curves and where entry conditions are easy, the forces of competition will *tend* to push the demand curves to a point of tangency with the downward-sloping portion of the average cost curve. This suggests that the same total output could be produced at a lower real cost by a smaller number of larger firms.

It is difficult, however, to draw any firm implications from this analysis about the welfare of consumers especially in the retail trades because much of the excess capacity which is generated is associated with the existence of peak demand. How much differentiation do consumers demand and how much are they prepared to pay for it in terms of the lost opportunities of a more standardized, lower cost system? Accepting the fact that consumers demand *some* differentiation, is the amount of excess capacity actually generated by the competitive process too large? Chamberlin regarded the 'tangency solution' in the case of large numbers of competing sellers as a 'sort of ideal', arguing that the elasticities of the individual demand curves form a 'rough index of buyers' preferences for the "product" of one seller over that of another'. This argument, however, is not tenable because consumers are not in fact given a choice of having *either* more standardization and lower prices, *or* more differentiation and higher prices. They are offered one or the other but not both.

With the existence of r.p.m., however, there is a much stronger presumption that too much surplus capacity will be generated. The maintenance of margins at a level higher than that which would prevail under freely competitive conditions protects the inefficient firms and promotes the entry of new ones. Small retail firms may also be encouraged by extensive delivery services, credit facilities, etc. supplied by wholesalers and manufacturers. Competition in service, therefore, is not restricted to distributive outlets but may extend back to the manufacturers.

This brings us to the last point about the effects of r.p.m.—the way in which it is related to manufacturers' competition. The importance of r.p.m. in this connection is that it strengthens manufacturers' price agreements. Price competition amongst retailers obviously endangers manufacturers' price agreements especially if this competition changes market shares. The inter-relationship between retailer and manufacturer competition and of the importance of r.p.m. in bolstering restrictive agreements amongst manufacturers is an important factor in several of the reports of the Monopolies Commission. To give just two examples. In its report on dental goods the Commission reported that '. . . manufacturers themselves claim that part of the value of resale price maintenance to them lies in the fact that if dealers compete in price the result very soon is a request for increased discounts (that is, for a reduction in the manufacturer's price)'. In the report on cigarettes the Commission argued that the 'manufacturers, who with few exceptions do not at present compete with one another in price for products of the same class, might be more willing to vary their own selling prices if there were no longer any standard retail prices'.

From this brief account of the main effects of r.p.m. we would expect that its breakdown would lead to a fall in distributors' margins, an increase in efficiency in the distributive trades accompanied by a speeding up of structural change, and some increase in competition amongst manufacturers.

The speed at which these changes will come about will of course vary. Thus the effect of the ending of r.p.m. on prices and margins will be fairly immediate and indeed the initial effect is likely to be more spectacular than the continuing one. The productivity gains to be expected, however, will show up only after a substantial time-lag. Both the price and productivity effects can be expected to be uneven as between trades because the scope for price reductions and the degree of 'pent-up' competition will show much variation. We have already indicated that the existence of r.p.m. did not mean that the more efficient were unable to expand relatively to their competitors. But r.p.m. did impose a more important constraint in some trades than in others. To what extent the disappearance of this constraint will result in the sort of changes listed above will also depend on such factors as the structure of the retail trades, the extent to which retailers' costs vary, and the desire of retailers to compete.

Even if the ending of r.p.m. had been the only major new factor affecting the distributive trades it would, therefore, be a difficult job to measure its effects particularly on the productivity side. In September 1966, however, the government introduced the Selective Employment Tax (S.E.T.), and this made any assessment of the situation much more complicated. We need, therefore, to develop some views about the likely effects of S.E.T. before we turn to some of the empirical evidence of recent changes in the distributive trades. The future of the tax is now under review, but regardless of how long it will last in its present form, a study of the effects of S.E.T. is in itself an interesting case study in the use (many would say abuse) of discriminatory fiscal policy.

3. *A Digression on S.E.T.*[11]

The White Paper which announced the Selective Employment

[11] S.E.T. was initially levied at a rate of 25s. a week for a full-time male and 12s. 6d. a week for a full-time female, and for part-time workers employed for

Tax stated that it was designed to achieve two main objectives. First, to improve the structure of the tax system by redressing the balance between services and manufacturing, and second to encourage a more efficient use of labour in services. It is with this efficiency aspect of the tax that we are concerned.

It is necessary to recognize at the outset that S.E.T. *could* have had a number of effects—an increase in prices, a fall in profits, an increase in productivity, a reduction in service, or of course some combination of these, and there is no reason to assume that the effects would be the same for all trades. Thus, for instance, the effect of the tax might have been to reduce profits, leaving prices, productivity and service largely unchanged, or it might have resulted in no change in profits but an increase in productivity and a decline in the amount of service. To proceed any further we need to look more closely at the competitive process in the distributive trades.

For most goods the distributor's price may be thought of either as a percentage addition to the cost of the goods, or as a percentage discount on the recommended retail price. Thus, for instance, in the case of a manufacturer who distributes his goods direct to the retailer, if the manufacturer's price is 100 and the retailer's price 125, the retailer's percentage mark-up on the cost of the goods is 25 per cent, and his percentage discount on the recommended retail price is 20 per cent. Over a wide range of goods this percentage mark-up or discount has shown a great deal of stability, so that when the cost of the goods from the manufacturer's increases, the application of a standard or conventional margin between the manufacturer's price and the retail price means that the *cash* margin increases.[12]

more than 8 hours a week the full rate of tax applied. In September 1967 this anomaly was largely removed when the rates applicable to part-timers working more than 8 and less than 21 hours a week were reduced to half that for full-time workers. After 1967 the rate of tax was increased on two occasions and in July 1969 it stood at 48s. and 24s. per week for full-time male and female employees respectively, with the category of part-time employees referred to paying one-third of the full-time rate. At the rates applicable in 1969 the tax typically added about 10 per cent to the payroll of retail firms. This of course was an average figure and there were substantial variations from one type of retailer to another. S.E.T. was halved in 1971 and finally abolished in 1973.

[12] Broadly speaking, manufacturers act in one of two ways. Either they quote an ex-factory (or delivered) price to wholesalers and retailers, and fix a recommended retail selling price by adding a percentage margin which is traditional for the commodity concerned, or their price quotations to wholesalers and retailers take the form of a discount—again based on traditional practice—on the recommended price. . . . This is not to say that the ratio (between the recommended price and the ex-factory price) is the same for all distributors. . . . But the ratio

An increase in the manufacturer's price to the retailer tends, therefore, to get passed on automatically in the form of higher prices to the consumer. Furthermore by applying a standard percentage mark-up to a higher base the increase in the retail price is bigger than the increase in the manufacturer's price. Thus, for instance, if as a result of an increase in manufacturing costs due, say to dearer imports following devaluation, the cost of goods to a retailer increases from 100 to 105, the application of a standard percentage mark-up of say 25 per cent means that the retail price increases from 125 to 131·25. The same result tends to occur in the case of any increase in manufacturing costs including an increase in the cost of labour. An important aspect of S.E.T., however, is that it did not apply to the production of goods and so did not increase the cost of goods to the distributors. The application of a conventional percentage mark-up, therefore, did not automatically increase the distributor's cash margin, so that there was a squeeze on profits. Clearly under such circumstances distributors could be expected to put pressure on manufacturers to widen margins by increasing the recommended retail price. Margins could most easily be raised in the case of trades where there is a great deal of vertical integration as, for instance, in footwear. In general, however, two factors made it difficult to pass on the tax. First, S.E.T. was introduced at a time when the breakdown of r.p.m. was increasing competitiveness in many trades, and when the prices and incomes policy was also acting as a restraining influence on price increases. Secondly, although the tax affected all distributors it did not affect them equally. It was less of a burden to those with a high sales/employee ratio, so that if the relatively inefficient firms attempted to pass on the entire tax they would lose trade to their more efficient competitors. The constraints on the wholesale distributor were particularly severe. His retail customers had to pay S.E.T. and would thus resent any attempt made by the wholesaler to increase prices. Furthermore the 'independent' wholesaler has to compete in varying degrees (depending on the trade) with manufacturers who distribute goods directly to retailers, and whose wholesale operations are in practice nearly always exempt from the tax. Where this competition is important attempts by the wholesaler to pass on the tax would clearly tend to result in a loss

for all distributors as a whole tends to remain constant unless affected by a major change in the circumstances of the particular trade. . . .' National Board for Prices and Incomes, *Distributors' Margins in Relation to Manufacturers' Recommended Prices*, Report No. 55, February 1969.

Margins are not always fixed in percentage terms. For cigarettes and petrol, for example, they are fixed in money terms.

of trade.[13] The tax, therefore, put pressure on distributors to look for ways of restoring their net profit position, so that they were induced to search for ways of reducing costs, and in particular to be more economical in their use of labour. The tendency of S.E.T. to increase labour productivity (i.e. the volume of sales per employee) could be explained by some combination of the following processes.

First S.E.T. may have had a 'shock' effect on firms, thus causing an increase in internal efficiency. This assumes of course that distributors were not operating at maximum efficiency before the tax.

In distribution the effect on internal efficiency is in practice indistinguishable from the second way in which distributors may react to a squeeze on profits, which is by reducing the amount of service offered with the goods. This may take the form of fewer sales assistants, less elaborate packaging, etc.

Thirdly, since S.E.T. did not affect the production of goods and thus did not increase the price of machines, labour became more expensive relative to capital so that there was an inducement to switch towards more capital intensive methods of distribution. The scope for substituting capital for labour within a given type of outlet, however, is very small, especially in retailing, and the main importance of this aspect of S.E.T. is seen in terms of the *further inducement* it gave distributors to change the type of service—from counter service to self-selection and self-service in retailing, and from the traditional methods of wholesaling to wholesaling on a cash and carry basis.

Fourthly, S.E.T. may have increased productivity by causing a reduction in the number of outlets so that a given volume of sales is concentrated on fewer outlets. This reduction in numbers comes about because a squeeze on profits results in the elimination of marginal outlets and also has the effect of reducing the number of

13 Professor Kaldor has put forward a different hypothesis as to why retailers could not pass on S.E.T. He sees the typical retail market as one of imperfect competition, i.e. a market with many firms producing differentiated products, and easy entry conditions. Firms are assumed to be profit maximizers and act independently in fixing gross margins, which are determined by the degree of competition as reflected by the elasticity of demand. The profit-maximizing price of a commodity equals marginal revenue (MR) e/e-1, where e is the elasticity of demand. At the profit-maximizing output, MR = marginal cost (MC), therefore price = MC e/e-1. Assuming that variable costs are constant up to full capacity so that MC = average variable cost (AVC), price = AVC e/e-1. Only variable costs, therefore, enter into the determination of price, and given these costs price is determined by the elasticity of demand. The remaining step in the argument is that labour in retailing is largely an overhead cost, i.e. there is little scope for varying the number of employees per unit of selling space. The cost of labour, therefore, does not enter into the determination of price so that S.E.T. left the profit-maximizing price of the firm unaltered.

new entrants. This effect is not limited to the small 'independent' distributors, indeed retailers with only self-employed labour were not affected, but applies to all outlets which are only marginally profitable, including for instance branches of multiple retailers. Co-operative societies in particular regarded S.E.T. as an important factor contributing to the closure of 'non-economic' outlets.[14]

There are two qualifications of some importance which need to be made to the foregoing analysis of the likely productivity effects of S.E.T.

First, S.E.T. must be seen as a special factor which accelerated already existing trends. Thus, for instance, the increasing cost of labour has long been a factor favouring the expansion of retail shops using less labour-intensive methods of selling, and is one of the factors underlying the growth of the market share of multiple retailers at the expense of the independents and co-operative societies, especially in the food trades. Again the number of shops has shown a long-term downward trend.

Secondly, there is the problem of the quality of service. More specifically, an increase in labour productivity as measured by the volume of sales per person engaged may be accompanied by a change in the amount and quality of service supplied to customers. When this is the case how much of the productivity gain is 'genuine'? It is not possible to answer this question in precise quantitative terms. However, it is not true to say that, on account of the service element, all productivity gains are only apparent and not real. This is seen most clearly in the case of the expansion of self-service and self-selection. So long as consumers have the choice of self-service or counter service, then the increase in productivity associated with the expansion of the former must be considered genuine. The same may apply when there is a switch from more service and higher prices to less service and lower prices. This is particularly likely where the change is associated with the breakdown of r.p.m., because the latter tends to generate excessive competition in service as far as the consumer is concerned. Clearly the *amount* of service offered in the initial position is very important.

The same consideration applies to a fall in the number of shops, and the concentration of sales in fewer outlets. A fall in the number of shops means a reduction in service as far as the customer is concerned if, for instance, he has to walk further to buy a packet of cigarettes. But if the decline in the number of outlets is accompanied by a fall in price this may be a preferred position from the consumer's point of view. The problem of course is complicated by several

[14] See W. B. Reddaway, *Effects of the Selective Employment Tax, First Report, the Distributive Trades* (HMSO, 1970), p. 142.

factors. A reduction in the number of shops in central shopping areas is less of a reduction in service than closures out of town. Another important consideration is whether the sales of the shops which have disappeared fall at peak or off-peak periods. One of the main advantages of more rather than fewer outlets is that at times of peak demand a larger number tends to increase the comforts of shopping.

A discussion in terms of the *number* of outlets only is of course an over-simplification. The *size* of the outlets is also important. Thus there may be no increase in the discomfitures of shopping at times of peak demand if a fall in the number of shops were accompanied by an increase in the size of the survivors. In the long run this does of course tend to happen. But there are important constraints which firms face in attempting to improve their shopping facilities when this involves expansion. Indeed commenting on the progressive abandonment of r.p.m. Professor Yamey concluded that 'Official controls over the expansion and adaptation of retailing facilities may well prove to be the most serious remaining constraint on competition and innovation in the distributive trades after the scope and extent of r.p.m. have been reduced'.[15]

C. THE EFFECTS OF THE BREAKDOWN OF r.p.m. AND OF S.E.T.

From the point of view of wanting a measure of the quantitative effect of either the Resale Prices Act of 1964 or S.E.T. it is rather 'unfortunate' that the effects of the other were being worked out at much the same time. It is important, however, to distinguish the effects on margins from those on productivity and the structure of the distributive trades.

Whatever else it may have done, S.E.T. was certainly not a factor which tended to *reduce* margins. Any such effect must therefore be attributed to the progressive abandonment of r.p.m., plus any other special factors, in particular of course the restraining effect on price increases of the Prices and Incomes Policy.

As far as productivity and structural change are concerned, however, both r.p.m. and S.E.T. were forces pulling in the *same direction*. The arguments which were put forward above lead us to expect gains in productivity on account of both policies, and both tend to bring about the same sort of structural change—such as an increase in concentration in the distributive trades, and further pressure on the independent wholesaler. The analysis of changes in productivity and

[15] B. S. Yamey (ed.), *Resale Price Maintenance* (Weidenfeld & Nicolson, 1966), p. 298.

structure, therefore, must be in terms of the joint effect of both policies.

1. Prices and margins

Since r.p.m. obstructs price competition it could be expected that its abandonment would lead in some trades at least to lower prices and margins. Some, and not all, because the likelihood of this happening depends on such factors as the nature of the goods sold, the degree of competition at the manufacturing end, the number of distributive outlets, the extent to which their costs vary, and the extent to which 'uniformity of action' amongst distributors has become firmly entrenched. These factors vary substantially from trade to trade so that a uniform effect is not to be expected. Apart from this the timing of the ending of r.p.m. varied between trades. Some trades decided to abandon the practice as soon as the Bill became law; others followed suit at a later date; others maintained the practice until the adverse decision of the Restrictive Practices Court in the case of confectionery (July 1967) and footwear (June 1968). It is well known, however, that the abandonment of r.p.m. has led to price reductions on a wide range of goods which have been highlighted by the practice of manufacturers of recommending retail prices.

Some evidence on the movement of percentage gross margins is given in Table 9.1, which shows for four broad categories of retail

TABLE 9.1. *Annual Movements in Percentage Gross Margins: Large Retailers*

Trade	% per annum compound	
	1965/66–1967/68	1961–66
Food	+1·71	+0·41
Clothing and footwear	+2·70	+2·17
Confectioners, tobacconists, newsagents	−1·12	−0·12
Household goods	−0·34	+1·88

Source: W. B. Reddaway, *Effects of the Selective Employment Tax*, p. 43.

trade the annual percentage movement in gross margins for the period 1965/66–1967/68 and also for the period 1961–66. The figures have to be used with caution especially since the resale price legislation relates to categories of goods and not retail trades. However they do show that in the two trades, food and clothing and footwear, where r.p.m. was relatively unimportant before 1964, percentage margins continued to rise. For confectioners, etc. and household goods, however, where r.p.m. was much more firmly entrenched, the evidence suggests a marked change in the movement of margins.

These effects on prices and margins are largely 'once for all' effects and when prices have stabilized at a competitive level margins are likely to move more closely in line with those of other goods. Furthermore it is worth noting that whereas in some trades the ending of r.p.m. has had little immediate effect because of the absence of competitive pressures, in others the benefits which consumers have obtained *could* be lost if, for instance, there is a marked increase in concentration at either the manufacturing or retailing end.

2. *Productivity*

In this section we describe briefly a simple method of estimating the effect of the ending of r.p.m. and of S.E.T. (hereafter referred to as the 'S.E.T.–r.p.m. effect') on productivity and then comment on the results. The analysis is restricted to the retail trades. To simplify the exposition still further a very simple statistical approach has been adopted, although this can be justified on the grounds that much more elaborate methods give much the same result. The basic data are shown in Table 9.2.

TABLE 9.2. *Output, Employment and Productivity, Retail Trades 1954–68 (Index number, 1954 = 100)*

Year	Output[1]	Employment[2]	Productivity
1954	100·0	100·0	100·0
1955	104·6	102·2	102·3
1956	106·1	102·9	103·1
1957	109·1	103·8	105·1
1958	111·5	103·0	108·3
1959	117·5	105·5	111·4
1960	122·4	107·2	114·2
1961	125·9	106·9	117·8
1962	126·5	107·0	118·2
1963	131·9	108·0	122·1
1964	136·0	108·0	125·9
1965	139·7	107·0	130·6
1966	141·7	105·9	133·8
1967	143·8	103·9	138·4
1968	147·1	101·4	145·1

Source: W. B. Reddaway, op. cit., Appendix F.

[1] Volume of sales at 1963 prices.
[2] Persons engaged on a full-time equivalent basis.

The method used to estimate the quantitative importance of this effect is as follows. First one has to arrive at an economically plausible explanation of productivity movements over a run of years up to 1964, i.e. before the factors we are examining were affecting the picture. Secondly, on the basis of this explanation of past events a prediction can be made of what productivity would have been in the years from 1965 onwards in the absence of the S.E.T.–r.p.m. effect. The predicted productivity levels can then be compared with the actual figures in order to give an estimate of the S.E.T.–r.p.m. effect on productivity.

It is reasonable to expect that over a decade, productivity would show an upward trend reflecting such factors as the adoption of new selling methods. Figure 9.1 shows that over the period 1954–64 there was indeed a very strong upward trend of 2·4 per cent per annum. It is also clear from the diagram that the trend itself gives a good

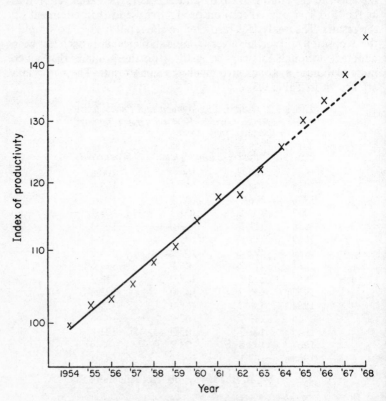

FIG. 9.1. *Trend of Productivity in Retailing, 1954 = 100*

explanation of the movement in productivity. However there are also deviations from the trend and these are in the main positive in years when the level of activity is high (e.g. 1955 and 1961) and negative in years when it is low (e.g. 1957 and 1962).

One way of accounting for this result is by reference to the degree of tightness in the labour market, on the grounds that the state of the labour market affects productivity by affecting the recruitment of additional labour. Thus, when the labour market is tight (as reflected for instance by a high level of vacancies) retailers are unable to recruit as many workers as they would like to have in relation to their sales, so that productivity tends to rise above trend. In a recession, on the other hand, retailers will find it easier to recruit the employees that they require because the labour market is easier, so that productivity will tend to fall below trend.[16]

On the basis of this simple analysis, therefore, our explanation of productivity runs in terms of a time trend and a variable which reflects the state of the labour market. More formally the equation fitted to the data from 1954 to 1964 is:

$$Y = a + bt + cV,$$

where: Y = productivity;
$\quad\quad t$ = time trend;
$\quad\quad V$ = the degree of tightness of the labour market as measured by the level of vacancies; and
$\quad\quad a, b,$ and c are parameters.

The results of the analysis are shown in Fig. 9.2. The first section of the diagram shows the actual productivity and the expected productivity which was derived by fitting the above equation. The second section shows the actual and predicted productivity for the years after 1964. The difference between the curves of actual and expected productivity shows, for each year, the cumulative effect of the S.E.T. and r.p.m. effect. In 1967 this amounted to a gain of 3 per cent and in 1968 a gain of 5 per cent, i.e. in 1968 the index of productivity was 145·1 as against an expected productivity index of 138·2.

Our estimate of the S.E.T.–r.p.m. effect on productivity, therefore, is that by 1968 it had resulted in a cumulative gain in productivity

16 An alternative explanation of the pattern of productivity deviations shown in Figure 9.1 could be given in terms of the level of retail sales. Thus, for instance, one could test the hypothesis that productivity would be above trend when retail sales are above their 4-year moving average and below trend when sales are below the 4-year moving average. Such a relationship does in fact exist and if it had been used instead of the labour market variable the result would have been to increase the estimated S.E.T.–r.p.m. effect on productivity.

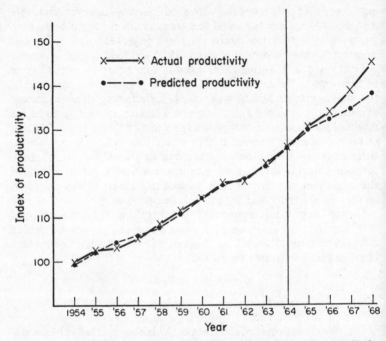

FIG. 9.2. *Actual and Expected Productivity in Retailing, 1954–68* (*Index numbers*)

of about 5 per cent. This result has been arrived at on the basis of one very simple statistical approach. Several other approaches, however, many of them of a much more elaborate kind, all put the cumulative productivity effect in 1968 somewhere between 4 and 6 per cent.[17]

It remains to comment on the results of this statistical analysis. Four points in particular need to be made. First, the reliability of the results are, of course, affected by the accuracy of the basic data. In retail trades there are in particular many problems in arriving at a series of figures for employment because of the importance of self-employment and part-time working about which information is incomplete. Secondly, the explanation of past events cannot be perfect so that the use of the past to predict the future inevitably gives results which are subject to a margin of error. Thirdly, there is the question of the relative importance of S.E.T. and the ending of r.p.m. in causing the gain in productivity. Perhaps some more detailed enquiries into the productivity movements of different categories of

[17] The same sort of quantitative effect also applies to wholesale distributors.

goods would throw some light on this question. If one or the other *had* to be chosen as the most powerful factor my own view would be to choose S.E.T. But a more accurate description of events might be that the two factors operating together were especially powerful and that either factor alone might not have had the effect it did without the presence of the other.

The fourth comment about the results is that one cannot be certain that S.E.T. and the ending of r.p.m. were the only abnormal factors affecting productivity after 1964. It has been suggested, for instance, that the investment boom in distributive trades in the period 1962–64, when gross fixed capital formation increased from £301 m. to £377 m., might have been a factor in explaining the exceptionally good productivity performance in the years 1966–68.[18] We have to be careful in using these figures because in retailing, where the renting of premises is very important, they may give a very misleading picture of capital employed. Assuming, however, that the capital formation figures do give a reasonable picture of changes in capital employed there are two further points which need to be made. First, investment itself may simply lead to more excess capacity without a gain in productivity. It has to be argued therefore that the investment boom of 1962–64 resulted in an acceleration in the exit of inefficient shops. Secondly, the capital formation figures show an investment boom in earlier years such as 1958–60, when gross fixed capital formation in distributive trades increased from £209 m. to £284 m., but this did not lead to any exceptional productivity performance after a lag of two or three years.

Finally, we should mention the 'shake-out' of labour which occurred after 1966. There has certainly been a change in the conditions of the labour market in recent years with, for instance, the number of unemployed being much higher in relation to the number of vacancies than could be expected on the basis of the pre-1967 relationship. One explanation of this change is that labour hoarding has become less important. This is a factor which has been emphasized mainly in connection with the manufacturing sector, and in this sector the productivity performance in 1967 is certainly consistent with a shake-out of labour having occurred in that year. As shown in Table 9.3 there was a small fall in output and on the basis of past experience very little gain in productivity could have been expected. In fact productivity increased by 3·0 per cent. The high productivity gain in 1968 also probably owes something to the 'shake-out' effect, although on the basis of past experience when output increased rapidly a big productivity gain in 1968 was to be

18 See for instance, Lady Margaret Hall's article in *The Times*, Monday, March 16, 1970.

TABLE 9.3. *Year to Year Changes in Output and Productivity UK, 1954–68, per cent.*

| | Retailing | | Manufacturing | |
	Output[1]	Output per person[1] employed (full-time equivalent)	Output[2]	Output per employee[3] in employment
1954–55	4·6	2·3	6·4	3·6
1955–56	1·4	0·8	−0·5	−1·1
1956–57	2·8	1·9	2·2	2·2
1957–58	2·2	3·0	−1·3	0·0
1958–59	5·4	2·9	6·0	6·8
1959–60	4·2	2·5	8·2	3·7
1960–61	2·9	3·2	0·2	−1·2
1961–62	0·5	0·3	0·4	1·3
1962–63	4·3	3·3	4·1	5·7
1963–64	3·1	3·1	8·9	7·3
1964–65	2·7	3·7	3·3	2·0
1965–66	1·4	2·5	1·5	1·2
1966–67	1·5	3·4	−0·2	3·0
1967–68	2·3	4·8	6·3	7·4

Sources: 1. W. B. Reddaway, op. cit., Appendix F.
2. National Income and Expenditure, 1969, table 15.
3. Annual Abstract of Statistics, and Ministry of Labour, Manpower Studies No. 1, HMSO, 1964.

expected.

To what extent, however, has the shake-out effect been an important factor in retailing and one which operated *independently* of S.E.T? Although the possibility cannot be eliminated completely it is unlikely to have been important. There *was* a 'shake-out' of labour in retailing in 1967 and 1968 but it was due to the S.E.T.–r.p.m. effect which we have already examined.[19]

3. *Changes in structure*

The effects of S.E.T. and the breakdown of r.p.m. on structure are of a much longer-term nature than those which have been examined so far. Consequently we have to be content with a few tentative suggestions about the likely course of events. There are two effects in particular which deserve some consideration and which are

[19] Another important difference between the manufacturing and distributive trades sectors is that in the former the annual productivity gain was already substantially higher in the period 1960/61–1965/66 than in the period 1955/56–1960/61, whereas for the latter this was not so. See Chapter 1.

closely related—the tendency towards greater concentration in retailing, and the effect on the independent wholesaler.

Both S.E.T. and the greater competition following the breakdown of r.p.m. are likely to accelerate the trend towards higher concentration in the retail sector. Both impose a squeeze on net profit which will accelerate the downward trend in the number of shops by causing more exits and by discouraging new entrants. Furthermore, the greater competition following the breakdown of r.p.m. will allow the more efficient firms to expand their market share more rapidly.

Another factor which may have an important influence in the same direction is a decline in service and less favourable terms which are offered to small shops, both by manufacturers and wholesalers. In trades where r.p.m. was firmly entrenched, manufacturers who find an increasing proportion of their trade being diverted to multiple retailers will tend to worsen the terms and service which they give to small retailers relative to those offered to multiples. Indeed they may be forced to do this because of the bargaining power of large multiple retailers. It is interesting to observe that several manufacturers who were approached during the S.E.T. enquiry said that they had made the terms to wholesalers *less* favourable as compared with the terms to national multiple retailers. The latter can usually obtain special discounts from manufacturers on account of their 'nearness to consumers' quite independently of the volume of goods taken. Where this occurs the small retailers who have to depend on wholesalers for supplies will become less competitive.

This brings us to the other main aspect of structure which is likely to be affected—the importance of the independent wholesaler. There has been a long-run tendency for the share of trade handled by wholesalers to decline, a trend which has been associated with the growth in importance of the multiple retailers. S.E.T. and the breakdown of r.p.m. put further pressure on the wholesaler. As already mentioned, the breakdown of r.p.m. could be expected to result in manufacturers giving more favourable terms to multiple retailers. We would expect S.E.T. to have been particularly important where wholesalers are in close competition with manufacturers since the latter's wholesale activities were normally exempt from the tax.[20]

It appears then that *in general* the S.E.T.–r.p.m. effect would be to increase concentration in retailing, and to reduce the importance of the independent wholesaler. However, two important points need to be added.

The first is the need to emphasize the diversity of experience. For

[20] The wholesaler's competitive position relative to that of the manufacturer's was also weakened by the fact that the wholesaler was not eligible for investment grants during the period 1966–70.

instance, the importance of manufacturers' competition which whole-salers have to face varies substantially from trade to trade. Again the amount of 'pent-up' competition released after the breakdown of r.p.m. varies from trade to trade depending on the initial structural and behavioural conditions at both the manufacturing and retailing ends.

Second, the survival of small retailers and independent whole-salers will depend on their ability to adapt themselves to the new conditions. Thus the more widespread adoption of self-service in small shops and the formation of voluntary groups of retailers has been an important development in a number of trades and especially in groceries. A more recent development has been the rapid growth of 'cash and carry' wholesalers. Wholesalers, too, are likely to be induced to speed up the process of rationalizing their activities, often by means of acquisition or merger.

The general effect of the breakdown of r.p.m. and the imposition of S.E.T. was therefore to cause an acceleration of productivity growth, and to add to the forces tending towards a higher level of concentration in retailing and to the decline of the independent wholesaler. However, the abolition of S.E.T. in 1973 inevitably weakened the strength of these forces. Indeed there is the question of whether there will to some extent be a reversal of the position towards the pre-S.E.T. situation. The answer to this depends very much on the mechanism by which S.E.T. affected the distributive trades. If it was through the acceleration of new methods of selling or by eliminating slack within firms then there is not much reason to expect any reversal to the pre-S.E.T. situation. But if the main impact was a reduction in service with given methods of selling or if it worked mainly through the elimination of marginal shops then some reversal of the situation is more likely.

In fact, employment in the S.E.T. paying industries increased after 1971, the year in which S.E.T. was halved. In the distributive trades, for instance, employees in employment in Britain increased by nearly $1\frac{1}{2}$ per cent between June 1971 and June 1972, after a continuous decline of over 10 per cent between 1966 and 1971. The halving of S.E.T. was only one factor contributing to this change. The volume of retail sales began to pick up in the first half of 1972 following the tax cuts in that year and the previous one, and the high rate of price inflation probably led to a significant widening of cash margins. But whatever the true explanation the employment and productivity trends in the distributive trades and other services following the abolition of S.E.T. will be just as interesting to examine as they were in the years following its introduction.

CHAPTER 10

The State and Industrial Development

A. INTRODUCTION

The policy measures discussed in the last two chapters cover only a part of the now very complicated inter-relationships which exist between industry and the State. There are several other ways in which the government intervenes in industrial affairs, the purpose of which is often to speed up the process of change. Thus, for instance, during the post-war period the government has used various forms of incentives to induce a higher rate of investment and thus, it is hoped, a faster rate of growth. Financial aid to industry is made available in a number of ways. Apart from financial aid for specific industries such as shipbuilding and aircraft, the Industrial and Commercial Finance Corporation offers assistance to small businesses, and the Finance Corporation for Industry provides loans for re-equipment and rationalization schemes. The government also plays an important role in research and development. Most of the government effort in this field is now the responsibility of the Department of Trade and Industry. The research and development resources which are the responsibility of the Department include the Industrial Research Establishments such as the National Physical Laboratory and the National Engineering Laboratory, the Atomic Energy Authority, and the National Research Development Corporation. The latter holds patents arising in the private sector and assists in the development and exploitation of selected inventions where it appears that they are not given sufficient backing from private sources.

These aspects of policy raise several complicated issues. With regard to investment incentives, for instance, how important are differences in the level of investment in explaining differences in the rate of growth? And given that investment is an important explanatory variable, how effective are investment incentives in inducing greater investment expenditure? Again, as far as research and development is concerned we saw in Chapter 2 that a high proportion of expenditure is concentrated in the aircraft industry, much of which, it is argued, could be more beneficially applied to other research-intensive industries such as electronics, chemicals, precision instruments and machinery. Government policy has been criticized not only on this account but also for overemphasizing basic research and for leading to a shortage of professional scientists and engineers in industry. The latter in turn has resulted in less effective research and development and in particular to a less effective application of research and development results.[1]

These are all important problems which require careful consideration. I wish to turn, however, to two other aspects of public policy towards industry, namely, the part played by public enterprises in shaping industrial structure, and regional policy.

B. PUBLIC ENTERPRISE

Where the government considers the performance of private enterprise to be grossly inadequate and not remediable by indirect action it can seek a solution through public ownership. It will not be possible to look in detail at the economic problems of the nationalized industries. This would take far too much space and since the circumstances of the nationalized industries vary so widely it would demand a separate study of each industry. The purpose of this section is to indicate briefly some of the more important implications of nationalization for industrial structure and performance. There are three issues of particular importance.

First, nationalization has a direct impact on industrial structure by increasing the degree of concentration. As far as subsequent performance within the industry is concerned the key question is whether the nationalized undertaking produces better results than would have been forthcoming under the structure which it replaced or by some alternative structure which could have been brought about under private or public ownership.

Secondly, and related to the problem of maintaining internal efficiency, there is the question of the extent to which nationalized industries should be allowed to diversify into new areas of activity and as such to behave in a similar way to large companies in the private sector.

[1] See Merton J. Peck, 'Science and technology', in Richard E. Caves and Associates, *Britain's Economic Prospects*, The Brookings Institution, 1968 (London: George Allen and Unwin). The government is not unaware of these problems. 'Within the Ministry of Technology's programmes, defence research and development has been reduced while the emphasis of past programmes on aerospace and nuclear work is being reduced in order to build up support for a wider range of industries'. The Ministry of Technology, *Industrial Research and Development in Government Laboratories, A New Organization for the Seventies* (HMSO, 1970), p. 8.

Thirdly, there may be wider indirect effects on industrial structure as a result of the price and investment policies of the nationalized industries.

These three aspects of public enterprise will be considered in turn. It will not be possible to refer at every point to each of the industries in the public sector so attention will be focussed on some of the areas which are currently of greatest interest.

1. The Effect of Nationalization on Industry Structure and Performance: the Steel Industry

The most immediate impact of nationalization is of course the effect it has on market structure. Nationalization may, as in the case of coal, result in a complete monopoly of domestic production but still leave the industry facing severe competition from close substitutes. The case of iron and steel is more complicated. The range of products which is produced is much wider, and nationalization left in being a very substantial private sector in the industry.

The British Steel Corporation, which was brought into being by the Iron and Steel Act 1967, acquired the assets of the fourteen companies, together with their subsidiaries, which produced not less than 475,000 tons of crude steel in the year ended June 30, 1964. This left a sizeable private sector consisting of more than 100 companies. The resulting division of production between the public and private sectors is shown in Table 10.1. The BSC has complete or near-complete monopoly in many of the carbon steel products, but the private sector has substantial interests, and in some cases the major share of production, in alloys and some of the finished carbon steels such as bright steel bars.

Even in areas where it has a dominating position the BSC has to face some competition from substitutes such as plastics, but more important is the growing importance of world trade in steel products and thus of overseas competition. In 1950 the proportion of steel production entering world trade was 11 per cent, by 1967 this proportion had grown to 18 per cent.

Furthermore, nationalization did not mean that the state acquired 14 companies which had hitherto been in active competition, at least not as far as price competition is concerned. From 1953 the Iron and Steel Board had been charged with the task of exercising 'a general supervision over the iron and steel industry with a view to promoting the efficient economic and adequate supply under competitive conditions of iron and steel products'. In fact, however, the maximum prices laid down by the Board became fixed common prices by agreement between the companies.

The absence of price competition would certainly have reduced

TABLE 10.1. *UK Steel Production in 1968 (share of the British Steel Corporation, per cent)*

Product	Carbon steels	Alloy steels
Crude steel	93·3	63·8
Semi-finished steel	93·9	71·2
Rails and accessories	99·2	—
Plates	91·3	79·6
Heavy rolled sections	84·9	—
Wire rods, etc.	58·2	56·6
Light sections and hot rolled bars	45·6	42·0
Bright steel bars	7·1	22·5
Hot rolled strip	83·1	} 27·6
Cold rolled strip	34·3	
Hot rolled sheet (non-electrical)	100·0	} 51·7
Cold rolled sheet (non-electrical)	100·0	
Electrical sheet	100·0	—
Tinplate and blackplate	100·0	—
Tubes and pipes	74·8	29·2

Source: National Board for Prices and Incomes, Report No. 111, *Steel Prices*, Appendix A.

any natural tendency for efficient firms to expand at the expense of the less efficient. But even if there had been more effective competition several factors would have made the required structural alterations difficult to achieve at least by internal expansion—the costliness and durability of plant, the development of profitable specialities by the large firms, forward integration which gave an assured outlet for some products, and the fact that the leading firms had plants of varying degrees of efficiency and interests in more than one region.

The structural weaknesses of the industry are illustrated by the fact that in the case of pig iron, for instance, it has been estimated that the entire UK output could in 1963/64 have been produced in twenty of the largest blast furnaces then being built, whereas the number of furnaces actually in production was, on average, 73.[2] With basic structural weaknesses of this magnitude the required degree of rationalization is likely to be achieved only through a substantial reduction in the number of firms. The fact that this was not achieved by merger or acquisition may have owed something to the weakness of competition and the threat of nationalization.

It would be a mistake, however, to imagine that nationalization

[2] C. Pratten, R. M. Dean and A. Silberston, *The Economies of Large-Scale Production in British Industry: an Introductory Study* (Cambridge University Press, 1965).

will lead quickly or automatically to a satisfactory solution. The most ardent supporters of nationalization point to the weaknesses of an industry's structure and performance, often by comparison with the superior performance of private enterprise in other countries, and seem to *assume* that the deficiencies will be rectified under public ownership. It is argued, for instance, that public ownership will allow investment to be properly planned so as to avoid over- and under-capacity, that production can, where desirable, be concentrated in a smaller number of works, and that it will be possible to adopt 'progressive' labour policies with the implication that damaging disputes will be avoided.[3]

All this *may* be achieved, and in particular considerable progress should be possible in rationalizing production by the phasing out of inefficient plant and the concentration of production in a smaller number of units using the latest techniques. But it is important not to lose sight of the difficulties. Periodic surpluses and shortages of steel products are likely to continue because of erratic fluctuations in the demands of customer industries and because new steel capacity is installed in large units. The progress of the industry towards greater efficiency may be impeded by government intervention. The government has in the past shown its willingness to prevent production from being organized so as to maximize efficiency by its decision in 1958, for instance, to build two new strip mills—one in South Wales and one in Scotland—instead of one. More recently, the British Steel Corporation's 1968 price review was referred to the National Board for Prices and Incomes which recommended that the proposed price increases should be abated by 25 per cent.[4] The Board was particularly concerned with the inflationary consequences and balance of payments effects of the proposed price increases and with the failure of the Corporation to devote sufficient attention to cost reductions. As to the distribution of the proposed price increases over the various products, the Board drew attention to the fact that the greatest price increases had been proposed where the Corporation has a predominant share of the market, so that the Corporation was accused of exploiting its monopoly position. The Corporation's comment was that however successful its profit improvement measures may be 'it is clear that their effect on results can largely be nullified if the Corporation is not permitted to base its prices realistically on its costs and competitive position'.[5] It also 'strenuously denied' the

[3] See for instance, Richard Pryke, *Why Steel?*, Fabian Research Series, No. 248.
[4] National Board for Prices and Incomes, No. 111, *Steel Prices*, HMSO, May 1969.
[5] British Steel Corporation, *Annual Report*, 1968–69.

charge that it is not paying sufficient attention to ways of improving efficiency.[6]

It is not possible to judge the merits of the Board's accusations of insufficient attention to efficiency and exploitation of monopoly power and that the Corporation has in these ways been operating against the public interest. There is, however, a danger that intervention to reduce profits will have adverse consequences on investment. In addition it is interesting to note that even during the difficult transitional period when the new management has been largely preoccupied with problems of reorganization the government has felt justified to intervene in the detailed restructuring of prices and marketing strategy.

In the longer term the crucial problem will be to *maintain* efficient management so as to secure satisfactory performance both in terms of cost minimization and of the discovery and adoption of new processes. This raises two important points.

First, there is the question of the best organization of an industry and in particular on the extent to which it is desirable to centralize decision-making. In the case of iron and steel it is certainly arguable that the government would have done better to have reorganized the industry on the basis of (say) five or six separate companies. This of course is not an issue peculiar to steel but one which applies to all large undertakings. Thus in the case of electricity generation a major problem is that of having all technical and research decisions made by a single small group so that any wrong decision is magnified. We have already drawn attention to this in Chapter 2 with reference to the different approaches in the United Kingdom and the United States to the organization of research in the field of nuclear power stations. Where nationalization results in the centralization of decision-making the advantages of competition, and of having two or more separate managements trying their own different ideas, are lost. Rather, efficiency has to be maintained without the spur of domestic competition in many fields but with the probability of at least some government interference. One thing is certain: size itself will not ensure success. The British Steel Corporation is now one of the four largest steel companies outside the Communist countries, and approximately the same size as Bethlehem Steel, the second largest US steel company. In the US, however, major innovations have often come from the smaller companies such as Armco Steel which introduced the wide strip mill and which is about half the size of the British Steel Corporation.

Secondly, the rate at which an industry is expanding is also relevant to the problem of increasing efficiency. In this respect the

[6] British Steel Corporation, *Steel Prices*, May 1969.

Japanese experience is interesting. Their steel industry is highly concentrated in six integrated steel-producing companies, five of them being amongst the eighteen largest outside the Communist countries. The present size of their companies, however, is due to the remarkable post-war growth record of Japanese steel production which has increased more than ten-fold since 1950. Clearly when an industry is experiencing such a rapid growth rate it is much easier to maintain efficiency by, for instance, maintaining an up-to-date stock of capital, than it is in a market where the rate of growth is comparatively slow.

2. *New Public Enterprise*

In the private sector a firm which is in a slow-growing industry can increase its own rate of expansion by diversifying into new lines. To what extent should nationalized industries be allowed to extend their interests in the same way and thus create new public enterprises? There have already been some significant movements in this direction. For instance, the National Coal Board has moved into the production of certain chemicals, and the Transport Holding Company had by 1968 interests in the manufacture of vehicles, travel and tourism, as well as road haulage and passenger transport.[7]

There certainly seems to be a strong case for allowing public enterprise to grow in this way. The changing pattern of demand and of market opportunities means that the successful firm is the one which is able to reduce its interests in declining sectors and expand them in growing ones. Success in exploiting new opportunities is a sign of good management and restrictions on fields of activity in which a firm is allowed to operate may have a detrimental effect on the efficiency of a whole organization. 'Artificial restrictions on growth would rapidly blunt the spirit of enterprise upon which profitability throughout the undertaking must depend and would bring about stagnation generally.'[8]

There is another argument in favour of allowing nationalized industries to diversify. Industries such as coal and steel are heavily represented in some of the less prosperous areas of the economy. Diversification could play an important role in the development of growth points in these areas by establishing groups of activities with close technical and marketing interdependence.

This, however, brings us back to the problems of organization. The success of the Transport Holding Company certainly seems to

[7] The Transport Holding Company ceased to exist in 1968 as a result of the government's reorganization of freight transport. It is now part of the National Freight Corporation.

[8] Transport Holding Company, *Annual Report*, 1963.

have owed a great deal to its form of organization. 'From the beginning the Holding Company has worked through a structure of subsidiary and associated companies. . . . The consequent freedom and flexibility throughout the organization as a whole, the resulting accountability and discipline, and the element of protection afforded against the more direct forms of abuse of public ownership have in the Holding Company's view been major factors in securing the success of the businesses concerned.'[9] If diversification were to become an accepted part of the behaviour of nationalized industries an organizational arrangement of this kind would be essential.

3. *Price and Investment Policies*

Apart from the fact that nationalization has an immediate impact on the structure of an industry, the price and investment policies laid down for nationalized industries may also have wider effects on industrial structure. During the 1950s several economists argued that the general instruction that nationalized industries should break even over a run of years resulted in prices being too low in relation to those in the private sector. There was, therefore, an over-expansion of demand for the goods and services produced by the nationalized industries and also of investment to meet this demand. A further factor, it was argued, tending towards the over-expansion of investment was that as compared to private firms the nationalized industries were getting their finance too cheaply.

The arguments usually ran in terms of a comparison of profitability or self-financing in the public and private sectors. 'The larger the nationalised sector the more important it becomes that this sector taken as a whole should make profits. The present nationalised sector is already large enough for it to be probable that the only general convention we have—that each industry should try to break even—is causing serious damage to the economy. . . . This is not to say that all nationalised industries should be expected to make some contribution to the finance of investment or government expenditure. But where it can be seen that a particular industry could make profits without any apparent 'distortion' of output then it seems manifestly wrong that it should throw the whole burden of finding the savings required for its own investment on to the government or the rest of the economy.'[10]

The danger of over-expansion of nationalized industries due to low prices and easier financial criteria than those prevalent in the private sector was mentioned in the 1961 White Paper on the

[9] Transport Holding Company, *Annual Report*, 1967.
[10] I. M. D. Little, *A Critique of Welfare Economics* (Oxford University Press, 1957), 2nd. edn., pp. 214–15.

Financial and Economic Obligations of the Nationalised Industries, which laid down objectives in terms of self-finance and rates of return on capital. There are several difficulties, however, associated with overall objectives of this kind. First, it may be possible to satisfy a given overall level of profitability at more than one level of output and with varying combinations of internal efficiency and monopolistic exploitation. That is, one way of meeting self-finance or profitability targets is by raising prices, and the extent to which this is possible depends on the industry's monopoly power. Secondly, a given self-finance target means that different rates of return have to be looked for on new investment in different industries depending on their capital intensity and rate of growth. Thus closely competing industries such as coal, electricity and gas would be set different rate of return targets on new investment whereas a proper policy would apply the same rate of discount in evaluating investment projects, with departures justified in those cases where there are large divergences between private and social costs and benefits. Investment projects then should be soundly based; the source of finance is a secondary problem. Thirdly, it is not clear which private rate of return is to be taken for comparison. Reference is frequently made to some average return in the private sector, but from the point of view of resource allocation there would seem to be a stronger case for at least giving much greater weight to returns achieved in those private industries which are close substitutes of the particular nationalized industry concerned. But in applying this to a particular circumstance and comparing coal with fuel oil, for example, there is the further difficulty that the latter is a joint product and the profit on it depends on how the oil companies allocate their costs, which in turn will be affected by the price of coal.

A similar concern for the proper appraisal of investment projects in nationalized industries is found in the 1967 White Paper.[11] There are three points in particular which it emphasizes. First, that nationalized industries should use consistent methods of investment appraisal and that they should use the same test rate of discount in evaluating projects—and one which is broadly consistent with the average rate of return looked for on low-risk projects in the private sector. Secondly, prices should reflect marginal cost, otherwise there is a risk of undesirable cross-subsidization and a misallocation of resources. Thirdly, it is not enough to ensure that prices reflect costs. There is need also to pay close attention to the costs themselves. Recognition of the importance of internal efficiency is the main reason for setting the nationalized industries financial targets. The

[11] *Nationalised Industries: A Review of Economic and Financial Objectives* Cmnd 3437, November 1967.

setting of financial targets may, however, mean that it will not be possible for the industry to set prices equal to marginal cost. Prices thus determined may yield a return on capital which is too low. In this case prices will have to be raised, this being justified on the grounds that more will be gained by ensuring managerial efficiency than is likely to be lost by possible resource misallocation. Thus the 1967 White Paper again demonstrates the government's concern about the demands made by the nationalized industries on the finance available for investment, and that these demands should not be inflated by faulty investment appraisal or internal inefficiency.

So far our comments have related to nationalized industries taken as a whole. The problem of misallocation of resources and the feasibility of intervention which can improve matters is seen most clearly, however, when nationalized industries are examined not as a group to be compared with the private sector but in relation to products which are close substitutes and complements. For the situation where intervention can most clearly improve matters is one where a product is a member of a group in which there are a few close substitutes, so that changes in relative prices have important allocative effects within the group, and where the demand for the output of the group taken together is inelastic, so that price changes in the group have relatively little effect on the rest of the economy. If, then, there are large discrepancies in the ratio of price to marginal cost within the group, a policy which brought relative prices and costs more into line would almost certainly improve matters.

Such a situation is approximated for instance in the transport sector, where a particularly important issue is traffic in towns and the demands for more road investment to accommodate the ever-increasing flow of private vehicles. In the cost–benefit analysis of investment in new roads the major item on the benefit side is the time saved as a result of relieving traffic congestion and, for a given cost, the greater the degree of congestion the greater the apparent 'return' on new investment. Congestion, however, is related to existing charges and these are well below the marginal social cost of private transport. This results in an over-expansion of the use of private transport which in turn means greater congestion which provides the main justification for more investment. Here is a clear example of a misallocation of resources resulting from the divergence of relative prices and relative costs of public and private transport.

In theory the logical solution is to increase the charges which private road users have to pay, the actual charges imposed varying according to the degree of congestion. Road pricing, however, would involve formidable practical problems as well as imposing considerable hardship on a large number of individuals. But there is no need to rely on this kind of policy. A vast improvement would be achieved by, for instance, banning private motor cars from the centre of towns and imposing restrictions on the delivery times for commercial vehicles. Such an approach would avoid the costs of levying a system of charges, and its appropriateness is also enhanced by consideration of the fact that congestion costs are only one of the social costs associated with traffic in towns.

C. REGIONAL POLICY

The reference just made to congestion costs brings us to the regional problem. Broadly speaking the problem may be summarized as a situation in which the Northern and Western regions of the United Kingdom have shown persistently higher rates of unemployment, higher net outward migration, lower income per head and lower growth of employment opportunities than the Midlands and the South. That differences exist between regions is not surprising in an economy undergoing continuous structural change. What is important from the policy point of view is the size and persistency of the discrepancies and whether or not the process of adjustment is tending towards a socially acceptable allocation of economic activity. We will first examine the background to post-war regional policy; second, examine the case for regional policy; third, suggest a suitable framework for action and finally look critically at post-war policy in the UK.

1. *The Background to the Regional Problems*

The regional problem is a multi-dimensional one, embracing problems such as rural depopulation, congestion in densely populated areas, and the secular decline of important industries. It is with this last aspect and the associated problem of depressed industrial areas that this section is concerned.[12]

In the 1920s the deep depression in the staple exporting industries —coal-mining, textiles, shipbuilding—resulted in heavy unemployment in areas where, because of the presence of natural resources or external economies, these industries were concentrated. There were several reasons why the required transfer of resources to expanding industries did not occur. The general depression meant that there

[12] The term 'depressed areas' is used to refer to the less prosperous regions of the country—Northern Ireland, Scotland, Wales, northern England and parts of north-west and south-west England. The degree of prosperity within these regions does of course vary a great deal, and to describe the entire regions as depressed is more a matter of convenience of expression than an accurate description of actual circumstances.

was no certainty of employment elsewhere—there was considerable unemployment in the South-east and the Midlands throughout the 1920s and 1930s. The depressed industries were very large and highly concentrated geographically so that the required reallocation of resources was exceptionally great. Furthermore, much of the labour and capital embodied in the industries was highly specific. The depressed areas had few links with the new growth industries and there was certainly little incentive for new firms to move into the areas. The expansion of electricity and road transport had greatly lessened the importance of the coalfields and the railways in determining industrial location. Labour was readily available elsewhere and other areas could offer much more attractive sites especially to the market-orientated industries producing consumer goods. All these factors meant that there were few alternative employment opportunities for labour in the depressed areas.

In the post-war period, whether due to government policies or to more fundamental economic factors, the problem of gross unemployment on a national scale seems to have been solved, and the high overall level of activity has undoubtedly been a major factor in easing the problems of the depressed areas. But due to the fact that demand is not evenly distributed between industries and that different forms of industrial activity are not evenly distributed between regions, the low *average* level of unemployment has continued to be associated with a fairly wide dispersion of regional rates of unemployment. Thus whereas the percentage of the working population out of work in the UK over the period 1960–70 averaged 2·1 per cent, in Northern Ireland it was 7·1 per cent, in Scotland 3·7 per cent and in Wales 3·3 per cent. The unemployment figures reveal only a part of the social and economic problems of the depressed areas, and in particular do not reflect such factors as the poor quality of much of the social capital. However, the problem of job opportunities is clearly an important one, and this is the aspect of the regional question on which attention will be focused.

What, in terms of employment opportunities is the basic problem of the depressed regions? A convenient way to start answering this question is to put forward two extreme views. On the one hand, it is argued that the basic problem is that the depressed regions have inherited an unfavourable industrial structure. What is required to solve the problem, therefore, is to attract new firms to the areas, the presumption being that after an initial period of adjustment these firms would not be adversely affected by any continuing cost disadvantages. On the other hand, it may be argued that the basic problem is not the inheritance of an unfavourable industrial structure, but the fact that they do not provide suitable locations for new growth industries. This view stresses the continuing cost disadvantages which would face new firms if, say, they were forced to establish themselves in the depressed regions, and it clearly leads, from the economic efficiency point of view, to very different policy conclusions.

Both views, however, contain an important element of truth. There is no doubting the fact that the depressed areas are, as compared to the average position for the UK, much more dependent on the large declining industries. The Welsh economy has an above-average proportion of employment in mining: Northern Ireland in agriculture, shipbuilding and textiles; Scotland in shipbuilding, and so on. On the other hand, it is equally clear that the concept of locational advantages and disadvantages is meaningful, so that it would not be sensible to adopt a policy of forcing firms indiscriminately to move to the depressed areas. The issues involved are empirical ones and answers are needed to the following questions. How much of the below-average growth performance of the regions is due to structural factors, and how much is due to the fact that all industries in these regions tend to have below-average growth rates because of locational disadvantages? What is the nature of the cost disadvantage which firms would encounter in the depressed regions; how important are these disadvantages and what types of firm are adversely affected in this way?

Various attempts at arriving at a quantitative answer to the first of these questions have been made. The method of estimating the relative importance of the structural and growth factors is to compare the actual growth of employment with a hypothetical growth rate. Thus one way of estimating the structural component is to measure the difference between what the rate of growth of employment in a region *would* have been if each of its industries had, over the period, grown at the national rate, and the rate of growth of national employment. And the growth component may be measured as the difference between the rate at which national employment would have grown if all industries had grown at the rates achieved in the region, and the actual rate of growth of national employment.

The calculation of hypothetical growth rates involves several problems which may result in serious error in estimating the relative importance of the structural and growth weaknesses. For instance, the results are dependent on the degree of disaggregation of the industry data. An analysis based on broad industrial groups such as textiles and mechanical engineering will bias the results against showing the importance of structural factors because of the structural variation between regions which is found within the industrial group. There are also important interdependencies between industries which are not allowed for. To give two important examples. The strategic importance of industries such as shipbuilding and motor vehicles, the former concentrated in the depressed areas and the latter in the Midlands and South, is not reflected in the method used. Both these are assembly industries and a large proportion of their inputs are supplied from within the region. The expansion of the motor vehicle industry has facilitated the expansion of other industries in the prosperous regions, and conversely the decline of shipbuilding has reduced the growth prospects of other industries to a much greater extent than is revealed by these studies. Again it has been noted that in the post-war years some of the fastest growing industries have been in the service sector. Industries such as financial, professional and scientific services in particular have shown a rapid rate of growth. The rate of growth of these services tends to be lower in the depressed areas than in the prosperous ones, and this would appear in the analysis not as a structural weakness but as a locational disadvantage. There can be little doubt, however, that at least part and probably a very large part of the relatively slow rate of growth of services in the depressed regions is itself *due* to structural weaknesses. These are industries for which demand is mainly local so that their rate of growth will be largely dependent on the industrial structure and income of the regions. The failure to allow for interdependencies of this kind will again result in an underestimate of the importance of structural factors.

However, quantitative studies have generally shown that the structural weaknesses of the regions have been an important factor in explaining differences in the regional and national growth rates in employment. Thus in a recent study covering various periods since 1921 A. J. Brown concludes that 'systematic structural effects seem to have been as important as, or more important than, systematic tendencies for particular regions to do well or badly in all industries together.[13] The relative importance of structural weaknesses, however, is not the same in all regions. For the period 1921–61 Brown discovered that the structural effect was the predominant factor explaining the below average growth of employment in Northern Ireland, Wales, the North and Yorkshire and Humberside, but that a general inferiority in growth performance was the main factor in the North-west and Scotland.

2. *The Case for Regional Policy*

The case for regional policy may be argued from two general standpoints. First, even if it were argued that a vigorous attempt to

[13] A. J. Brown, *The Framework of Regional Economics in the UK* (Cambridge University Press, 1972), p. 146.

change the pattern of industrial location brought about by market forces would result in a loss of efficiency and a somewhat lower measured rate of growth of national product, a regional policy could still be defended on social and cultural grounds. In this case a judgement would have to be made on how much of an efficiency loss was acceptable for the purpose of pursuing these non-economic goals. Second, however, there may be an economic case for regional policy, the basis of which is the argument that the market mechanism will not bring about a satisfactory adjustment to an optimal position. This proposition requires more detailed consideration.

We may start by examining the process of adjustment brought about by market forces, and then proceed to examine why it may not give a satisfactory solution. In terms of the labour market, and assuming some degree of wage flexibility, a situation where there are large differences in the degree of excess demand for, or supply of, labour between regions will result in regional earnings differentials, with earnings in general being higher in the regions with the tightest labour market conditions. These differentials will be an inducement to workers to move to the more prosperous areas. They will also affect the location decisions of firms in so far as lower earnings act as an inducement to firms to establish themselves or to expand in the less prosperous areas. Alternatively, the adjustment process may be viewed mainly in terms of the relative *availability* of labour and jobs in different regions. In this case the pattern of movement would be the same but the emphasis would now be on job opportunities and the availability of labour rather than on earnings differentials. In practice the role of earnings differentials in inducing movement will vary from one occupation and industry to another depending, for instance, on the extent to which trade union action has secured uniformity. However, whether it is wage differentials or job opportunities which are most important in explaining the actual working of the labour market, is there any reason to believe that the process will result in a smooth and rapid adjustment to an optimum position? A number of reasons have been put forward to suggest that it will not.

First, the adjustment process will at best result in a socially desirable allocation of resources, but only after a long period of adjustment during which a large number of people suffer considerable hardship. The extent, for instance, to which labour mobility can be relied upon to equalize the degree of excess demand for labour between regions is reduced by a number of factors. The degree of mobility of certain sections of the unemployed workforce may be very low as a consequence of having acquired skills which are specific to the declining industries, and also due to social and cultural factors which 'tie' households to particular regions. Furthermore, the employment problem of the less prosperous regions is only partly reflected in the relatively high level of unemployment. In addition the *activity* rates in these regions, that is the proportion of the population of working age which is in the work force, tend to be significantly lower than the national average—a consequence of the low employment opportunities. A further manifestation of the different labour market situations is found in the form of a general tendency for labour productivity, especially in the service industries, to be lower in the less-prosperous areas. In retailing, for instance, there is a clear positive relationship between labour productivity as measured by sales per person engaged and the degree of tightness of the labour market.[14]

Second, the decline and expansion of regions may be a *cumulative* process. For instance, the workers who move away from the less prosperous areas are likely to contain a disproportionately high number of the younger, more skilled, and enterprising members of the population. Emigration will in turn have adverse income effects. Migration means that a region suffers an immediate loss of income equivalent to unemployment pay and this will also have a small multiplier effect. The decline in income is also likely to lead to a fall in induced investment both in the private and public sectors which will reduce income levels still further and make the region less attractive to new firms. While these factors are hardly likely to attract new firms to the less-prosperous areas, the new developing areas enjoy several advantages; notably, increasing returns to scale associated with industrial expansion, and a more up-to-date stock of social capital. Both of these are very powerful factors drawing firms to the expanding areas.

The process of adjustment brought about by market forces may, then, lead to a cumulative process of decline and expansion, with the expanding areas attracting the more adaptable resources from other regions of the economy thus making them less attractive for new developments. Since the labour force has in fact been growing in absolute terms in all regions, the above should be expressed in terms of relative rates of change, but this does not destroy the basic argument that the market mechanism is not likely to bring about a rapid adjustment to a new equilibrium position. The post-war evidence in the United Kingdom supports this view, since in spite of heavy migration there has been little tendency for the labour market conditions in different regions to be equalized.

Third, the argument that the market process will fail to result in an optimum allocation of resources is reinforced by the fact that

[14] See K. D. George, *Productivity in Distribution*, University of Cambridge, Department of Applied Economics, Occasional Papers, No. 8.

the decisions made by employers and employees are based on a consideration of private costs and benefits which may diverge from those which are borne by society. More specifically, expansion in the prosperous areas will eventually result in congestion costs which are not reflected in the costs borne by individuals and firms. The fact that location decisions are based on actual charges which fall short of marginal social cost means that expansion in the prosperous areas will proceed beyond the social optimum point.

This then, is the economic case for a regional policy. The analysis also suggests what benefits an effective policy would give. First, an allocation of resources between regions which is nearer to the social optimum. Second, a lower overall level of unemployment associated with a given rate of price inflation.[15] Third, the fuller utilization of the labour force will be associated with an increase in output which is due not only to a lower overall rate of unemployment but also to increased activity rates and higher labour productivity in the now less-prosperous regions.

3. *A Framework for Policy*

Although the foregoing analysis suggests that there may be economic benefits to be gained from a regional policy, this does not mean that the policy actually pursued by the government will succeed in achieving them. In particular it should be emphasized that costs *do* vary between locations, and the effectiveness of policy may be severely weakened by a failure to distinguish between locations which are suited to the development of new industries and those which are not.

Mention has already been made of the increasing returns to scale enjoyed by expanding industries. This provides a very powerful argument in favour of developing 'growth points' in the less-prosperous regions. Such growth points need not, of course, be suitable for all types of industrial activity. Indeed a general policy of diversification for its own sake regardless of the economies of specialization and concentration is not desirable. The establishment of an 'isolated' firm which purchases its inputs from outside the region is less beneficial than one which has close technical interrelationships with other firms in the area, apart from the undesirable increase in transport which is generated. It may be argued that the government need not or should not decide which locations are suitable for efficient

---

[15] The argument that a more even distribution of activity between regions will improve the 'trade-off' between the rate of unemployment and the rate of inflation is based on a non-linear relationship between the rate of inflation and the degree of tightness of the labour market, with earnings being more sensitive to tight labour market conditions than to slack ones.

growth, but instead should define very broad areas, such as the whole of Wales or Scotland, which are eligible for financial assistance, and that the location decisions of individual firms will select the natural growth points. The number of new developments coming into a region, however, is limited, and with such a policy there would be a danger that the new developments would be spread too widely, thus sacrificing external economies of scale. Furthermore, the selection of growth points is likely to lead to more efficient public investment in transport and other services, which in turn makes the area attractive to new firms.

The reference to public investment draws attention to the importance of forward planning of the areas which are selected for development. Congestion costs and loss of amenities are not developments peculiar to the South-east and the Midlands, and long-term planning of the growth areas is essential if more urban sprawl is to be avoided. Such planning is made more essential by the increasing importance of commuting, a trend which is already very evident for instance in South Wales. The planning of growth areas, therefore, must consider not only the expected expansion in industrial activity, but also what this implies in terms of the demand for housing and places of recreation. 'Economic success must be related to a pattern of living which people find tolerable. . . . From a national point of view, then, one can see a "geography of opportunity" in terms of growth points. . . . Related to this one has a "geography of desire" in terms of pleasant and well-planned places to live and to take recreation.'[16]

The framework for regional policy which is suggested, therefore, involves the selection of locations which are suited to efficient industrial growth, and planning the investment in social capital in these locations and the adjacent residential areas on the basis of the expected industrial development and population growth. It is unrealistic to assume of course that policy can be exclusively concerned with the planned development of growth areas. There will be areas of need which are not within easy access of growth areas, and where, because of immobility, a serious wastage of resources will result without some new development. There is no ideal solution, but given the limited resources which will be devoted to regional development the most efficient policy is one which concentrates these resources on those areas best suited to sustained economic growth.

4. *Policy in the United Kingdom*

Post-war policy in the United Kingdom has varied a great deal in

[16] C. F. Carter, 'The Hunt Report', *Scottish Journal of Political Economy*, November 1969.

forcefulness. In the immediate post-war years government control of
factory space was used to the advantage of the Development Areas
which were also assisted by loans and grants, the provision of basic
public services and the reclamation of derelict land, under the
Distribution of Industry Act 1945. During the 1950s, however,
although the Government could still influence the direction of
industrial expansion by use of industrial development certificates it
made very little use of this power. Controls on industrial location had
in fact largely disappeared and financial inducements to industry

TABLE 10.2. *The Movement of Manufacturing Industry, Transfers[1] and
Branches[2] 1945–65*

Host region	1945–51 Number of moves	%	1952–59 Number of moves	%	1960–65 Number of moves	%	1945–65 Number of moves	%
Peripheral areas[3]	463	49·6	214	23·8	475	40·3	1,152	38·2
South-east and East Anglia	220	23·6	456	50·6	384	32·5	1,060	35·2
Rest of England	250	26·8	231	25·6	321	27·2	802	26·6
Total	933	100·0	901	100·0	1,180	100·0	3,014	100·0

[1] The transfer of establishments from one area to another, involving the
cessation of activities at the first location.

[2] The opening of a second or subsequent establishment, not necessarily an
organizationally subsidiary one.

[3] The peripheral areas correspond closely to the areas where government
inducements have been available.

were modest. The recession of 1958 and the growing difficulties faced
by industries such as coal-mining, textiles and shipbuilding caused
attention to be focused again on the fundamental weakness of the
industrial structure of the Development Areas. During the 1960s,
therefore, industrial development certificates were again used more
forcefully to restrict expansion in the South-east and the Midlands,
and financial inducements became very much more important.

Valuable information relating to these three broad phases of
post-war regional policy is contained in a study of the movement
of manufacturing industry.[17] Some of the relevant information is

[17] See R. S. Howard, *The Movement of Manufacturing Industry in the United
Kingdom 1945–65* (Board of Trade, 1968).

summarized in Table 10.2. Over the whole period 1945–65 the number of movements, both transfers and the establishment of branches, was just over 3,000, of which 38 per cent were to the peripheral areas. In the two period 1945–51 and 1960–65 when regional policy was fairly forcefully applied, the percentage of the total movements going to these areas was 50 per cent and 40 per cent respectively. In the intermediate period, however, the figure was only 23 per cent. It appears, therefore, that the location decisions of firms may have been substantially influenced by the forcefulness of government policy.

This study also brings to light some other interesting facts. First, over the whole period, there were almost as many moves to the South-east and East Anglia as there were to the peripheral areas, 78 per cent of them originating in Greater London. The proportion of moves which took the form of transfers, however, was very different. In the case of moves to the South-east and East Anglia, 58 per cent were transfers, whereas only 17 per cent of the moves to the peripheral areas were of this kind. Furthermore, the absolute number of transfers to these areas was very small in the 1950s when there were only 16, compared to 113 and 71 in the earlier and later periods respectively. The high proportion of moves to the development areas which take the form of establishing a new branch is of some importance to the long-run viability of the development in these areas, because when there is an overall decline in demand for a firm's products it will frequently be the branch in the development area which suffers most.[18]

Second, it is also interesting to see where the moves to the peripheral areas originated. Information on this is given in Table 10.3. Greater London was the most important single source, accounting for 28 per cent of the moves. Another 25 per cent, however, originated in the 'Remainder of England', which contains such regions as the North-west excluding Merseyside, and Yorkshire, which although not classified as Development Areas suffer from much the same sort of problem.

The patterns observed in the above analysis are supported by more up to date information for the period 1966–71. This period saw a further major reinforcement of regional policy, and 45 per cent of manufacturing movements went to the peripheral areas. London, the South-east and East Anglia continues to be the most important source of moves with 49 per cent of the total, compared to 39 per cent over the years 1945–65, but again a substantial proportion, 20 per cent, originated in the 'remainder of England'.

[18] See, for instance, B. J. Loasby, 'Making Location Policy Work', *Lloyds Bank Review*, January 1967.

TABLE 10.3. *Origin of Moves to the Peripheral Areas, 1945–65*

Origin	Number of moves	Employment '000
Greater London	320	115
Rest of South-east and East Anglia	139	60
West Midland conurbation	92	39
Rest of West Midlands	41	29
Peripheral areas	95	16
Remainder of England[1]	287	96
Unallocated	12	6
Abroad	166	77
Total	**1,152**	**438**

[1] North-west less Merseyside, South-west less Devon and Cornwall, Yorkshire and Humberside, East Midlands.

TABLE 10.4. *Changes in Regional Disparities in Unemployment, Net Migration and Personal Income per Head*

Region	Unemployment % 1958	Unemployment % 1967	Net migration '000 1956–61	Net migration '000 1961–66	Personal income per head (% of UK average) 1954/65	Personal income per head (% of UK average) 1964/65
Northern Ireland	9·3	7·7	−93	−38	64	64
Wales	3·8	4·1	−22	+5	87	84
Scotland	3·7	3·9	−142	−194	93	88
Northern	2·4	4·0	−30	−37	93	82
North-west	2·7	2·5	−60	−13	102	95
South-west	2·2	2·5	+91	+108	87	91
UK	2·1	2·5				

Source: Gavin McCrone, *Regional Policy in Britain* (George Allen & Unwin, Ltd., 1969), Chapter 6.

There seems little doubt that variations in the forcefulness of regional policy do have a significant effect. How effective, however, has the policy been in 'closing the gap' between the Development Areas and the rest of the country. At first sight it would appear that the information shown in Table 10.4 suggests that there has not been a marked improvement. The biggest improvement up to the mid-1960s was in Northern Ireland where there was a fall both in the level of unemployment and in net migration. Unemployment, however, is still at a very high level. In Wales and Scotland although the rate of unemployment was higher in 1967 than in 1958 there was a slight decrease in the extent to which it exceeded the national average. In some regions, however, the situation in certain respects was worse in the mid-1960s than it was in the 1950s. In the Northern region, for instance, the unemployment situation had significantly

TABLE 10.5. *Total Cost of Special Regional Assistance to Industry, Over and Above That Available Nationally, Great Britain*

	£ million					
	1963–64	1965–66	1967–68	1968–69	1969–70	1970–71
Government factory building and loans	24	22	25	32	46	36
Grants under Local Employment Acts	6	20	21	23	38	34
Investment grants	—	—	72	85	90	90
Free depreciation	—	45	4	—	—	—
Regional employment premium			34	101	105	110
S.E.T. premium	—	—	—	25	25	—
Total	**30**	**87**	**156**	**266**	**304**	**270**

Source: Expenditure Committee (Trade and Industry Subcommittee), *Economic and Exchequer Implications of Regional Policy* (HMSO, May 1973).

worsened, and in Scotland net outward migration was higher in the period 1961–66 than in the period 1956–61. In so far as regional policy up to the mid-1960s had been effective it seems that it was mainly to prevent the regional disparities being worse than they actually were.

Even this of course could be quite consistent with regional policy having had a substantial positive impact on employment opportunities in the regions. Thus the growth of employment opportunities resulting from regional policy may be obscured in the unemployment figures because of the loss of jobs in declining industries. In measuring the impact of policy, therefore, it is more instructive to examine the extent to which the policy has resulted in extra employment in the assisted areas.

A major strengthening of regional policy occurred after 1963. The total cost of special regional assistance in Britain from 1963–64 onwards is summarized in Table 10.5. The most striking fact is the large increase in total aid to industry from £30 million in 1963–64 to £156 million in 1967–68 and £304 million in 1969–70. The major additions to the financial inducements have been investment grants and the regional employment premium. Together they accounted for £200 million worth of assistance in 1970–71 and to 74 per cent of all financial inducements.

What sort of impact did this much more active policy have on the supply of jobs in the assisted areas? One detailed study of the effects has estimated that over the period 1963–70 the total number of extra jobs resulting from the more active regional policy was of the order of 200,000.[19]

It seems clear that by the end of the 1960s financial inducements, mainly in the form of investment grants and the regional employment premium were very important in creating new jobs in the Development Areas. The debate concerning the effectiveness of alternative policies in creating extra job opportunities, however, continues.

There is one general factor which is important in determining the effectiveness of a given expenditure on regional development, and that is the overall level of activity in the economy and business expectations concerning future demand conditions. A high level of activity and favourable expectations about future demand will, as compared with a recession and unfavourable expectations, be associated with a larger number of expansion projects, with the likelihood that it will be relatively easy to induce firms to expand in the less-prosperous areas. The fact that the much more active policy after 1963 coincided with a strong expansion in the economy was undoubtedly important in contributing towards its success in the early stages.

Apart from this there are a number of other interrelated issues. First, before the introduction of the regional employment premium concern was frequently expressed that the emphasis on financial inducements in the form of loans and grants for investment expenditure was undesirable because of the tendency which such inducements had to encourage the more capital-intensive firms to expand in the Development Areas. There is certainly very little to be said in favour of such a strong bias towards capital intensive projects. However, too much emphasis has been placed on relative degrees of capital intensity, and not enough on the degree of complementarity between firms. Thus it is more important to consider whether a firm has close technical links with others already established in a development area than it is to examine its capital–labour ratio. This argument of course is related to the case for growth points, and the view that this is the best way of achieving self-sustained development. If this view is correct it also implies that a concentration of government assistance

[19] See B. Moore and J. Rhodes, 'Evaluating the Effects of British Regional Economic Policy', *The Economic Journal*, March 1973.

on the areas most favourable to growth will result in the *need* for incentives disappearing more quickly.

Second, financial inducements have in the main applied to the industrial sector of the economy. But in recent years some financial inducements have been extended to the service industries. In 1970 service industries in Development Areas were given the benefit of free depreciation and in June 1973 the Government announced financial measures in the form of grants and loans to encourage the movement of services into the Development Areas. This extension of financial inducements to services is to be welcomed. It is the service sector which has shown the fastest increase in employment over the last two decades, and financial inducements to services appear desirable not only from the point of view of increasing the number of job opportunities in Development Areas but also to assist in establishing a greater *variety* of job opportunities.

Third, controversy has also surrounded the extent to which financial assistance discriminates between efficient and inefficient firms. Up to 1966, assistance was mainly in the form of extra allowances which could be set against tax so that only profitable firms benefited. The system of investment grants introduced in 1966 applied to all firms irrespective of their profitability as long as they undertook investment in assets which were eligible for assistance. One of the main justifications for the change was that the grants would assist the small and rapidly expanding firms whose profits were not high enough to benefit fully from the old system of allowances. More important from this point of view is the regional employment premium which is an unconditional subsidy to all manufacturing establishments in Development Areas, and has thus been criticized in giving assistance to inefficient as well as efficient firms and to firms that do not, as well as those that do, increase employment. The intention of the subsidy was to increase the competitiveness of firms in the Development Areas by reducing unit wage costs. The result would therefore be a regional devaluation and an increase in output and employment in the assisted areas. A reduction in prices, however, is only one possible response to a subsidy of this kind. It is also possible that part of the subsidy could be absorbed in higher wages, and also, and much more likely, that it would be used by firms to widen their profit margins. The latter would still result in increased output and employment if the higher profits were used to increase investment or non-price competitiveness. The exact effect of the subsidy on employment depends on the relative importance of these alternative responses.[20]

---

[20] An analysis of the estimated effect of the regional employment premium

Whatever the precise mechanism by which the regional employment premium works, however, there is no doubt that its overall effectiveness has been weakened. When it was introduced in 1967 it was as a fixed money payment per employee and its real value has therefore been greatly eroded by inflation. In addition, in 1970 the Conservative Government confirmed its intention to phase out the subsidy in 1974. This has probably resulted in businessmen further discounting the benefits of the subsidy in so far as future production and employment plans are concerned.

Fourth, there is the question of financial inducements versus controls. Control on new developments in the most congested areas in the prosperous regions has been exercised mainly by means of industrial development certificates and office development permits. In addition there has been a dispersal of civil service work from London.[21]

Control of office development is particularly important in Central London where it is the most important creator of new jobs. Office development control is thus crucial in dealing with the problems of congestion. However, it was not until 1964 that office building was brought under control with the introduction of Office Development Permits (ODPs) which had to be applied for to the Board of Trade by all companies wishing to build an office in London in excess of 3,000 square feet.[22] By this time a major boom in the granting of planning permissions for office building in Central London had seemingly come to an end. Net planning permissions (i.e. gross permissions less schemes for replacement demolitions and 'change of use') reached a peak in 1955 when 5·5 million square feet of new office space was approved. The figure remained above 3 million square feet from 1954 to 1960. The early 1960s saw a marked decline and in 1963 the figure was only 800,000 square feet. By the time controls were imposed, therefore, planning permissions for new office development were already low by the standards of the previous ten years. Nevertheless, in the first three years of the operation of the ODP system the area of new office space for which planning per-

in creating new employment on alternative assumptions about its effect on prices, profits and wages, is found in A. J. Brown, 'The Green Paper on the Development Areas', *National Institute Economic Review*, May 1967.

[21] For details see *The Dispersal of Government Work from London* (HMSO, June 1973).

[22] By July 1966 all office developments in the South-east and West Midland regions were subject to control. Outside the London Metropolitan Region, however, the exemption limit was raised in July 1967 from 3,000 square feet to 10,000 square feet.

mission was granted sunk to a very low level, averaging only 100,000 square feet per annum.[23]

This sharp fall in planning permissions in the 1960s has not been accompanied by an equivalent reduction in new office space *made available* because of the long time-lag between the granting of planning permission and the completion of new buildings. Thus, for instance, whereas the annual average office space granted planning permission fell from 3·5 million square feet in the period 1948–64 to 0·6 million in 1965–68, the new office floor space completed fell by much less—from an annual average of 3·0 million square feet to 2·0 million square feet. The continuation of a strict enforcement of ODP policy would of course have a marked effect on the addition to office space when the backlog of planning permissions had worked itself out, but already by 1968 there seems to have been some relaxation in the restrictions on new planning permission in Central London. In view of the importance of congestion costs a relaxation of restraints on new development in Central London is to be deplored. Furthermore, to be effective, a policy of dealing with congestion would have to apply to a much wider area than London itself, because strict control there but not in adjacent areas will lead to a large number of 'short-distance' movements which might do little to relieve congestion and indeed may even accentuate it.

With the present array of policy weapons there is certainly a strong case for maintaining a tight control of new development in the most congested areas. It has been suggested, however, that the most appropriate way of dealing with the social costs of congestion would be by the imposition of a tax rather than a system of controls and financial inducements. In its most general form this suggestion amounts to a regionally differentiated payroll tax which would replace the existing system of controls and differential subsidies. Thus 'if we wish to correct the artificially low cost to the individual of services in the expanding areas it would seem more logical to do so by raising these costs than by lowering those elsewhere. More important, the subsidies relate to the amount of investment and the tax to the amount of employment. Both are, of course, only approximations to the social costs involved, which depend on the population in the area and the extent to which it uses the services in question, but the payroll tax seems to provide much the closer approximation.'[24] More recently a limited application of the idea had been made in the form of an argument for a congestion tax which would exist alongside the financial inducements. Such a tax would apply to 'the

[23] I am grateful to Mr J. Rhodes for this information on office development in Central London.

[24] M. J. Farrell, *Fuller Employment*, Hobart Paper 24, p. 27.

conurbations in prosperous areas and their immediate surroundings where an additional tax reflecting the cost to the rest of the community of each taxed unit's presence there would be appropriate'.[25]

Clearly more evidence is needed on the effectiveness and administrative feasibility of different policy weapons before any firm conclusion can be reached on their relative merits.[26] But apart from the question of the most effective package of inducements and controls there are some more general points which need to be made concerning the basis of a successful regional policy.

First, the regional problem is one which ideally requires long-term planning of policy. In fact policy has, to a large extent, been dictated by short-term considerations. To some extent this has been due to differences of opinion between governments about the desirability of specific policies, but whatever the real cause it has certainly meant that the effectiveness of policy in general has been reduced. Attention has already been drawn to the fact that the declared intention of the Conservative Government to abolish the regional employment premium has probably diminished its effectiveness. In addition, following the period 1966–70 when there was a big increase in the size of the financial inducements and when assistance became less selective in relation to efficiency and the creation of new jobs, a start was made in October 1970 towards a return to a greater emphasis on selectivity. Investment grants were abolished and instead, for firms in the Development Areas, there was a return to free depreciation on expenditure on new plant and machinery and higher initial allowances on new industrial building. However, in 1972 investment grants were restored for firms in Development Areas although at only half the level of those existing in 1970. Short-term policy changes of this kind are bound to weaken the overall impact of policy.

Second, policy in the UK may be criticized for failing to concentrate resources on developing those parts of the Development Areas which are most suited to development and thus for reducing its effectiveness by spreading the assistance too widely.

Finally, by dividing the country into 'black' and 'white' regions policy makers failed to see the long-run consequences for the so-called 'intermediate' or grey areas. We have already noted that a substantial proportion of the moves to the Development Areas in the period 1945–71 originated in the intermediate areas. Following

[25] A. J. Brown, Note of Dissent in the *Hunt Committee Report on the Intermediate Areas*, Cmnd. 3998, 1969.

[26] For a strong criticism of investment grants and the regional employment premium, see T. Wilson, 'Finance for Regional Industrial Development', *The Three Banks Review*, September 1967.

the Hunt Committee Report the Government has introduced some measures of assistance for the intermediate areas but they are hardly likely to be sufficient at their present level to offset the general tendencies inherent in existing policy. A complete reappraisal of regional policy is thus required which takes into account the long-term growth prospects of all regions. The need for such a reappraisal is made all the more urgent by virtue of our membership of the European Economic Community. There is certainly a danger that within the EEC the underlying economic forces will operate more strongly to the disadvantage of some of the Development Areas. If this danger materializes it will raise the most fundamental question of all: what total sum will we be prepared to spend in subsidizing particular regions?

INDEX

Absolute cost advantages 96, 98
Acquisitions (*see* Mergers)
Adams, Walter 92 & *n*
Advertising:
  and concentration 90–1, 100, 125–6
  and economies of scale 125–6
  and growth of manufacturer-dominated industries 124–6, 134
  and market structure 124–32
  and other product differentiation activities 100, 113, 126
  and price competition 114, 125
  and profitability 124
  and the large retailer 127
  as an entry barrier 96–7, 124, 156
  expenditure by industry 80–1
  factors influencing size of 81–2
  growth of expenditure on 156
  taxation of 156
Alchian, A. A. 104*n*
Allocative efficiency 39, 75–6, 78, 80, 136–43, 204
Armstrong, A. G. 21*n*, 34, 35 & *n*

Bain, Joe S. 73 & *n*, 86*n*, 87, 169
Barriers to entry 94–9
  absolute cost advantage 96, 98
  and growth 99, 124
  and monopoly policy 94, 97–8, 155
  and technological change 99
  anticipated reactions to entry 96
  as a determinant of profitability 117, 119–24, 134
  economies of scale 95–9
  product differentiation 94, 96, 99
  to new and existing firms 12, 82, 94, 96
Baumol, William J. 104 & *n*, 106 & *n*, 136*n*
Blair, J. M. 40*n*, 50*n*, 68*n*, 100 & *n*

Brown, A. J. 206 & *n*, 217*n*, 219*n*
Burn, Duncan 57*n*
Business goals (*see* Management goals)

Capacity:
  adjustment to increases in demand 45, 72, 77–8, 129, 138
  and mergers 63
  and peak demand 77–8, 138, 177
  excess 45, 77–8, 92, 99, 137, 139, 176–7
Carter, C. F. 210*n*
Catherwood, H. F. R. 172*n*
Coase, R. H. 51*n*
Collins, N. R. 118 & *n*
Comanor, William S. 123*n*, 129*n*
Companies:
  Allied Breweries 38, 144, 145*n*, 160*n*
  Armco Steel 198
  Associated Electrical Industries 131
  British Insulated Callender's Cables 144
  British Steel Corporation 195–8
  Courtaulds 37, 52, 53, 115, 152, 156, 159
  English Electric 131
  General Electric 38, 131
  Kodak 114, 151
  Marks & Spencer 52, 60
  Mitsubishi Electric 156
  Mitsubishi Heavy Industries 156
  Pilkington 53, 114, 115, 128, 156
  Procter & Gamble 97–8
  Transport Holding Company, 199 & *nn*, 200 & *n*
  Wall Paper Manufacturers Ltd 159
  Westinghouse Electric 156
Concentration (*see* Seller concentration)

221